HEROES

HEROES

The Champions of
Our Literary Imagination

BRUCE MEYER

HarperCollins*PublishersLtd*

Heroes
© 2007 by Bruce Meyer. All rights reserved.

Published by HarperCollins Publishers Ltd.

First Edition

All illustrations are from the collection of
the author, except for the photo on page 24:
Northrop Frye, September 26, 1984,
© Library and Archives Canada. Reproduced
with permission of Library and Archives
Canada. Source: Library and Archives
Canada/Credit: Harry Palmer/Harry Palmer
fonds/PA-183431.

Every attempt has been made to obtain
permission to reproduce copyrighted works.
In the event of an inadvertent omission or
error, please contact the publisher.

HarperCollins books may be purchased for
educational, business, or sales promotional
use through our Special Markets Department.

HarperCollins Publishers Ltd
2 Bloor Street East, 20th Floor
Toronto, Ontario, Canada
M4W 1A8

www.harpercollins.ca

Library and Archives Canada Cataloguing in
Publication

Meyer, Bruce, 1957–
Heroes : the champions of our literary
imagination / Bruce Meyer.

ISBN-13: 978-0-00-200091-8
ISBN-10: 0-00-200091-1

1. Heroes in literature.
2. Literature—History and criticism.
I. Title.

PN56.5.H45M49 2007   809'.93352
C2007-901317-1

HC 9 8 7 6 5 4 3 2 1

Printed and bound in the United States
Set in Bembo
Design by Sharon Kish

This book is for Ernie, Margaret, Carolyn, Kerry, and Katie . . .
and in memory of my father, Homer Meyer

Il temporal foco e l'eterno
Veduto hai, figlio; e se' venuto in parte
Ov' io per me più oltre non discerno.
Tratto t' ho qui con ingegno e con arte . . .
—Dante, *Purgatorio*, Canto XXVII, 127–30

To strive, to seek, to find, and not to yield.
—Alfred, Lord Tennyson, "Ulysses"

CONTENTS

MAKING HEROES OUT OF DUST

I n classical mythology, Hero was a priestess of Aphrodite, the god-dess of love and beauty. She was named for Hera, Zeus' wife, and lived at Sestos, on the Hellespont, the narrow channel in present-day Turkey that separates Europe from Asia. On the opposite shore, at Abydos, lived her lover, Leander. For Hero to preserve her stand-ing as a holy person in her community, she had to conduct her affair with Leander with the utmost discretion. Each night, under the guise of lighting a pyre to honour the gods, she would build a signal fire to guide her lover on his one-mile swim between the two continents. Before dawn each day, he would make the swim home again, this time guided by the light of the sun rising before him. But one night, in an act of treachery by a jealous god, a storm dowsed the beacon, leaving Hero's swimming lover to the darkness. Leander lost his way in the swift current, circling round and round until, exhausted, he gave up his life to the cold waters.

So inspiring and heroic was Leander's nightly dip that in 1810, Lord Byron re-enacted it—in the company of a British military

---

In this engraving by Gustav Doré, Dante greets his beloved Beatrice at the threshold of the Garden of Eden in the Purgatorio.

officer who almost drowned in the process. The legend also touched Virgil, Ovid, and Christopher Marlowe, each of whom saw the lighting of the beacon as a symbol of the human determination to love in a universe that would dash hope and desire. Hero's is a story about the power of love to bridge mighty currents and draw continents together; it's also proof that the idea of the hero is as ubiquitous and universal as love itself.

Whenever I begin to question the role of the hero in literature, I find myself returning to Dante. Dante is peculiar in that he makes himself the hero of his own epic poem. Indeed, he never misses an opportunity to tell his readers about himself. He wants us to know who he is and what he has experienced, not just in his journeys through hell, purgatory, and paradise, but in what was the here and now of medieval Italy. Dante wants us to know that his life has gone very, very wrong. He is a man who is lost in the world and in himself. And to help get him back on the right path, he chooses as his guide not only the poet Virgil but all of Western literature as he knew it. He believes that literature—the classics, the Bible, and everything else his mind can contain—can correct the deviation in course that would destroy a lesser soul. In the end, he finds more than he set out to attain—a greater world and a greater self.

Whenever I reread Dante's *Divine Comedy,* I am always impressed that he has created a character who is the image of himself. Put yourself in his worn, exile's shoes for a moment. Imagine that you have suddenly been turned out of political office and disgraced by foes you cannot answer. Your home has been seized and destroyed. Your wife, whose family has orchestrated your downfall, disowns you and you cannot see your children. Your books and scientific instruments, the work of a lifetime, have been confiscated. Your writings have been burned in the public square. The church to which you directed your soul has cut you off without hearing your side of the story. You are alone and cold in a world where home, place, and the security of faith are the only anchors. You have two options: you can despair and perhaps end your days, broken in hope and spirit, or you can imagine something greater than yourself. Taking the second option, you seize the entire universe in your mind and evolve it as a dramatic and complex structure through which you can learn to understand the world and yourself. And then, with faith in the power of your own imagination, you place yourself as the protagonist in the middle of a grand schema designed by God Himself. Out of the perils of your own suffering, you choose the most heroic option of all, making yourself the hero of your own story.

The Dante who visits hell, purgatory, and paradise in his "vision" is looking inward in an attempt to understand both the world of human character and the landscape of his own soul. As he reaches the threshold of God in the *Paradiso,* words fail him. Language is insufficient not merely because he is facing the infinite nature of divinity, but because he has come to the end of himself. There is no place further for him to go. He has at last reached an understanding of who he is as a human being, and he cannot put it into words:

> How weak are words, and how unfit to frame
> My concept—which lags after what was shown
> So far, t'would flatter it to call it lame!
>
> Eternal light, that in Thyself alone
> Dwelling, alone dost know Thyself, and smile
> On Thy self-love, so knowing and so unknown!

Dante proves that the process of learning about oneself is a heroic enterprise. The school of human character works beyond language. It is a realm where the individual is transformed by all he has encountered, and to articulate that transformation in precise terms is impossible.

In Canto XVII of the *Paradiso,* Dante is given the chance to meet his all-time hero, his ancestor Cacciaguida, who died defending the spiritual centre of Dante's world, Jerusalem. At the conclusion of his interview with his illustrious forebear, Dante admits that his greatest fear is that he will lose the immortality he might acquire through his literary work. He's not being egotistical. He believes that what he has written has a point, and he does not want it to go out of fashion, the way so many others have done. He laments:

> Through Heav'n I've learned things, such that if retold,
> They'd leave an acrid taste of many a lip;
>
> Yet, if I am truth's friend, and am not bold,
> My name, I fear, will live but brief measure
> With those who'll call these days the days of old.

Cacciaguida laughs at his worried descendant, and gives Dante some fatherly advice on the durability of truths and virtues: "Make thy whole vision freely manifested, / And where men feel the itch, there let them scratch." In other words, people will always go looking for truths. But guidance is not something that one person can impose upon another.

Purgatory is where souls learn their way back to God. When they exit purgatory, the transformation is complete. The individual is changed. He has learned what he has to learn about himself, and is able to set that to work as a means of coping with life and its challenges. He comes into an understanding of his strengths and weaknesses. This process of life-long learning concludes not with a cap-and-gown ceremony, but with the completion of our personal narratives, that moment when we reach beyond ourselves into either divinity or nothingness. Dante seems to suggest that we are recreated according to the image of ourselves that we wish our stories would present. Literature can be terrifying because it offers us the possibility of encountering our own potential. The careful reader—the critical mind, as St. Augustine suggests in the *Confessions*—is someone who can put distance between what he is reading and how he is affected by what he reads.

The hero is a universal concept that fascinates and even badgers us as human beings. Even if we choose to turn away and declare, as Douglas Coupland does in *Generation X,* that there are no more heroes, these figures are still there to carry the narrative. They reside at the centre of the action, representing the human point of view in the reader's imagination. They are an image of ourselves, and they enable the narrative to function as a human and humane construct in our imaginations. Heroes are the firing pin in a story that ignites our mechanism for absorbing the world, and they are ingrained in the psychological and imaginative fabric from which humanity is woven. They are the story's point of relativity. The world is always ready to present us with models that point us to who we think we must become. We may reject as old-fashioned this process of identifying something of ourselves or our experience in a narrative, but it is working on us nonetheless. When we tell our children stories, it is not only because we want them to know about the past, but because we want them to look into those stories and discover details for their own developing identities. I saw this at work during my daughter's formative years, when she would ask me to tell her stories of my own childhood, of the people I had known and the events I had lived through. I realized that she was seeking imaginative touchstones for her own experiences. She was looking for measures against which to set her own life as it developed. But the point was not to find lessons in the stories. What she wanted were the stories themselves, the structures and substance of my own past, so that she could transform her experiences into the material of her own narrative. Life works us over and constantly delights us with the stories we learn from others and the stories we tell ourselves.

What I have attempted to do in this book is to examine the types of heroes that Western, and in particular English, literature presents to readers. I am exploring here the possibilities of human behaviour that define those characters who most actively work on our imaginations. I have chosen to start with the most recognizable—yet most overlooked—image of the hero: ourselves. The common hero is a very modern concept. He rises out of the ashes of a civilization that was humiliated by the sight of Homeric warriors clashing in the dust of Troy. The great misfortune in most discussions of heroes is that their authors are immediately drawn to characters like Achilles and Ajax, the muscled brutes whose outsized humanity borders on a psychotic belief that the world's problems can be solved through violence. But in the twentieth century, there emerged a new code for the hero in the simple figure of ourselves as problem-solver. This stately yet diminutive figure rises, through knowledge, courage, and perseverance, to face the challenges of a world that is still worth communion with. In examining these characters, I was constantly reminded that the hardest thing to imagine is ourselves.

This book progresses from the figures with whom we are most familiar to those who seem like apparitions. These are the tragic, the dark, and the saintly heroes who remind us of our own pitfalls and possibilities. I would like to think that these heroes are the expressions of our souls, the highs and lows that we reach through good fortune and bad. Beyond these characters, I have allowed the literary imagination to guide me. The hyperbolized epic hero lives large and seeks a reality that is even larger, yet he is still grappling with the most basic human concerns: love, home, identity, and justice. And although the epic hero is someone who is both touched and tainted by divinity, he is still essentially human in his outlook and his capabilities. He dwells on earth and is as much a product of dust as the common man. The divine hero, by contrast, offers us a glimpse of an existence that is untouched by the limitations of life. These figures hold the promise that the more we learn to grow towards that which is beyond us, the more likely we are to learn how we, too, can overcome our limitations. The divine hero is a target rather than an expression. Jesus is **a role** model beyond the grasp of the average

The archetypal nineteenth-century view of Norse heroes, such as those who populate Wagner's operas. Note the weapons, the donning of skins, and the attachment of the characters to animistic appearances.

human being, but he is nevertheless the destination of which we dream. There has to be something beyond what we know, or knowledge would cease to function as a propelling force for the human spirit. The divine hero is what we would wish to see as the very best in ourselves. And even if we fall short of such impossible standards, we are still able to perceive an image of our own humanity that is better than what we see at first glance.

My intention in this book is to present something more than a catalogue of types. What intrigues me is the way heroic characters respond to the challenges they meet in life. Each challenge is as individual as the characters themselves. W. B. Yeats once claimed that there were twenty-eight different types of personalities in the world. He was not merely being facetious; he was attempting to understand human motivation because he believed that we are what we do, both existentially and imaginatively. In the *Poetics,* the ethically minded Aristotle suggests that the hero is someone who commands our attention and our devotion because he is good. But the idea that the hero speaks for the goodness in our nature omits the possibility that he can be someone far less than perfect—someone with flaws, desires, foibles, and weaknesses like us. Seen in this light, heroes reassure us that weakness is not an impediment to success, and that it is okay to be ourselves. They affirm that we have the right to celebrate ourselves in literature and to admire, if only fleetingly, even our failings. Thomas Carlyle, in *On Heroes and Hero-Worship,* attempted to define the traits that make an individual noteworthy. He examined Dante, Shakespeare, Napoleon, and others, and asked himself what he found in them that was so attractive. There was, he suggested, something more than human about them, a spark almost of divinity that was worth adulation and attention. Carlyle was fascinated by characters who, through deeds or ideas, captured our imaginations and made us want to become like them. This act of hero-worship is something that seems very natural to us, especially in our most playful and self-forgetting states. Heroes have the potential to take us out of ourselves.

Each day when we open the newspaper, we encounter narratives of people just like us, momentary heroes who come and go with the times. Narrative reminds us that a thread of events links us together in the moment when we exist. It reminds us that our lives follow a pattern, with a beginning, a middle, and an end, and that along the way, we encounter moments of significance. Literature, however, takes a more long-term approach to the question of what makes a human being unique, and what captures and holds our attention as readers. What interests me is how literature—poetry, fiction, drama—keeps returning to the same set of behavioural patterns and the same recurring characters. It is my aim in this book to examine this pattern and these characters. These, it seems, remind us of the possibilities that are inherent in every personality, and the paths that define who we are and how we present ourselves to others.

We do not become the heroes we encounter in literature unless we choose to do so, or unless our minds short-circuit and trick us

Engraved by G. Greatbach from the Somerset Portrait

HISTORIES

A nineteenth-century frontispiece from an edition of Shakespeare,
suggesting the range of the bard's imagination.

In this print by Gustav Doré, Dante is led through hell by his guide and singing master, the Roman poet Virgil. Hell is composed not just of souls in torment, but of stories without endings.

into thinking that we are someone else. Cervantes' great hero, Don Quixote, falls victim to his own reading. He transforms himself into a knight straight out of a second-rate, late-medieval romance, and he suffers as a result of it. Quixote works on the assumption that literature edifies. The Don Quixotes of the world permit the fence between reality and imagination to erode. But the way to build that fence, to strengthen our sense of discernment, is to study literature as something both beautiful and objective, to learn to appreciate just what an author has done to present us with a detailed examination of the possibilities inherent in a human personality. For all the Quixotic notions of blurred boundaries, there is still the idea that heroes can pass along some useful knowledge that will enable us to see beyond the confines of our own lives.

Perhaps there is, beneath every story of every character, an active sense of wish-fulfillment, where the character attains the personality he wants to have. Authors write from the knowledge that when they create a character, that character has to convey a sense of completeness to be accepted by the reader. What transforms a character from being merely the centre of the narrative action to the level of a hero is that he or she exceeds what is expected. Heroes conquer not only the machinations of the plot and the situations in which they are involved, but also the reader. The hero is someone who is seen by others as they wish to be seen: the self created by the imagination.

Heroes fascinate and attract us. We should know who they are so that when we encounter them, we will recognize them as possibilities of human expression. They hold our attention for the span of a poem, the duration of a drama, or the world of a novel because they intrigue us and tease us with the depth of the "other." Through them, we are able to get to know someone else, not just because they are oversized or grandly replete in armour or sitting in a state of awe above the world. Through them, we are able to discover a broader concept of what it means to be human, what it means to strive and fulfill the dreams we dream and obtain the answers to the questions we ask. We can entertain a host of characters in our minds and be transformed only by those we truly wish to emulate. We protect ourselves from that which we do not wish to acknowledge as ourselves. We see in them what we most fear or most admire. As they function within the context of a literary text, heroes are the avenues to the selves we entertain in our imaginations—a reflection of all the possibilities we envision, both good and evil—and they remind us not only of what we could become but of who we are in our own narratives.

1 THE SHADOW IN THE LABYRINTH
The Universal Hero

I n the storied labyrinths of the human imagination, a figure wanders the twists and turns of the narrative, searching for the solution to the puzzle. He carries with him his courage, perhaps a dagger, and a lifeline that will enable him to vanquish the unimaginable and reclaim his rightful place in the world. But just who is that figure who walks those corridors? What drives him to overcome the obstacles set before him? What allows him to succeed where others would fail, where our mortal fears would overcome us, and where our courage would falter? What does he learn that would enable us to rise to similar challenges? What faith in our own abilities does he inspire? What does he give us that we do not realize we possess? There are as many answers to these questions as there are readers. The hero has more than a thousand faces—he is as unique and individual as each one of us.

What makes heroes so hard to define is that each one is both unique and highly personal. Heroes reflect the values and the personality traits that make us individuals. They represent the dreams we long

---

Alfred, Lord Tennyson, circa 1860, presumably holding a volume of Arthurian romance.

to fulfil and our need to face and overcome obstacles as we proceed to the next chapter. To say that there is a formula for the hero in our literature would be wrong; the broadest statement that can be made about heroes is that they are emanations of what we value and what we find fascinating.

From childhood, we try to put a face on that figure in the labyrinth, although the corridors are almost pitch black and the hero changes shape with every thought. That figure may be protean, but we choose to love him because there is something in him that assures us that our dreams can triumph over the realities we face, and that we can win out over our limitations. The more we listen to stories, the more we become attuned to our own possibilities. The heroes are there to guide us through the passages of narrative.

As a child growing up in Toronto, I loved to hear stories about the past as I put faces to those who had gone before me, and breath to the dust that inhabited the memorial shrines of frames and photo albums. Sunday dinners were the place where stories were shared— some again and again. I never grew tired of them. My favourite was one my grandmother used to tell about three children she had taught at a Chinese Sunday school in Toronto during the First World War. I always loved to hear their narratives because I could relate to the characters in them.

The first child, a young girl about ten years old, came to the Sunday school because she desperately wanted to improve her English. She was precocious and memorized vast passages from the Bible, for which she won a prize. When she was given the chance to choose any book as her reward, she chose a copy of *Gray's Anatomy*. She grew up, won a scholarship to medical school, and became the first Chinese woman doctor in the city. She inspired generations of young women to follow in her footsteps, and became a revered figure in the city for her contributions to the improvement of health and society.

Her little brother had the romantic in him. When he, too, succeeded in the memorization competition, he chose as his prize Tennyson's

Idylls of the King, a nineteenth-century series of long poems about chivalry, honour, and adherence to one's faith. He dreamt of being a soldier, but as he grew up, he was confronted with race barriers in the Canadian army—Chinese need not apply. When the Second World War broke out, he repeatedly attempted to enlist. He was finally taken when he agreed to learn Japanese and parachute behind enemy lines on a suicide spy mission. Of the eight young Chinese-Canadian men sent on the high-risk mission, only he and two others returned. He became the most decorated Chinese-Canadian hero of the Second World War, and spent the rest of his life revered not only in his own community but in Canadian society generally.

The third child, a little girl who loved to participate in the small pageants and plays that the Sunday school produced, was forced to return to China after the death of her father. When she got there, she found it foreign and unfamiliar. Girls were not allowed to participate in public plays, and she wrote to her friends in Toronto that she felt she did not belong. Nonetheless, she persevered. She put her skills in drama to the test when a motion picture company opened in Shanghai. Because of her command of English, she was able to learn the craft of movie-making from the American directors who had come to assist in establishing the studio. She made number of feature films and became the darling of the screen, the Mary Pickford of China. Nothing seemed beyond her abilities. She even took flying lessons in an age when Amelia Earhardt was capturing the imagination of the North American public. Those new skills were most needed when the Japanese invaded China.

The actress's lover, a Chinese film producer, was captured by the Japanese, sentenced to death, and interned in a prison camp. Determined to rescue her man from the firing squad, the actress disguised herself as an old male peasant. Armed with a pistol concealed in a basket, she gained entry to the camp and escaped with her lover to a nearby airfield. She then shot her way onto a Japanese plane and flew it safely to the Chinese lines. Her exploits became front-page news when she and her lover reached Australia, and she sent the press clippings to her friends in Toronto. She had taken a role that would have made for high drama on the silver screen and made it a reality.

The stories of those three children have replayed themselves in my imagination for years, and I have been trying to analyze just what it was about them that fascinated me so. One was a healer, one a soldier, and one a screen icon who lived in real life the parts she had played for the camera. But to categorize them thus does not explain why they were so important to me.

Thomas Carlyle, the nineteenth-century historian and man of letters, struggled with the same issue: How do we define the hero if we approach the problem through the process of classification? In one of the first volumes to address the question of the nature of the hero, *On Heroes and Hero-Worship* (1841), Carlyle simply made a list of figures from the past who had captured his imagination. As a historian guided by spirit and intellect more than by reason, he omitted men of science—perhaps because he saw that science in his own age was still in a fallible state of evolution—and focused instead on saints, statesmen, and lowly types like writers and theologians. He began the book with a discussion of "The Hero as Divinity," which suggests that he placed God at the centre of things, and that he viewed heroes as individuals who yearn for something greater than what common experience offers. Dodging the issue of the Judeo-Christian God, which would have led him deep into a theological quagmire, Carlyle wrote instead about the Norse god Odin—a bearded, justice-dispensing figure from a tradition displaced from Carlyle's own age but close enough in behaviour to conjure the God of his own religion. Still, Odin's daring deeds, in Carlyle's view, suggested that the Norse deity was more like Hercules or Apollo from the classical pantheon than he was the creator-God of Genesis or the law-giving Yahweh of Exodus. To Carlyle, the "consecration of valour [was] not a bad thing!" Heroes, he believed, should exercise self-sacrifice, valour, and violence as part of their social code.

Thomas Carlyle, the father of hero theory, depicted here in his later years in the garden of his Chelsea home on Cheyne Row.

Clearly, Carlyle was fascinated by the ways in which our literary imagination set the rules for how heroes should behave. For the chapter he called "The Hero as Prophet," he chose to consider Muhammad, the founder of Islam. For "The Hero as Poet," he gave us Dante and Shakespeare. For his discussion of "The Hero as Priest," he cited Martin Luther and John Knox, the helmsmen of the Reformation. Samuel Johnson, Jean-Jacques Rousseau, and Robert Burns make an odd trio in "The Hero as Man of Letters." One set language into order with the construction of the first English dictionary; the next redefined man in nature, both physically and politically, and helped to trigger the French Revolution; and the third defended the common man in all his passions and foibles. And finally, for kingly champions, Carlyle, seemingly torn between populism and authoritarianism, chose Oliver Cromwell and Napoleon.

In the end, Carlyle was only able to conclude that heroes fascinate us because we worship them. What his choice of heroes suggests, however, is that he appreciated strong leadership in democracy, even at the cost of democratic freedoms. It appears that he valued faith, creativity, spirituality, and daring. And above all, he admired those who imposed their own unique versions of order on the challenges they encountered. As he cast his worshipful eyes upon these figures from the past, Carlyle overlooked the human element in favour of super-human accomplishments. To succeed is not good enough for the Victorian historian. One must exceed.

Carlyle's enthusiasm was contagious. The lectures that formed the basis for his book were sold-out events, the hottest tickets in London. Everyone, it seems, was fascinated with the question of what makes a hero a hero. There had to be a formula, and numerous writers and scholars became determined to find it. In 1871, the British anthropologist Edward Tylor began to study the similarities among hero myths throughout the world. The ubiquity of the same events in a hero's life—his birth from noble parents, his unusual education, and his propensity for being at just the right place at just the right time to save his people—suggested to Tylor that there *was* a pattern. This triggered a small scholarly industry in search of the "hero pattern" that would occupy anthropologists and psychologists for several generations.

In 1909, Otto Rank, a disciple of Sigmund Freud, became fascinated with the childhood lives of heroes. In *Myth of the Birth of the Hero,* Rank claimed that his actions are largely an Oedipal reaction to his father, and that the quest he undertakes is really an attempt to usurp the father figure. Alternately, Rank asserted, the hero is someone who suffers from latent memories of birth trauma. His struggles in the world are actually attempts to work out the problems he encountered at the time of his birth. The theory works for Oedipus, the unfortunate heir to the throne of ancient Thebes who kills his father and marries his mother. His story, argued Rank, proves that myths are our attempts to work out solutions to the miswiring of the human psyche. Rank's theory is questionable, however. Some heroes do not have their childhood described as part of their stories. In the *Odyssey,* Odysseus' childhood has no bearing whatsoever on his actions. Other heroes are simply presented to the world as adults, like Arthur, who emerges magically from the sea in Tennyson's *Idylls of the King.* Still others, including Beowulf and Moses, are low-born and rise through society by adoption. Heroism, as an expression of what Freud called the Oedipus complex, reduces the stature and nature of the hero's adventures to mere sexual responses to early childhood traumas. The Jungians thought they had a better explanation.

The Jungians believed that the child's forging of consciousness, although itself a heroic act of the highest degree, was something that the hero inevitably outgrew. They argued that the real heroic pattern—the feats, quests, and challenges that heroes encounter—is a matter for adult experience. Joseph Campbell went further, asserting that the hero need not be high-born. This led to the twentieth-century idea of the anti-hero, characters of low birth like Arthur Miller's Willie Loman in *Death of a Salesman* and James Joyce's Leopold Bloom in *Ulysses.* A Jungian himself, Campbell made the case that myth consists of a series of repeated situations or motifs called archetypes, which are engrained on a collective unconscious shared by all human beings.

Campbell defined the hero as "someone who has given his or her life to something bigger than oneself." In *The Hero with a Thousand Faces* (1949), he examined the universal hero as he appears throughout world mythology. He focused on the lifecycle of heroes from epic poetry and myth. The adult adventures, he concluded, not the childhood hurts and desires, are what make the hero heroic. His stature is predicated on the idea that his life is a journey. That journey begins with a departure, a "call to adventure." The appearance of divine assistance marks the character as someone who has been called to a higher purpose. The hero then undergoes a period of initiation, a time of trials and temptations when he learns about himself as a physical being, as well as a psychological, spiritual, and intellectual creature. This preparation period is followed by a great challenge, usually combat with an evil force that seems indestructible. The hero marshals all his skills and talents to solve the puzzle presented by such creatures as Theseus' Minotaur, Hercules' Hydra, or Christ's devil in the desert. Having vanquished the creature and solved the puzzle, the hero returns enlightened to the place where he began, completing the cyclical pattern of the journey.

In a national epic such as Virgil's *Aeneid* or a "romance" like the Arthurian legends or J. R. R. Tolkein's *Lord of the Rings,* the hero sets off in pursuit of his goals, even though he is aware that he may not succeed. The entire fate of a nation or race rests upon the hero's shoulders. There is a period when supernatural or divine beings school him in the talents he will require to complete his task. At this point, the hero is often armed with special weapons. Virgil's Aeneas carries forward the shield that bears the future history of Rome. (Virgil places a special emphasis on this union of individual and equipment in the opening lines of the *Aeneid* when he announces, "I sing of the arms and the man.") Tolkein's Frodo Baggins is given special elfin gifts that will make him immortal and invisible—tools that in a tight moment can make a mere mortal into a divine being. Thus prepared, the hero embarks on a long journey, during which he suffers moments of doubt. What enables him to overcome the obstacles he faces is that he learns from his environment and from himself. The knights in *The Quest of the Holy Grail* discover that heroic action consists not only of what they do, but of what they think. The mind is as much a landscape as the forest or wasteland through which the hero pursues his goal. His inner life is as much a struggle as his outer life.

The period of self-discovery and of learning self-control—a demand that T. S. Eliot places upon his nameless hero in "The Waste Land" when he concludes that the salvation of Western society lies in man's ability to "give, sacrifice and control"—is followed by a titanic struggle with the ultimate obstacle. This obstacle is generally evil, like Tolkein's Sauron or, in the *Aeneid,* the indigenous inhabitants of Latium, who stand in the way of the establishment of the new Troy. The final battle is a savage one, and a great price is paid for the victory. Friends and companions often fall. Losses are sharp, poignant, and bitter. The hero may even lose something precious to himself—a part of his identity. It is the price that must be paid. But the reader, like the hero, is determined that there can be no failure. The hero *must* triumph.

In Campbell's hero pattern, something wonderful yet unique to the nature of stories works its magic on the reader if she or he is willing to stand back from the narrative and watch for it. The reader has psychologically wagered that the hero will overcome the obstacles and provide a resolution that guarantees his own survival and the triumph of the reader's aspirations. Sigmund Freud, in his essay "Writers and Day-dreaming," points out that there is an egocentric quality to heroes in stories. He notes:

> The feeling of security with which I follow the hero through his perilous adventures is the same as the feeling with which a hero in real life throws himself into the water to save a drowning man or exposes himself to the enemy's fire in order to storm a battery. It is the true heroic feeling, which one of our best writers has expressed in an inimitable phrase: "Nothing can happen to *me!*" . . . Through this revealing characteristic of invulnerability we can immediately recognize His Majesty the Ego, the hero of every day-dream and every story.

Freud's point is that in the process of following a hero through a story, the reader blurs the distinction between his own identity and the hero's. He appoints and subconsciously acknowledges the hero as his delegate within the narrative. The hero becomes a stand-in, going where the reader fears to tread. By cheering for him, the reader is really cheering for himself. Everyone likes success.

When the hero triumphs, the story generates a profound feeling of resolution and happiness. When the hero fails, however, and the reader realizes that his delegate has met catastrophe, there is a spontaneous outpouring of grief, a catharsis. This is the moment of tragedy. And yet, a reader will resolutely stick with a story even when the inevitability of failure is a stated fact. In *Chronicle of a Death Foretold,* a novella that Gabriel García Márquez originally published as a serialized journal of an actual murder, the first paragraph states that the chief character is going to die that day:

> On the day they were going to kill him, Santiago Nasar
> got up at five-thirty in the morning to wait for the boat the
> bishop was coming on. He'd dreamed he was going through
> a grove of timber trees where a gentle drizzle was falling, and
> for an instant he was happy in his dream, but when he awoke
> he felt completely spattered with bird shit.

Reality, especially when it involves mortality, is always a hard pill to swallow. The literary imagination of the reader—that zone in the mind where stories come to life—is a spokesperson, as far as Freud was concerned, for our egos, the sense of self that believes the self is immortal.

It is no accident that so many hero stories involve characters who flirt with immortality. The most important and death-defying character of the Western literary imagination, Christ of the New Testament, is the one hero in a broad tradition of ancient heroes who is able to overcome death. The appeal of Christianity and the Christian mythology is based on a faint-hope clause that implies we can live forever by adjusting the way we think about ourselves, the world, and our relationship to forces in the cosmos. Other heroes, especially those in the classical tradition, are essentially failures because they succumb to their own mortality. What makes these characters attractive, however, is that their larger-than-life accomplishments give the reader hope that the hero's success will be endless. The Pagan Classical view of the universe is essentially tragic, whereas the Judeo-Christian world-view suggests that life is eternal, and that everything will eventually come to a survivor's resolution. The end result of mankind's great journey through time is his arrival at a metaphorical home, the proximity to God that was lost at the beginning.

According to Campbell, the hero's journey is complete when he returns home to a world that is eerily different from the one he left behind. In literature, this moment is called the denouement, the point when the reader reflects upon the events of the journey and its outsized experiences to try to make sense of a sequence of episodes that are, individually, beyond belief. Stories do not necessarily drive either the hero or the reader towards moral reflection, but they do push both the character and his observer into making some attempt to understand what has happened and how each has been changed by the events. In this sense, heroes are metaphors for process—for how things change and how the innate mechanisms of human nature evolve in order to survive.

Campbell's observations are quite obvious in the epic structures that repeat themselves throughout Western literature. Although his ideas were based largely on the mythology and iconography of king-ship, Campbell was astute in his ability to see that the patterns of heroic behaviour that are so self-evident in literature have their basis in the fundamentally human spiritual desire to endure and to prevail. When applied to traditional epic or mythological heroes, those fig-ures who inhabit the core stories of religions and national psyches, the pattern works well. The problem with Campbell's theory—and with the various attempts to articulate a hero pattern, whether Freudian or Jungian—is that the identity of the hero has been confused with the events of his story. Is the hero the maker of the story, or is the story the maker of the hero?

The literary critic Northrop Frye struggled, with considerable success, to answer this question in his *Anatomy of Criticism,* a work

*The twentieth-century
critic Northrop Frye as
photographed in 1984.*

that examined the various narrative structures in poetry, fiction, and
drama. Frye noticed, in the second chapter of the *Poetics* (a defining
work that has influenced both readers and authors throughout the
ages), a frequently overlooked passage in which Aristotle observed
that there were various types of characters in literary works:

> Since imitative artists represent men in action, and men who
> are necessarily either of good or of bad character (for as all
> people differ in their moral nature according to the degree
> of their goodness or badness, characters almost always fall
> into one or the other of these types), these men must be
> represented either as better than we are, or worse, or as the
> same kind of people as ourselves.

What troubled Frye about Aristotle's observation was that it conveyed
an unfashionable moral reading of how a figure in a work behaves,
and how the reader interprets him or her. Goodness and badness,

to Aristotle, created a kind of class division in literature. The good people were noble, by their behaviour and also by their birth. Those who were bad were of the lower classes, debased by lack of breeding, station, and education. To counter Aristotle, Frye set about dividing the hero in literature into five key types: the Mythic Hero, the Romantic Hero, the High Mimetic Hero, the Low Mimetic Hero, and the Ironic Hero.

The Mythic Hero is someone close to Campbell's definition of the hero, a figure who follows a pattern of behaviour and tradition. The Mythic Hero is divine or semi-divine in nature—like Jesus, for example, a ubiquitous figure in world literature and world mythology. Because he is not a mortal man, Frye argued, he is cut off from experiencing tragedy and the philosophical and physical pain that is associated with it.

The Romantic Hero, while extraordinary, is still very much a human being, and thus subject to tragedy, suffering, and downfall. This category of hero includes such literary characters as Homer's Odysseus and Lancelot, Arthur, and Galahad, from Tennyson's *Idylls of the King.* The Romantic Hero is essentially a voyager who is tested by events and experiences so he can learn from the pressures of the world and become an improved character. This is what drives characters like Galahad, a figure who represents a model for others to follow.

Frye's High Mimetic Hero is patterned on other, more formidable heroes. He is someone who assumes a leadership role, either willingly or reluctantly, as Jason does in Apollonius of Rhodes' *Voyage of the Argo* or the semi-divine Aeneas in Virgil's epic poem. But what sets the High Mimetic Hero apart from his predecessors is that he is the product of an age that does not believe in or have access to magic or divine intervention. He is on his own. Shakespeare comes close to creating a High Mimetic Hero in *Henry V,* though Henry, following the Battle of Agincourt, is quick to point out that the stunning English victory was the product of God's intervention and not soggy French ground or very accurate English archers. During the very awkward scene in which Henry attempts to woo his prize of war, Princess Katherine, we see that the High Mimetic Hero is at the mercy of his passions. The tongue-tied Harry fumbles his way towards a union of politics and desire, and demonstrates that as a human being he is unschooled in the art of love. What is more important, however, is that the High Mimetic Hero is open to criticism, both from the reader and from other characters within the work. At one point, Henry must confront and address the charges of two foot soldiers who cannot see the virtue of dying for a king's cause. Henry is also subject to considerable scrutiny when he orders the execution of his French prisoners in retaliation for the slaughter of the English boys who were guarding a baggage train. Was Henry V a war criminal, various critics have asked? The question remains unanswered.

The Low Mimetic Hero is essentially the modern anti-hero, a common man who is as much a part of the realm of the everyday as the reader. He is a figure who suffers, who knows life from the ground level. He is Leopold Bloom in James Joyce's *Ulysses* or Willy Loman in Arthur Miller's *Death of a Salesman*. As the most recent of heroic creations, he has his origins in comedy, where he acts as a mirror not only of nature, as Hamlet would suggest, but of the audience. The great contradiction built into this definition is that the Low Mimetic Hero bears little resemblance to previous examples of the hero. His job is to keep things together or die trying. His failures reflect the reader's own shortcomings, and his successes represent a remote hope for happiness that might be enjoyed by all. One example of a Low Mimetic Hero that Frye failed to mention is Dante, the protagonist pilgrim of hell, purgatory, and paradise in *The Divine Comedy*. Dante is more than an observer: he is a common man who has become the most fantastic voyager. The great thrill of his journey is that it takes place in his mind, and his greatest power is his imagination, an attribute that all readers possess in some degree.

The final type of hero in Frye's catalogue is the Ironic Hero, someone low-born who nonetheless endures all the trials and tribulations of the world. He is Huckleberry Finn in Mark Twain's novel of the same name, the idiot child Benjy in William Faulkner's *The Sound and the Fury,* or Ishmael in Melville's *Moby-Dick.* If Frye proved anything by categorizing literary heroes in *The Anatomy of Criticism,* it was that literature, more than philosophy or anthropology, could explain how individuals will react when confronted with a situation or plot dynamic, and how their true natures will emerge as a result of their reactions. But the hero is much more than a mouthpiece for response in literature. Lurking just beyond the boundaries of Frye's argument is the suggestion that the hero reflects the possibilities that lie embedded in the human imagination. Behaviour is only one aspect. Character is only one aspect. The hero is a state of being, a projection of the terror of possibility that exists within the imagination, and the expression of potential that lies within the mind. There is a tremendous sense, as unfashionable as it may be to say so, that the hero is a manifestation of the desires that each of us possesses. And when we identify or sympathize with a hero, we have not only established a form of communion and communication, but also discovered something of ourselves that makes us want to learn more.

Literature is the one of the most concrete expressions of the imagination. It owes a debt to who we are as human beings, and has borrowed distinctly from myths that have been passed down to us through thousands of years. But it has evolved its own life and its own complexities. Western literature, especially its great works, provides us with a catalogue of possible definitions for the hero— definitions that we live with and live through, either consciously or unconsciously, on a daily basis. The common individual, the tragic hero, the dark hero, the infernal, the saint, the demigod, and the deity—each one of the literary types discussed in this book presents us with an image of who and what we are in the landscape of our own imaginations.

In a world that is becoming increasingly individual, personal, private, and less conscious of ritual, the last preserve of mythology appears to be the book and its offspring—television, radio, and film. Literature has maintained and kept fresh the expression of human desires and imaginative structures. It provides us with a spectrum of heroic types, recording their behaviour and showing how the heroic spirit is continually reawakened, regenerated, and reformed.

Anthropologists and mythologists have traditionally explored the hero from the perspective of male-dominated myths, rituals, and beliefs. Neither Rank nor Campbell takes into consideration the fact that anyone, male or female, can be a hero. Despite Campbell's profound and groundbreaking attempts to understand the hero at the core of the universal imagination, his arguments are extensions of theories of kingship and paternity.

The universality of the word "hero" suggests that it is a central concept of the imagination. It is an English word that etymologically remains faithful to its origins in the Indo-European family of languages. The root is the Greek word *heros,* and it carries almost exactly the same meaning and connotations that we see in the word today. When they applied it to a woman who possessed the qualities associated with the hero, the Greeks feminized the word as *heroine.* This feminized version became popular as a critical term, particularly in France during the seventeenth century and in England from the eighteenth century on, when playwrights and novelists began to place women as characters in their narratives. This verbal demarcation between a male hero and a female heroine was a significant impetus for writers such as Charlotte Brontë and Jane Austen, who decided to make their main characters stronger and more assertive than their male counterparts. In *Jane Eyre,* Brontë uses her heroine to assert the equality of men and women. For Jane, life is heroic, and entails taking action against a world that would suppress an individual's identity and thwart the imagination. She says:

It is vain to say human beings ought to be satisfied with tranquillity: they must have action; and they will make it if they cannot find it. Millions are condemned to a stiller doom than mine, and millions are in silent revolt against their lot. . . . Women are supposed to be very calm generally: but women feel just as men feel; they need exercise for their faculties, and a field for their efforts as much as their brothers do; they suffer from too rigid a restraint, too absolute a stagnation, precisely as men would suffer; and it is narrow-minded in their more privileged creatures to say that they ought to confine themselves to making puddings and knitting stockings, to play on the piano or embroider handbags.

By playing against gender expectations, such marvellous characters as Jane Eyre and Jane Austen's Elizabeth Bennett in *Pride and Prejudice* opened a whole new role for women in both literature and society. The distinction between male and female characters who possess heroic attributes became so blurred that by the latter part of the twentieth century, the word "hero" had acquired gender-neutral connotations. This went a long way towards challenging the assumptions of Campbell and others who perceived the heroic as an exclusively male domain. Nowadays, a hero can be anyone, regardless of gender.

Wherever the roots of the classical tradition touched Western civilization, from French (*heros*) to Italian (*eroe*) to Spanish (*heroe*) and Portuguese (*heroi*), the idea of the hero as a semi-divine, outsized human being capable of wondrous achievements rooted itself in the languages. (Even the German word for hero, *Held,* suggests a heroic, superhuman tenacity—the ability to hold on at all costs.) Nowhere is this clearer than in the epic struggle of the Anglo-Saxon hero Beowulf against the embodiment of evil, the monster Grendel. In one of the climactic scenes in *Beowulf,* the hero grips the monster's arm so tightly that he tears it from the creature's body, slaughtering the dreaded beast and preserving the sanctity of society, the meadhall, for civilization:

Then he discovered, who had done before
so much harm to the race of mankind,
so many crimes—he was marked by God—
that his body could bear it no longer,
but the courageous kinsman of Hygelac
had him in hand—hateful to each
was the life of the other. The loathsome creature felt
great bodily pain; a gaping wound opened
in his shoulder-joint, his sinews sprang apart,
his joints burst asunder. Beowulf was given
glory in battle—Grendel was forced
to flee, mortally wounded, into the fen-slopes,
seek a sorry abode; he knew quite surely
that the end of his life had arrived,
the sum of his days.

The hero, in this context, is someone who is capable of defending ordinary people against those elements in the universe that are
beyond their ability to answer. The hero brings order out of chaos,
stands for life (Freud's *Eros*) in the face of death (*Thanatos*). What we
see metaphorically in the stories of heroes is the struggle of life to
overcome death.

The *Oxford English Dictionary* offers four definitions of the word
"hero." First and foremost, it says a hero is "a man of superhuman
qualities favoured by the gods." In that phrase, the dictionary calls to
mind the classical hero who populates the epics and legends that have
so powerfully inspired Western literature. This definition has shaped
our expectations not only of how literary characters ought to behave,
but of how our politicians, our police, and even our sports heroes
and parents are expected to perform. The ramifications of these high
expectations can be felt all the way through literature. Characters
like Don Quixote are both delightful and pathetic as they struggle to
bear up under the weight.

Heroes are individuals of whom a great deal is demanded, and nothing less than a divine performance will do. When they fall short, no matter how noble the cause or how honest the aspiration, they are written off as failures. Merely mortal characters like Frodo Baggins or Jason in *The Voyage of the Argo* are singled out for great deeds because fate or some higher source of authority has chosen them for their tasks and challenges. In answering those challenges, they must, as Virgil's Aeneas does, put aside their own lives, desires, egos, and agendas to pursue a higher purpose. They must abandon all sense of limitation to achieve the impossible. Human beings, after all, are human because they live with their own limitations. To escape them, as the characters of Christ and Buddha do in their stories, is to reach a heroic plateau where life takes on an entirely different function, becoming a doorway between this world and the world beyond. And when this occurs, the hero himself becomes a portal through which we are allowed a glimpse of divinity.

The dictionary also states that a hero is "an illustrious warrior." This definition underscores just how important literature, legend, and oral epic can be in shaping the way a broad term is set in our minds. The warrior hero—someone who is willing to do battle and risk his life for a cause—has come down to the present age as a figure who stands between us and disaster, and who represents our aspirations in mortal combat.

This second definition was driven home to me with bitter irony on the night of September 11, 2001. I was watching a news broadcast of the final moments of New York's twin towers. Firefighters and police were on the scene, attempting to take control of the situation. The firefighters, resplendent in their armoured helmets and gear, some with axes in hand, made their way up the smoke-filled staircases. "They looked," remarked one survivor, "just like Greek warriors in all their equipment."

As the initial shock of the event wore off, I was left with the puzzle of why the image of Greek warriors had sprung into that survivor's mind. The answer lies in the impact that Homer's epic poem of the Trojan War had on the Western imagination. In the *Iliad,* the gods are caught in a standoff and no resolution seems in sight. As Homer's characters, both Trojan and Greek, present themselves on the battlefield to die, they go forward with the awareness that they are the inheritors of the traditions of the Heroic Age. (The Heroic Age is a period in classical literature that begins with Perseus' slaying of Medusa, a beast whose very appearance can turn mortals into stone.) With each successive hero who presents himself in classical mythology—Theseus, Bellerophon, Jason, and Hercules—the assumption grows that individuals can turn the tables on hopeless situations. But with tragic irony, Homer tells us that the grandsons of Hercules, the son of a supreme god, die on the battlefield at Troy. And Zeus eventually trades the life of another son, the almost immortal Achilles, to end the slaughter on the bloody plain before the gates of Troy. What emerges from the *Iliad* is a metaphor of self-sacrifice, the idea that there are those in every society who are willing to die to defend their beliefs, their families, and the things they love.

By dying for others, heroes gain glory. The concept of glory, from the Latin *gloria,* means "exalted renown, honourable fame; adoring praise and thanksgiving." The verb "to glory" comes from a different Latin root: *gloriari,* meaning "to boast." Readers of Norse mythology know that Valhalla, the place of heroes, is "a hall in which heroes who have died feast with Odin." It's a place very similar to the meadhall, the core of society that Beowulf was struggling to protect in his combat with Grendel. In Irish mythology, the afterworld of the hero is Tir-nan-Og, the land of the forever young, a place where youth, plenty, and perpetual happiness abound. The classical equivalent is Elysium, the sacred land that lies far to the west of the known world; that's where all the generations, past and future, come together for games, concerts, and unlimited Roman delights. Death, Western and Eastern traditions suggest, is not such a bad thing. Soldiers, literature tells us, are remembered long after their passing. But in the contemporary world, death is increasingly seen as an end to everything, rather than simply an altered state of being. The omnipresence of science has created suspicious and cynical readers who question whether the idea of the hero as "an illustrious warrior" is valid, especially if he pays for his glory with his life.

Dead heroes present a very different picture in literature. Their narratives are concluded, and yet they take up positions of prominence and high standing. They take on the trappings of divine heroes because they are ritualized and transformed into concepts for adoration and idealization. Their deaths, and what we make of them, cause these figures to transcend reality in our imaginations. The soldiers who suffered the horrific hardships of the trenches in the First World War were treated worse than animals going to slaughter. Yet after they perished, they were elevated by the same society that had once deemed them expendable for the most abstract of causes: God, king, and country. Certainly dead soldiers, in a tradition that can be traced back to Virgil's *Aeneid,* are worthy of remembrance. But Wilfred Owen, in "Anthem for Doomed Youth," reminds his readers that they would have had a considerably different view of the soldiers had they witnessed the horror of war directly and not through the filters of imaginative distance. Like Hercules, whose mortal flaws were burned away by the poison of the centaur's blood in the shirt that killed him, dead heroes assume a kind of inviolate iconographic status. They cross from the flawed realm of the mortal to the objective, remote, and mysterious realm of the semi-divine. In the *Iliad,* Homer elevates his dead heroes by showing readers that death increases the value of an individual, transforming mere mortals into powerful shades that represent virtues rather than inadequate combat skills.

The idea of the transformative power of death carried through even to the early years of the twentieth century; following the First World War, the celebration of dead heroes became a national preoccupation for Allied countries. The poet Laurence Binyon, who had spent the war in the reading room of the British Library, was commissioned to write a piece to honour those who had not returned. The poem he created—"For the Fallen"—has become familiar to us all as part of the annual ritual of remembrance in many Commonwealth nations:

> They shall grow not old, as we that are left grow old:
> Age shall not weary them, nor the years condemn.
> At the going down of the sun and in the morning
> We shall remember them.

Even Binyon's poem underwent a transformation. It is now titled "Requiem" in the plans for most November 11 ceremonies. Binyon had not intended his poem to become a transforming vehicle for the dead of the First World War. He merely wanted to create an Iliadic rendering of the war, to capture the view of the proceedings that had appeared to him as he sat in the British Library.

In the latter part of the twentieth century, the view of dead heroes changed substantially. They ceased being spectres whose presence informed our behaviour and became witnesses who sought to warn us of the thanatic powers at work in times of destruction. Writing from Palestine in 1943, the English soldier-poet Keith Douglas stressed that to write about war, one must witness it directly. Douglas felt that war poetry, the poetry of dead heroes, demanded a kind of honesty that only combatants could bring. For him, reality passed through a sniper's scope, not through the pages of Homer. He wrote:

> I never tried to write about war, with the exception of a
> satiric picture of some soldiers frozen to death, until I had
> experienced it. Now, I will write about it, and perhaps one
> day cynic and lyric will meet and make me a balanced style.
> Certainly you will never see the long metrical lines and
> galleries of images again.

Douglas wrote these lines in the wake of the Battle of El Alamein in North Africa. In writing about what he actually saw, he brought to his poetry a non-literary directness, an avoidance of ritualizing conventions about how the dead are transformed by literature. He opted instead for the reality of a conflict where men killed one another brutally.

In the poem "Vergissmeinnicht," written in Tunisia in May 1943, Douglas recalled coming upon a tank his unit had destroyed three weeks earlier. Inside, he found the bloated corpse of its German driver and a photograph of the soldier's girlfriend, which she'd signed "*Vergissmeinnicht,*" or "Forget me not." Wrote Douglas:

> But she would weep to see today
> how on his skin the swart flies move;
> the dust upon the paper eye
> and the burst stomach like a cave.
>
> For here the lover and the killer are mingled
> who had one body and one heart.
> And death who had the soldier singled
> has done the lover mortal hurt.

As if foreseeing his own death—which came just over a year later, during the D-Day landings—Douglas wrote about the deaths of others, perhaps to understand just what he would soon face himself. For him, the dead were not heroic figures but foreshadowings, and through contact with them, he faced the frailty of his own humanity and came to appreciate the value of his own life. What dead heroes teach us is the sanctity of life itself, and the need for it to be defended and celebrated.

So what else is a hero? According to the third definition, he is the "chief male character" in a story. In literature, this character is often given a gender-neutral term: protagonist. The word "protagonist" is made from two Greek words: *proto,* meaning "first" or "prime," and *agonistes,* meaning "contestant." This would seem to suggest that the hero is someone who finishes in first place, though the story of how the term came into being proves that you could be a protagonist and still finish out of the running.

In classical Greek theatre, playwrights usually took the lead role in their productions. Women were not allowed to act, so all the characters were played by men. In Athens, one of the likely sources for the term "protagonist," dramas were written and produced as part of an annual competition. The lead character was literally the "prime contestant." Not only was the *proto-agonistes* caught up in the dramatic action, as a hero pitted against a fatalistic universe bent on reducing him to tragedy, but he was also competing to have his own play chosen the best of the year. What the hero suffered, especially in tragedies, was "agony," a word that comes to us from the Greek *agon,* meaning "contest." The third definition of the hero reminds us that heroes struggle against the problems and imperfections of the world. Observers of the drama were able to learn from the hero's actions and sufferings while being spared the realities of his pain.

Sophocles, the man behind some of the most profound dramas in Western literature, including *Oedipus the King* and the heroine-centred *Antigone,* seemed to summarize the fate of the protagonist when he declared that "to live greatly is to suffer greatly." Sophocles knew something about suffering. He was forced to give up a career on the stage because his voice was too thin to fill the ancient amphitheatres through the heavy, thick masks—called persona—that actors used to portray different characters.

Donning a mask to represent an alter ego has long been a hallmark of many heroes. From Gaston Leroux's phantom beneath the Paris opera house to radio and television's Lone Ranger or Zorro, heroes have suppressed their own identities and chosen to achieve their ends anonymously. The mystique of the "masked man" caught the attention of the Irish poet W. B. Yeats, who suggested that heroes don

Milton, in a nineteenth-century engraving, dictating Paradise Lost *to his daughters. In reality, the cottage at Chalfont St. Giles, where he wrote his epic, had extremely small windows. Milton did not need physical light because he was blind.*

masks to hide their own inner conflicts and to focus their attention on external duties. Yeats noted, "We make out of the quarrel with others, rhetoric, but of the quarrel with ourselves, poetry."

The essay in which Yeats made his comment, "Per Amica Silentia Lunae," an occult piece composed towards the end of his illustrious literary career, takes its title, which translates as "through the friendly silences of the moon," from a line in Virgil's *Aeneid*. What Yeats sought to examine in the essay was the way that the soul's nobler aspects struggle with the dark animus he called "the Daemon," or what some, other than ourselves, want us to be. The hero, Yeats believed, dons a mask to hide the dark nature lurking deep inside himself. We see that dark hero emerge in such fascinating and infernal characters as Marlowe's Doctor Faustus, Milton's Satan in *Paradise Lost,* Brontë's Rochester in *Jane Eyre,* and Victor Frankenstein in Mary Shelley's *Frankenstein*. To Yeats, these figures were not simply manifestations of the inner turmoil of the human psyche, a Noh theatre of the self. They come out badly when the ideas of what constitutes heroic behaviour become lost in the translation from inner life to outer expression. Yeats writes:

> I thought the hero found hanging upon some oak of Dodona
> an ancient mask, where perhaps there lingered something of
> Egypt, and that he changed it to his fancy, touching it a little
> here and there, gilding the eyebrows or putting a gilt line
> where the cheekbone comes; that when at last he looked out
> of his eyes he knew another's breath came and went within his
> breath upon the carven lips, and that his eyes were upon the
> instant fixed upon a visionary world.

The adoption of a mask or alternative identity explains why some heroes aspire to god-like status. They can become something other than themselves. Supernatural skills assist the hero in crossing that important boundary between mortal mediocrity and divine superiority—think of Superman leaping tall buildings at a single bound. In hagiographies—biographies of the lives of saints—miracles, acts of transcendence, and demonstrations of enormous courage are the reasons certain individuals are admitted to sainthood. They literally assume an identity based on holiness and act out roles in imitation of Christ, according to a text or script.

It is no accident that a form of literature known as lives—originally short biographical studies of men of achievement by classical authors such as Plutarch and Suetonius—became the medium of choice for telling the stories of saints. When the Christian church needed to create an aura of mystery and power around those who followed the teachings of Jesus, these lives became the *acta sanctori,* or "records of holiness." In the thirteenth century, Jacobus de Voragine created the closest thing to a bestseller with a book called *Legenda aurea,* or the *Golden Legend,* which chronicled the stories of those who lived in an exemplary fashion. More than a collection of ripping yarns about martyrs and Christian teachers, the *Golden Legend* could be read aloud in church on the feast of each saint to encourage the congregation to go forth and emulate his or her actions. In this way, saints became role models, the Wheaties heroes of an age before breakfast cereals.

When the Renaissance idea of a human-centric universe gripped Europe with all its energy and enthusiasm two centuries later, authors like Giorgio Vasari turned to the hagiography to imbue the new exemplary figures of the age—artists—with an air of mystery. In *Lives of the Artists,* a work that became a bestseller in the early sixteenth century, figures such as Michelangelo, Leonardo, and Raphael were portrayed as the very best that mankind could produce. They also embodied qualities that the age considered heroic. They became celebrities, talking back to popes and princes, and setting their own standards for behaviour, just as modern movie stars do. Since the Renaissance, lives have served as a handy barometer of what an era considers to be heroic. For Samuel Johnson, who wrote *Lives of the Poets,* the successors of Shakespeare were the heroes of the English-speaking world. For Lytton Strachey, his *Eminent Victorians* were the apotheoses of a society that gave birth to the strange, uncertain, and existential uneasiness of the twentieth century. Even John F. Kennedy got into the act. On the road that would eventually take him to the White House, he penned *Profiles in Courage,* a book that would inspire a generation of young Americans to believe that they could change the world through commitment, talent, and above all, daring.

The fourth definition of a hero offered by the dictionary underscores what Carlyle was saying when he declared that his fascination with heroes was a form of secular worship. The dictionary notes that a hero is "a man admired for achievements and noble qualities." Albert Einstein, the great figure of twentieth-century science and a man himself worthy of the fourth definition, touched on this idea when he paid tribute to Marie Curie following her death. Speaking at the Roerich Museum in New York in 1935, Einstein tried to sum up what made the pioneer of radioactivity such a heroic figure. He said:

I came to admire her human grandeur to an ever-growing degree. Her strength, her purity of will, her austerity toward herself, her objectivity, her incorruptible judgement—all these were of a kind seldom found joined in a single individual. She felt herself at every moment to be a servant of society, and her profound modesty never left any room for complacency. She was oppressed by an abiding sense for the asperities and inequities of society. . . . The greatest scientific deed of her life—proving the existence of radioactive elements and isolating them—owes its accomplishment not merely to bold intuition but to a devotion and tenacity in execution under the most extreme hardships imaginable, such as the history of experimental science has not often witnessed.

In his praise for Curie, Einstein is offering more than a catalogue of rhetorical terms. He sums up the complex nature of the hero. The hero is admirable and noble, he suggests, because she is able to marry intellect to physical ability and a sense of selflessness. Words such as "tenacity," "servant," and "incorruptible" could be applied to any pro-tagonist of myth, and they evoke the Germanic *Held* and the Greek *heros*. Between the lines, Einstein is suggesting that any human being who possesses such attributes can achieve great things: each of us is capable of enduring our own hardships, harnessing our own intuitive abilities, and achieving our own levels of devotion to serve others.

So who exactly is that shadowy figure in the labyrinth? Who is the one moving stealthily with a dagger in one hand and a golden thread in the other in search of the challenge that will test his skill, his strength, and his courage? The answer may lie with those three Chinese children who were my childhood heroes. They answer the definitions of the hero that the dictionary provides and meet the pat-tern that Campbell presents. In reality, however, they were not heroes at all, but simply children who had dreams that seemed beyond the reach of their own immediate circumstances. They had incredible odds to face: a society that spoke a different language, a culture that was resistant to accepting them, and the gap that stood between who they were and what they wanted to become.

All three children grew up and went on to do remarkable things, to live lives that they had imagined into being through the power of their own minds and through their own desires to make their stories into realities. They had fulfilled the hero pattern. They had conquered their obstacles. My imagination attached itself to those children because they were heroes to my scale. They were children just like me. They inspired me because they offered me hope that somewhere in my own journey, I might discover, buried within me, qualities that would sustain me in times of challenge. If they could succeed, perhaps I could as well. After all, in the world of stories and the imagination, anything is possible.

Heroes in literature are not just human-shaped vehicles for dramatic action. In the labyrinthine twists and turns that narratives present, we look for a pair of eyes to guide us through the darkness of the unturned page. We are uncertain of what we will encounter around the next corner. Will it be the failure of the hero or the moment when he learns how to succeed? Will there be loss or resolution? Will our hopes be dashed or satisfied? Will we know the hero once the book is closed and re-encounter him or her in our dreams? When we stare into the hero's eyes, if only for that instant when we are lost in the maze of the story, there is a glimmer of recognition. The hero's face is our own.

2 EVERYONE HAS A PART TO PLAY
The Common Hero

I
n a speech he gave on January 6, 1941, with the threat of war looming over America, President Franklin D. Roosevelt defined the "Four Freedoms" for which his nation stood. They were freedom of speech and expression, freedom of religion, freedom from want, and freedom from fear. The Four Freedoms were the defining principles for Roosevelt's idea of a public service administration, a government that would serve the people. This idea was a direct response to events that were happening in other areas of the world—where the people were serving the will of their leaders, rather than the other way around. As fascism spread across Europe, and country after country fell to Hitler, Roosevelt felt it necessary to articulate a new sense of individualism—a step beyond what the Declaration of Independence and the Constitution had framed. What he envisioned was a philosophy that could be shared by every person in America, and indeed by all human beings. He realized that the world had changed. It was now a place where individuals would be called upon to fight for their own security, their own rights, and their own destiny.

Aristotle, the Greek philosopher, sought to put into order both the imaginative world and the characters who populated that high-born world, by examining the nature of epic and tragedy.

By the end of that year, the United States had declared war, and the country was beginning a long uphill climb in its struggle against the Axis powers. The entire population was mobilized to work towards a victory that would belong to every individual. Everyone had a part to play. While soldiers headed overseas, those at home worked in munitions factories or bought war bonds. Even the arts were enlisted. The conductor of the Cincinnati Symphony Orchestra decided to commission a piece of music to honour and glorify the fighting men and women of America for the opening of the symphony's 1943 season. The conductor, Eugene Goossens, approached a young composer whose populist leanings had already drawn him considerable attention. Goossens wanted the composition—a short fanfare—to speak in musical terms to the enormity of the struggle for freedom, liberty, and individual self-determination that lay before the nation. He felt that never before in history had these values been challenged to such a degree. A new type of music was needed to answer the new heroism that was being called for.

Goossens and the composer bandied about various names for the short piece, which would last approximately as long as a popular radio song. Suggested titles included *Fanfare for a Solemn Ceremony* and *Fanfare for Four Freedoms*. These seemed either overbearing or overly political. At the same time, the composer, a meticulous craftsman, kept redrafting and rescoring the work. The season opening passed, and the piece was still not ready for performance. Finally, the short fanfare for timpani, brass, and gong had its premiere, in March 1943. It was the perfect moment. "I [am]," said the composer, Aaron Copeland, "all for honoring the common man at income tax time." In fact, with a sly eye to his own populist vision of American society, he dedicated the newly christened *Fanfare for the Common Man* not to the servicemen and -women of America, but to those who would pay for the war out of their own pockets: the American taxpayers.

Fanfare for the Common Man has become an anthem for the emergent and redefined hero of the late twentieth century. It speaks to the dignity of common people doing uncommon things to rise above the challenges of a complex world. The piece was played at numerous memorial services following the events of September 11, 2001, as a tribute to those who gave themselves in service to human needs. Copeland viewed the hero as someone who walks among us and, in fact, lives within each of us. This notion—articulated on a grand scale in statements like Roosevelt's Four Freedoms speech and Ralph Bunche's defining principles for the United Nations—was more than just a response to a *Zeitgeist;* it became almost universally accepted in modern society. The question is, how did the common man become a hero?

On February 10, 1949, in the Morosco Theatre in New York, the playwright Arthur Miller first presented his modern tragedy, *Death of a Salesman.* The American stage had never seen a play quite like it. *Death of a Salesman* defied convention even as it echoed all the major notes that literature had been sounding for centuries about the way individuals respond to a universe that would crush them. To watch *Death of a Salesman* in performance is a chilling exercise in shared frailty. The protagonist, Willy Loman, is a weary and life-worn individual who has reached the end of his tether after years of adhering to the work ethic at the heart of the American economy. Having spent his life as a salesman "out there in the blue, riding on a smile and a shoeshine," Willy watches as his dreams of financial and social success for himself and his sons collapse around him. In the second act, he explains to an employer who has rejected him just what his life as a salesman has been like:

. . . I met a salesman in the Parker House. His name was Dave Singleman. And he was eighty-four years old, and he'd drummed merchandise in thirty-one states. . . . And when I saw that, I realized that selling was the greatest career a man could want. 'Cause what could be more satisfying than to be able to go, at the age of eighty-four, into twenty or thirty

different cities, and pick up a phone, and be remembered
and loved and helped by so many different people? Do you
know? when he died—and by the way he died the death of a
salesman, in his green velvet slippers in the smoker of the New
York, New Haven, and Hartford, going into Boston—when
he died, hundreds of salesmen and buyers were at his funeral.
. . . There was respect, and comradeship, and gratitude in it.
Today, it's all cut and dried, and there's no chance for bringing
friendship to bear—or personality. You see what I mean?
They don't know me any more.

Willy's desire to be a salesman is really a profound need to be recognized and championed as a distinct individual, a hero like his own hero. Willy wants to be someone of importance, someone whose actions have meaning to the lives of others. The strange paradox in the American dream is that it tells individuals they can make a difference even as it sets so many on the same course that individualization becomes almost impossible.

Miller sounds the same warning that Alexis de Tocqueville did in *Democracy in America* in the nineteenth century. De Tocqueville, the French aristocrat who visited the United States in 1831, argued that the ultimate product of a democratic society would be mass mediocrity rather than enlightened individualism. A levelling effect would produce a plentiful though uninspiring culture. (At its most frightening, the de Tocquevillian prophecy has produced post-war subdivisions where each house is identical to the next.) To his credit, Willy Loman almost achieves his dream of personal success, but coming close is just not good enough. The tragedy for Willy is that there is no way out of his predicament. He cannot be heroic according to the terms that he has set for himself. What Willy does not realize, but Miller did, is that tragedy is the simple inevitability faced by those who dream and fall short.

Writing in the *New York Times* a few weeks after the premiere of

Death of a Salesman, Miller explained why the play was having such an enormous impact on its audiences. In an essay titled "Tragedy and the Common Man," he theorized that few tragedies were written in the modern era "due to a paucity of heroes among us." Heroes were no longer venerated figures who stood above society (and therefore had farther to fall when their lives came crashing down around them). Pointing to the fact that we live in an age when "the skepticism of science" has drawn the "blood out of the organs of belief," Miller suggested that modern individuals like Willy Loman "are often held to be below tragedy." Tragedy, he argued, is somehow "above us" in the way that the great heroes of classical literature—Oedipus or Orestes, for example—were above the common man. He was determined to change that. He wrote, "I believe that the common man is as apt a subject for tragedy in its highest sense as kings were."

Literary convention from Homer and Aristotle on had always dictated that tragedy was the preserve of the high-born, the kings, princes, and generals who helped shape the fate of nations. But Miller made it valid for the little man—the "low man"—to support the enormous weight of tragic consequence, and in so doing, he proved that a major shift had taken place in the way that twentieth-century audiences understood tragedy. In Miller's own lifetime, most of the monarchies of Europe had disappeared. The fall of a prince became almost a twentieth-century cliché. When King Farouk of Egypt was deposed in 1952, he remarked that someday there would be only five kings left in the world: the four in the deck of cards and the one on the throne of England. The old literary distinction between the high-born and the low-born had ceased to function as a basis for tragedy.

In the classical world, high-born characters had the advantage over those from the lower social ranks. These upper-crust individuals acquired their standing in literature because they displayed both social position and the nobility of mind that enabled them to make the right choices when confronted with dilemmas. In the first book of the *Nicomachean Ethics,* the philosopher Aristotle stated that such individuals were worthy of our attention because they possessed a conscientious nature. Earnest and energetic, they were known as *spoudaios,* "serious," and they set a high moral standard for the community to follow because they not only lived by the laws but also made them. They were the ancient equivalent of role models, figures with natural leadership abilities. In the *Aeneid,* the *spoudaios* character is Aeneas, the Trojan prince who guides his band of refugees through an arduous series of tasks to achieve the security of a reborn Trojan homeland. The gods place the responsibility for the fate of his nation squarely upon his shoulders, and Aeneas remains one of the great moral paragons in Western literature, an exemplum for everyone from Roman schoolboys to Latin-educated Western leaders of the early twentieth century. What the *spoudaios* provided for Western literature and culture right into the latter part of the last century was the notion that leaders were figures of imposing stature, courage, and dedication who lived by a higher moral principle. When they triumphed, they proved that good could guide an individual to great achievements. When they fell—like Oedipus, Hamlet, and Coriolanus—they won the pity of readers because they appeared to suffer as a result of their excellence. (Such suffering is known as tragic irony.) The audience was left with the moral non sequitur of watching noble characters fail for their adherence to principles like faith, goodness, truth, and justice. The sufferings of the upper classes became models for all suffering. As an enlarged or hyperbolized figure who was bound up in events both personally and communally, the *spoudaios* exposed human flaws. Celebrity and royalty, even in ancient times, meant living life under a microscope, and tragedians such as Aristotle exploited this to teach their audiences lessons about the nature of suffering and how people should behave in the face of it. Suffering in this context became the domain of "serious" or noble characters. What was left for the lower classes was the "inserious" exposure of human flaws found in comedy.

According to Aristotle, the opposite of a *spoudaios* was a character of low moral standards, someone who was defined as "slight" or "base"—the low man who is Miller's Willy Loman. The word applied to such individuals was *phaulos*. Aristotle argued that *phaulos* characters were "low" because they pursued small goals rather than great ones. They were concerned with the daily minutiae, the nitty-gritty details of life, rather than with large questions of goodness, love, justice, courage, and truth. They were the Leperellos, not the Don Giovannis; the Sancho Panzas, not the Don Quixotes. These figures could be dismissed as laughable were it not for the fact that they represent something essentially fallible and human. The *phaulos* resides at the heart of Robert Burns's famous poem "To a Louse," where the Scottish bard remarks, "O wad some Pow'r the giftie gie us / To see oursels as others see us!" Comedy is driven by the idea that the common person—the groundling of Shakespeare's Globe Theatre or the workman of Athens—can look up on stage and recognize his own foibles and quirks, and laugh at the exaggerations of daily life. Comedy is not merely about the reconciliation of opposites. It's about the realization that there is something rough and unpolished in everyone: the Freudian ego untamed by the veneer of education or civilizing values.

The comic tradition, as evolved by classical playwrights like Aristophanes, spared no one from the lower ranks of society from its penetrating scrutiny. Classical comic playwrights went so far as to categorize the various types of non-heroic personalities that could be encountered within the realms of farce and social satire. Chief among these was a stock figure known as the *eiron*. He is a clever self-effacer who, through an assumed simplicity, triumphs over the loud-mouthed and bombastic *alazon,* the braggart impostor whose worldliness gets the better of him. The *eiron* is a character who, despite travails and hardships, rises above his situation through faith, courage, and adherence to modest principles of honesty and truthfulness. In *The Canterbury Tales,* Chaucer assumes the position of an *eiron*—someone who appears to be less intelligent than he really is—as he describes the personalities he encounters on the pilgrimage road from Southwark to the shrine of Thomas à Becket. In doing this, Chaucer was drawing on a long-standing tradition in Western literature of masking one's true meaning by appearing to say the opposite. The word *eiron* comes down to modern times as the notion of irony.

Among the other character types to appear in classical comedies were the *agroikos,* a country bumpkin whose churlish yet good-natured observations contain an element of earthy truth; the *pharmakos,* a scapegoat or victim; and the *vice,* a trickster figure. Tom Hanks's Forrest Gump—with his musings on life being like a box of chocolates—is an example of a modern *agroikos.* The *pharmakos,* by contrast, is forced to endure inexplicable suffering, and he evokes pathos in the audience or reader. Herman Melville's Billy Budd endures so much at the hands of his master-at-arms, Claggart, that he eventually lashes out at his tormentor and kills him. Budd's suffering is compounded by a stutter that prevents him from adequately defending himself. The *vice* manipulates situations and relationships between characters to move the plot to its comic resolution. Shakespeare's Puck, from *A Midsummer Night's Dream,* is a remarkably inefficient *vice,* causing problems among the lovers in the enchanted forest, turning Bottom into an ass, and generally giving sprites a bad name.

The *phaulos* are the cogs within the machine, not the grand designers of the mechanism. They are the Mechanicals, or common tradesmen, of Shakespeare's *Midsummer Night's Dream*—men like Peter Quince, the carpenter; Nick Bottom, the weaver; and Robin Starveling, the tailor. It is hard to imagine a world that could function without such people. They hold a mirror up to the common man to remind him that he is worthy of his own humour, and that he should not take himself so seriously as to let matters reach catastrophe. Little people, the assumption always went, did not suffer anything worse than humiliation or indignation. Because *phaulos* did not live greatly, they did not suffer greatly. The painful dignity of tragedy always seemed beyond the reach of the common man.

The *spoudaios* and the *phaulos* dialogue throughout Western literature, usually to great comic effect, though they rarely challenge each other's roles in philosophical discourse. This does happen, however, in Act IV, Scene I, of Shakespeare's *Henry V.* On the night before the Battle of Agincourt is to be waged, a disguised King Henry takes a walk among his troops and talks openly with the men whom he expects will die with him in the coming battle. When the king's conversation with a pair of soldiers—Williams and Bates—comes around to the topic of whether his cause is just, Williams voices the thoughts of many soldiers who deliver themselves for service into the hands of a leader. He says:

> But if the cause be not good, the King himself hath a heavy
> reckoning to make, when all those legs, and arms, and heads,
> chopped off in battle, shall join together at the latter day and
> cry all, "We died at such a place"; some swearing, some crying
> for a surgeon, some upon their wives left poor behind them,
> some upon the debts they owe, some upon their children
> rawly left. I am afeard there are few die well that die in battle,
> for how can they charitably dispose of anything when blood is
> their argument? Now, if these men do not die well, it will be
> a black matter for the King that led them to it. . . .

Henry responds to Williams's concerns with what amounts to a refusal to accept responsibility for the fate of those who have chosen, of their own free will, to serve. "The King is not bound to answer the particular endings of his soldiers, the father of his son, nor the master of his servant; for they purpose not their death when they purpose their services," he asserts. In other words, no one told them they had to be there. This is little solace. Henry then points out that the soldier's fears are those of someone who is answering to a baser

The real Henry V, from an eighteenth-century English engraving.

instinct. He lectures Williams on the faults of being a *phaulos*:

> Every subject's duty is the King's, but every subject's soul is his
> own. Therefore should every soldier in the wars do as every
> sick man in his bed, wash every mote out of his conscience;
> and dying so, death is to him advantage; or not dying, the
> time was blessedly lost wherein such preparation was gained;
> and in him that escapes, it were not sin to think that, making
> God so free an offer, He let him outlive that day, to see His
> greatness, and to teach others how they should prepare.

The Aristotelian idea that the noble life of the *spoudaios* is something that has to be learned has been drilled into Henry. He is the
product of a good classical education, and he holds to the line in the
sand between those who are high-born and those who are low-born.
Luckily for Henry, and for Williams and Bates, the English losses
in the Battle of Agincourt are minimal. The three men live to fight
another day, emerging out of the battle into the comedy of the final
acts of *Henry V.*

The answer that Williams wanted to hear to his question would
not be uttered completely until the twentieth century, when a young
British army officer examined the nature of heroism, glory, and
the conventional response to tragedy in Western literature. In what
remains an *annus mirabilis* in English literature (as the poet laure-
ate C. Day Lewis put it), the poet turned officer penned a startling
number of pieces between his enlistment in January 1917 and his
death in 1918, approximately one week to the hour before the end
of the war. In the course of that year, he reinvented the way modern
readers perceived war, and in doing so, he challenged notions of
heroism that dated back to Virgil, Aristotle, and Homer.

Wilfred Owen never lived to see his work in print, yet he had a
premonition that his poems would speak to future generations and
lay the groundwork for a redefinition of the hero. In a short statement

The horrors of war as evident in depictions of the classical era. Even Mannerism cannot erase the brutality that resides at the heart of epics such as the Iliad *and the* Aeneid.

that would become the preface to his *Collected Poems,* Owen tried to convey to his readers what he wanted his words to achieve:

> This book is not about heroes. English Poetry is not yet fit to speak of them.
>
> Nor is it about deeds, or lands, nor anything about glory, honour, might, majesty, dominion, or power, except War.
>
> Above all I am not concerned with Poetry.
>
> My subject is War, and the Pity of War.
>
> The poetry is in the pity.
>
> Yet these elegies are to this generation in no sense consolatory. They may be to the next. All a poet can do today is warn. That is why the True Poets must be truthful.

In poems such as "Dulce et Decorum Est" and "Strange Meeting," Owen sought to trace and understand the roots of the insanity that was "deflowering Europe." In a letter he sent from France in August 1914, when he was working as a tutor prior to his enlistment, he acknowledged that his role in the conflict would be more than that of a mere soldier. Owen was a dispassionate observer who felt tremendous empathy for his fellow soldiers, and tremendous contempt for

Keith Douglas, the Second World War poet, being reviewed on parade in North Africa by Winston Churchill. The photograph was taken in 1943 by the grandfather of my student Robin Parkes. Douglas is the moustached officer on the right.

the society and the lies of literature that had led an entire generation to its slaughter:

> I am furious with chagrin to think that the Minds which
> were to have excelled the civilization of ten thousand years,
> are being annihilated—and bodies, the product of aeons of
> Natural Selection, melted down to pay for political statues.

Owen's main complaint as an artist was with what amounted to Aristotelian values. The high-minded idealism of the *Nicomachean Ethics*—with its desire to create ennobled young minds that could strive for that elusive status of the *spoudaios*—was simply being thrown away with a blithe indifference that contradicted the core principles of civilization. But what struck him more was the nature of tragedy that Aristotle had outlined in the *Poetics*, and that so many artists from Virgil to Shakespeare had attempted to articulate and redefine through their works. The hero in Western literature was defined by tragedy, and tragedy was defined by Aristotle's reading of Sophocles and other classical playwrights. In the *Poetics,* Aristotle argued that in tragedy, a character always makes an unfortunate and irreversible discovery. That discovery leads to a calamity of catastrophic proportions, a disaster from which there is no turning back. In other words, tragedy is a rough learning process. The inevitable end of a tragic hero is a fall from life itself. During that fall, the protagonist attempts to make some sense out of what is happening, and to convey that sense to the audience as best he can. What troubled Owen was that what he saw surrounding him in the trenches of the Western Front was senseless, and he felt there was no point in offering thought as a response to absurdity.

The poetry, Owen declared, was in the pity. But what exactly did he mean by pity? Surely there was something more to the experience of the trenches than "sorrow and compassion aroused by another's condition"? Owen appears here to be referring directly to what Aristotle had to say on the subject of fear and pity in the *Poetics.* For Aristotle, a number of narrative conditions had to be met before an audience would feel compassion for a suffering protagonist. He wrote:

> Now if a man injures his enemy, there is nothing pitiable
> either in his act or in his intention, except in so far as suffering
> is inflicted; nor is there if they are indifferent to each other.
> But when the sufferings involve those who are near and
> dear to one another, when for example brother kills brother,
> son father, mother son, or son mother, or if such a deed is
> contemplated, or something else of the kind is actually done,
> then we have a situation of the kind to be aimed at.

In one of the most memorable poems of the First World War, "Strange Meeting," we encounter a soldier who seems to have escaped out of battle expressly to offer a philosophical response to events that fall well within the Aristotelian concept of "thought." In the dark regions where the soldier finds himself, he meets a man he'd killed the day before, and together they try to make sense of their situation as logic and memory falter:

"Strange friend," I said, "here is no cause to mourn."
"None," said that other, "save the undone years,
The hopelessness. Whatever hope is yours,
Was my life also; I went hunting wild
After the wildest beauty in the world,
Which lies not calm in eyes, or braided hair,
But mocks the steady running of the hour,
And if it grieves, grieves richlier than here.
For by my glee might many men have laughed,
And of my weeping something had been left,
Which must die now. I mean the truth untold,
The pity of war, the pity war distilled.
Now men will go content with what we spoiled
Or, discontent, boil bloody, and be spilled.
They will be swift with swiftness of the tigress.
None will break ranks, though nations trek from progress.
Courage was mine, and I had mystery,
Wisdom was mine, and I had mastery:
To miss the march of this retreating world
Into vain citadels that are not walled."

A miasma settles over the world of the poem, as if both the characters and the reader are incapable of understanding what has happened. For Owen, reality defied explanation. But he, like many writers who experienced the First World War, realized that culture—and its imaginative voice, literature—had done little to prepare him for what he would see. The maxims that had been passed down in the conversation of literature for almost three thousand years no longer fit the reality at hand. Art had failed to honour reality, and the consequences were horrific.

One of those maxims, a phrase drawn from the Roman poet Horace, was *Dulce et decorum est pro patria mori,* which translates as "It is sweet and good to die for one's country." It seemed a bitter lie to Owen. In the poem "Dulce et Decorum Est," he describes the death of a young soldier who cannot fit his gas mask on his head in time to protect himself from a lethal cloud of chlorine. Owen describes, in detail more graphic than anything Virgil offered, the gasping chokes of the soldier as death overtakes him. He concludes by admonishing those at home, who perceived the war through the pages of literature, for reducing it to a maxim:

> If you could hear, at every jolt, the blood
> Come gargling from the froth-corrupted lungs,
> Obscene as cancer, bitter as the cud
> Of vile, incurable sores on innocent tongues,—
> My friend, you would not tell with such high zest
> To children ardent for some desperate glory,
> The old Lie: *Dulce et decorum est*
> *Pro patria mori.*

The eerie coincidence here is that Horace himself had fled from Pompey's defeat at Philippi, in Greece, to save his own skin. The lie at the heart of the accepted truth is what troubled Owen. His view was that poetry needed to tell the truth, no matter how upsetting or unpoetic it proved to be. Owen's claim that the poetry was "in the pity" sounded a note of shared suffering that was almost akin to American blues music, or what the Canadian poet George Elliott Clarke calls "the philosophy of the cry." Blues, in its most essential form, is simply one common man sharing his suffering with others in what amounts to a Wordsworthian poetic of pain. In her novel *Jazz,* a *cri de coeur* of life and death in Harlem of the 1920s, Toni Morrison recreates a jam session through the voices of her characters.

Like instruments in an ensemble, the characters offer spontaneous emotion to express the pain of life and to warn others of the perils of misplaced beauty. What resides at the heart of Owen's poetry is a soldier's blues, the sharing of suffering to send a message to all who would listen. That message was a warning. His poetry was meant to signal the many ways that generations had been lied to about the nature of war and the meaning of the hero. But as he wrote his preface, he doubted whether future generations would understand what he was attempting to say. For Owen's own generation, the warning went unheeded. The only consolation was the possibility that someone, someday, would listen, and start looking at poetry not as beautiful lies but as essential truths.

The works that had formed the backbone of the classical education, especially the *Iliad* and the *Aeneid,* were translated in such a way as to perpetuate the noble lie that it was sweet and good to die for one's country. The definitions of glory inherited by those of Owen's generation from the Western canon had implied that honour, might, majesty, dominion, and power were good things, no matter what form they took. This misapplication of these abstract concepts, in retrospect, was really the voice of a society demanding that each person assume the mantle of dignified seriousness and behave like a *spoudaios.* And a large part of that preparation came from reading Homer's *Iliad.*

The *Iliad* entered the English language in 1598 via a translation by George Chapman, the same poet who completed Christopher Marlowe's unfinished love epic, *Hero and Leander.* (This was also the same George Chapman whose translations of Homer's epics so impressed John Keats.) Chapman's *Iliad* was presented in a poetic language that was stylish, reserved, and almost ritualistic, with a healthy dose of Elizabethan melancholy thrown in for good measure. The opening lines speak to the relationship between gods and men—a relationship that is, at best, tragic, and that reduces human beings to subjects and victims. Chapman wrote:

Achilles' baneful wrath—resound, O goddess—that impos'd
Infinite sorrows on the Greeks, and many brave souls los'd
From breasts heroic; sent them far, to that invisible cave
That no light comforts; and their limbs to dogs and vultures gave:
To all which Jove's will gave effect; from whom first strife begun
Betwixt Atrides, king of men, and Thetis' godlike son.
What god gave Eris their command, and op'd that fighting vein?

His lines are cast in the alexandrine measure—the hexameter, or six beats to the line, that reflected the original plodding nature of Homer's Greek. Chapman's *Iliad* speaks to the archetypes of the hero pattern that Joseph Campbell articulated, especially the *nekusis*, or the harrowing of the underworld, the voyage into death that plays such an important role in the Western mythos. In a *nekusis*, a word derived from the Greek for "to swim," a hero expands his stature and his understanding by making a trip to the underworld, an experience of death within life. He returns from his journey more enlightened and often bearing a message for the conscious world. Hell, Chapman tells us, is full of heroes, and it's the only real destination for those who are sucked away from the light of life by war. To be heroic, in this context, is to have one's soul torn away.

When Alexander Pope took his turn at translating Homer's epic, he dismissed Chapman's approach as mere Elizabethan theatrics, the stuff of Senecan revenge tragedy. Pope turned instead to a different poetic form, using the five foot iambic line, the measure of discourse and the natural pattern for modern English speech. Pope wanted his version of the *Iliad* to speak directly to readers, to persuade them that death in battle was a good thing, the highest calling of an educated and ennobled mind. This eighteenth-century version is full of high idealism and an awareness of political stratification. It is a class-conscious effort determined to remind its readers that what separates the *spoudaios* from the *phaulos* is adherence and obedience to the social and political structures of power:

Achilles' Wrath, to Greece the direful spring
Of woes unnumbered, heavenly Goddess sing!
That Wrath which hurl'd to Pluto's gloomy reign
The Souls of mighty Chiefs untimely slain;
Whose limbs unbury'd on the naked shore
Devouring dogs and hungry vultures tore:
Since Great Achilles and Atrides strove,
Such was the sov'reign doom, and such the will of Jove!
Declare, O Muse! in what ill-fated hour
Sprung the fierce strife, from what offended pow'r?

The generation of English readers who perished on the Western Front had Pope's translation drummed into them at the grammar schools. The unique, yet sad, fact about the art of translation is that each generation reinvents the original text according to the needs and perceptions of the time. In Pope's case, he had no way of knowing just how his version of the *Iliad* would impact on a generation of Edwardian schoolboys almost 150 years after he produced it. Pope believed, however, that serving a power structure—sacrificing oneself for the hierarchy—was the true path to high personal standards. Order, security, loyalty, might, majesty, dominion, and power were all equated with glory.

The same opening lines rendered in the recent translation by Robert Fagles are as close as modern English can come to expressing what Homer actually said. The Fagles translation does not hide the fact that Homer's poem is about unbridled anger, and how that savage emotion can destroy everything in its path:

Rage—Goddess, sing the rage of Peleus' son Achilles,
murderous, doomed, that cost the Achaeans countless losses,
hurling down to the House of Death so many sturdy souls,
great fighters' souls, but made their bodies carrion,
feasts for dogs and birds,

and the will of Zeus was moving toward its end.
Begin, Muse, when the two first broke and clashed,
Agamemnon lord of men and brilliant Achilles.
What god drove them to fight with such fury?

The frankness of the language and the rhetorical question at the conclusion redirect Homer's epic to its original intention: the idea that human beings, regardless of their class or background, are victims when rage gets out of control. For Fagles, the *Iliad* is not about power or melancholy, but about what happens when order breaks down. This translation carries Homer's poem beyond mere tragedy, and it echoes the warning that Owen sounded during his hectic year of writing prior to his death.

In the larger sense, Owen's death was not meaningless. His warning became a clarion call that was heard by almost every poet of the twentieth century. T. S. Eliot's "The Waste Land" and its companion poem, Ezra Pound's "Hugh Selwyn Mauberley," asserted that civilization was not really civilizing if it was involved in destroying an entire generation. Pound and Eliot—and later poets, like Keith Douglas in the Second World War and Denise Levertov during the Vietnam War—took Owen seriously. They made it their conviction to guarantee that every individual in society was aware of the difference between noble ideas and noble actions.

The other great impact of Owen's poetry on Western literature was that it questioned the classicism that had separated comic and tragic characters. In Owen's view, the war was fought not by chivalric princes or heroic kings in the tradition of Roland or Beowulf, but by weavers, carpenters, bellows menders, tinkers, joiners, and tailors. It was a bloody struggle, and the weight of it had fallen squarely upon the shoulders of the common man. Tragedy was now something that was borne by the masses, not simply by the privileged few.

Perhaps this was what Miller meant when he wrote, in his essay "Tragedy and the Common Man," that in an age without kings, the focus of great literature was "the heart and spirit of the average man." Recognizing the great shift from the *spoudaios* to the *phaulos,* Miller declared:

> The possibility of victory must be there in tragedy. Where pathos rules, where pathos is finally derived, a character has fought a battle he could not possibly have won. The pathetic is achieved when the protagonist is, by virtue of his witlessness, his insensitivity or the very air he gives off, incapable of grappling with a much superior force.

Miller was echoing the same post-war optimism voiced by William Faulkner in the year that *Death of a Salesman* was produced. In 1949, Faulkner, in his Nobel Prize speech, announced that "man would not merely endure, he would prevail."

The potential triumph of the common man engenders an optimism that is peculiarly American; it's a literary note that was sounded most clearly by the poet whose ideas rest at the heart of twentieth-century American literature, Walt Whitman. Whitman's sense of the individual was founded upon the belief that through his verse, he was acting as a spokesperson for a humanity that sought to celebrate itself. In the opening lines of "Song of Myself," from *Leaves of Grass,* Whitman announced: "I celebrate myself, / And what I assume you shall assume, / For every atom belonging to me as good belongs to you."

Whitman's empathetic individualism took America by surprise. In 1855, he self-published the first edition of *Leaves of Grass,* earning himself very little recognition beyond an exuberant letter from the philosopher Ralph Waldo Emerson. Emerson saw in the Brooklyn bard the manifestation of the American spirit—the same spirit he had been searching for in his transcendentalism, a philosophy that recognized the divinity that inhabits both nature and mankind. Emerson's views were influenced by English Romanticism, and in particular by the poetry and philosophy of William Wordsworth,

William Wordsworth, co-author of Lyrical Ballads, *who declared that poetry was "a man speaking to men," and who was partly responsible for triggering the modern notion of the anti-hero as a spokesperson for the common dictum.*

who in his famous preface to the second edition of *Lyrical Ballads* in 1802 had defined the poet as "a man speaking to men." In one of the most important documents relating to the elevation of the common man, Wordsworth declared that he had chosen as the subject for his poetry "incidents and situations from common life," in the hope that he could relate them "in a selection of language really used by men." Low and rustic life, he stated, was where the individual could find "the essential passions of the heart." Wordsworth realized that poetry of the common man redefined the very nature of the art form itself. For him, it was no longer about the idealization of salon subjects, but about the stuff of common experience that could be shared by all:

> Taking up the subject, then, upon general grounds, I ask what
> is meant by the word Poet? What is a Poet? To whom does
> he address himself? And what language is to be expected

from him?—He is a man speaking to men: a man, it is true, endowed with more lively sensibility, more enthusiasm and tenderness, who has a greater knowledge of human nature, and a more comprehensive soul, than are supposed to be common among mankind; a man pleased with his own passions and volitions, and who rejoices more than other men in the spirit of life that is in him; delighting to contemplate similar volitions and passions as manifested in the goings-on of the Universe, and habitually impelled to create them where he does not find them.

In other words, to Wordsworth, a poet was simply a human being living large, emotionally, intellectually, and spiritually. In this context, poetry became "the breath and finer spirit of all knowledge." And any person could become a poet, especially if his aim was to speak for the common experience. That was the case with Walt Whitman.

Whitman, to Emerson, was the idealistic, frank, and enthusiastic embodiment of what Wordsworth had been trying to achieve with his lonely walks through nature and his portraits of unfortunate rustics. And Whitman did not let Emerson down. In "Song of Myself," he dignified the voice of the *phaulos,* describing himself as "one of the roughs, a kosmos. / Disorderly, fleshy, and sensual . . . / eating, drinking and breeding. / No sentimentalist . . . no stander above men and women / or apart from them . . . no more modest than immodest."

To some extent, Whitman realized that he was kicking against a mindset that had been reinforced throughout the history of Western literature. Poets were expected to champion virtue, and virtue belonged to the nobility, not the rabble. To drive home the point that his was a poetry of the common man, Whitman posed for the picture that became the frontispiece of the second edition of *Leaves of Grass* wearing a hat, some baggy pants, and a workman's shirt open at the collar. His stance is relaxed, and his left hand rests in his pocket as if he is listening intently to a conversation he is having with his reader. This denial of formality drew him instant notoriety. So did his almost Eastern-style belief in the richness of the many over the nobility of the few. To Whitman, "the many" comprised countless individuals, each one unique and fascinating to the poet's eye. He wrote:

Through me many long dumb voices,
Voices of the interminable generations of prisoners and slaves,
Voices of the diseased and despairing, and of thieves and dwarfs,
Voices of cycles of preparation and accretion,
And of the threads that connect the stars—and of wombs, and
   of the fatherstuff,
And of the rights of them the others are down upon,
Of the deformed, trivial, flat, foolish, despised,
Fog in the air, beetles rolling balls of dung.

As a six-year-old child, Whitman had thrown his arms around the Marquis de Lafayette, one of the leaders of the American Revolution, when the man had paid a visit to New York. Whitman believed that he was a champion for those who had never been considered important by society. He declared that "all men ever born are also my brothers . . . and the women my sisters and lovers." No one, in Whitman's perception, was beneath dignity.

Several years before Whitman expressed his ideas of democratic individualism in "Song of Myself," an English novelist in a lonely parsonage on the edge of the windswept Yorkshire moors began composing a thrilling tale of romance and adventure among the common people. By 1848, she had penned a novel that would champion the female *phaulos*. Charlotte Brontë's story of the rise of an orphan girl from rags to riches was not new for its time. In novels like Daniel Defoe's *Moll Flanders,* female heroes had triumphed, by luck or by determination, over fear and the obstacles that society placed in their path. *Jane*

Charlotte Brontë, the author of Jane Eyre, *looking very independent following the success of her novel that rescued her from a life of sickness and despair.*

Eyre, however, was different. It is a Victorian Cinderella story, with the protagonist overcoming the obstacles of education, station, and finance through the power of her own will and her own intellect. But *Jane Eyre* is also a fictional platform for Brontë to champion the same rights of women that had been fought for in the previous century by writers like Mary Wollstonecraft. Like Whitman, who sought to celebrate himself and by doing so celebrate the many, Jane Eyre is in search of the abundance of actual and imaginative life that seems to both enrich the individual and define her. During her stern, puritanical education at an aptly named school, Lowood, Jane comes to realize that there is much in the world that is worthy of her celebration:

> My world had for some years been in Lowood: my experience
> had been of its rules and systems; now I remembered that the
> real world was wide, and that a varied field of hopes and fears,

of sensations and excitements, awaited those who had courage
to go forth into its expanse, to seek real knowledge of life
amidst its perils.

Such statements embrace the joy of discovering that a wider realm of
experience exists for those who are willing to overcome their fears.
The political chains that Jean-Jacques Rousseau wrote of in his *Social
Contract* and that Karl Marx mentioned in the *Communist Manifesto* are
metaphorical in Jane's case. They are chains of fear—fear of both society and one's role in it. Brontë transforms the chains from political to
imaginative constraints, the same "nets and snares" that James Joyce's
Stephen Dedalus contends with in *fin de siècle* Ireland. Ultimately, it's
a question of daring. Can an individual step outside the traditional
boundaries of society, and even the imagination, and declare that he
or she is worthy of the enlightening discoveries that Homer assigns
to his *spoudaios* hero in the opening lines of the *Odyssey?* Jane Eyre
and Walt Whitman ask themselves if they dare to discover life, and
both answer in the affirmative.

Jane Eyre is a *Bildungsroman,* a novel that charts the growth and
development of an individual consciousness. It records the liberation
of a mind that wants to dream and see dreams come true. When
Jane is an orphan, living with her unpleasant aunt and her equally
unpleasant cousins, she finds solace in works of literature that reflect
her state of loveless desolation:

Nor could I pass unnoticed the suggestion of the bleak shores
of Lapland, Siberia, Spitzbergen, Nova Zembla, Iceland,
Greenland, with "the vast sweep of the Arctic Zone, and those
forlorn regions of dreary space,—that reservoir of frost and
snow, where firm fields of ice, the accumulation of centuries
of winters, glazed in Alpine heights above heights, surround
the pole, and concentre the multiplied rigors of extreme
cold." Of these death-white realms I formed an idea of my

own; shadowy, like all the half-comprehended notions that float dim through children's brains, but strangely impressive. The words in these introductory pages connected themselves with succeeding vignettes, and gave significance to the rock standing up alone in the sea of billow and spray; to the broken boat stranded on a desolate coast; to the cold and ghastly moon glancing through bars of cloud at a wreck just sinking.

When Jane discovers on the day of her wedding that her groom to be, Rochester, is already married to Bertha, the madwoman in the attic, she flees into a scene of icy depravation and desolation. Snow, ice, and the numbing of the spirit become symbols throughout *Jane Eyre* for the thwarting of her aspirations. Society—indeed nature—seems to be out to stop Jane from making the great leap from her imagination to the real world. Her inner world is in tumult, but she struggles to believe in possibilities, even though the real world constantly crushes her. Brontë suggests that life inside Jane is similar to life in a state of revolution:

> How all my brain was in tumult, and all my heart in insurrection! Yet in what darkness, what dense ignorance, was the mental battle fought! I could not answer the ceaseless inward question—*why* I thus suffered; now, at the distance of—I will not say how many years, I see it clearly.

Time heals Jane's wounds. After wandering onto the icy moors, she is taken in by the kind-hearted family of a missionary, who nurse her back to health. Then, through one of those useful coincidences that populate Victorian novels, Jane discovers that her rescuers are actually her long-lost cousins. The cousins reveal her true identity to her: she is an heiress to a large fortune made from the Madeira wine trade. Jane eventually returns to Rochester, who is now blind, and becomes the eyes, ears, and mistress of the remains of a title and an estate. Jane's Cinderella story is complete. She ascends from the ranks of the *phaulos* to those of the *spoudaios*. At the end of the novel, Jane offers an explanation for her journey that would make Aristotle proud: "I know what it is to live entirely for and with what I love best on earth." She learns how to love and to hold on to what she loves, but above all, she learns how to survive and overcome.

What sets *Jane Eyre* apart from other novels is that it is the story of a woman, written by a woman, where the protagonist is fully drawn and achieves her own declaration of independence through the power of the intellect. The key to equality, in Brontë's view, was the liberation of the imagination in a society that thoroughly distrusted the power of dreaming. Brontë was fighting the vision of an old society, a society that had been taught to perceive the world according to norms and values that had been transmitted through literature. What she challenged was the idea that texts themselves can only venture so far in what they present as viable expressions of the imagination. As writers like William Blake discovered, the imagination becomes dangerous when it challenges the status quo. Yet Brontë—along with other nineteenth-century novelists, like Gustave Flaubert—believed that the best vehicles for expressing the value of the imagination as an active agent of change were fiction, poetry, and drama. Virginia Woolf, in *A Room of One's Own,* sounded this same message almost eighty years after the publication of *Jane Eyre.* Like Brontë, Woolf declared that if women were to achieve equality in society, they first had to make the voices of their own imaginations heard through literature. (Interestingly enough, Arthur Miller had originally intended to title Willy Loman's story *The Inside of His Head.* Miller said that he wanted to show just what went on inside the brain of an average man—the dreams and imaginings that so often seemed to be at odds with one another.)

Those heroes who portrayed the upstart assumptions of the *phaulos* were labelled anti-heroes by literary critics. By definition, the anti-hero is a character in a modern work of literature who displays attributes opposite to those traditionally ascribed to heroes. The anti-hero has been viewed as inept, stupid, at times dishonest, a vagabond, a clown—in short, a *phaulos*. The term has been applied to many characters, including James Joyce's Leopold Bloom—a figure of such common proportions that he would be insignificant if not for bearing the weight of a tremendous narrative. Joyce even made a community of anti-heroes from the characters in *Dubliners,* uniting them through a series of images of the Eucharist, as if they were joined in an act not only of community but of communion, a sharing of suffering. Anti-heroes also populate the plays of Samuel Beckett, especially *Waiting for Godot,* where Vladimir and Estragon, two tramps who seem to have fallen from a Renaissance *commedia dell'arte,* wait for someone of importance to show up. Godot, a shadowy *spoudaios,* of course never arrives. In one of the final and most moving speeches in the play, Vladimir attempts to take stock of his absurd situation:

> Was I sleeping, while the others suffered? Am I sleeping now? To-morrow, when I wake, or think I do, what shall I say of to-day? That with Estragon my friend, at this place, until the fall of night, I waited for Godot? That Pozzo passed, with his carrier, and that he spoke to us? Probably. But in all that what truth will there be?

What lies at the heart of Vladimir's speech is not an ennobling search for truth, but the recognition that his life has been defined by the suffering of others, and that such suffering is shared by the masses, not just borne by the select few.

The modern reinvention of the conventional hero in all its forms—the tragic hero, the epic hero, the infernal hero, the saint, and the super-natural hero—would seem to suggest that heroes are now ubiquitous. And perhaps that is the virtue of the common hero. There is nothing in him that the average reader cannot also find in himself. Common heroes are accessible and speak for the democratized individual, whose

Walt Whitman, depicted here in a photograph from the later stages of his life, when his reputation as a spokesperson for the people had been affirmed by his considerable popularity among American readers.

rights are by law inalienable. In the denouement of *Death of a Salesman,* Charley stands over the grave of Willy Loman and offers a eulogy that could apply to all heroes from literature:

> Nobody dast blame this man. You don't understand: Willy was a salesman. And for a salesman, there is no rock bottom to the life. He don't put a bolt to a nut, he don't tell you the law or give you medicine. He's a man way out there in the blue, riding on a smile and a shoeshine. And when they start not smiling back—that's an earthquake. And then you get yourself a couple of spots on your hat, and you're finished. Nobody dast blame this man. A salesman is got to dream, boy. It comes with the territory.

At the conclusion of "Song of Myself," Walt Whitman implied that the idea of the hero was not so much disappearing as it was dissipating over a very broad spectrum. The common hero, the voice of one among many that inhabits his poetry, had become ubiquitous:

> I bequeath myself to the dirt to grow from the grass I love,
> If you want me again look for me under your boot-soles.

> You will hardly know who I am or what I mean,
> But I shall be good health to you nevertheless,
> And filter and fibre your blood.

> Failing to fetch me at first keep encouraged,
> Missing me one place search another,
> I stop somewhere waiting for you.

Whitman remained steadfast in his belief in the common man right to the end of his life. In his will, he asked that the door of his crypt be opened at sunset each day so that his spirit might walk among the people.

3 TAKING ARMS AGAINST A SEA OF TROUBLES
The Tragic Hero

In 1812, a noted English poet gave a series of lectures in which he attempted to elucidate Shakespeare's more enigmatic protagonists. Although the actual text of the lectures is lost, an auditor by the name of J. P. Collier took copious notes and later reconstructed what the poet had to say. What fascinated him was that Shakespeare created so many characters who called into question the very nature of the hero in a dramatic work. And it was Hamlet who most puzzled the poet:

> The first question we should ask ourselves is—What did
> Shakespeare mean when he drew the character of Hamlet? He
> never wrote anything without design, and what was his design
> when he sat down to produce this tragedy? My belief is that
> he always regarded his story . . . as the ground upon which he
> was to work. What then was the point to which Shakespeare
> directed himself in Hamlet? He intended to portray a person,
> in whose view the external world, and all its incidents

William Shakespeare, author of Hamlet, *caught in a moment of literary inspiration—a rare depiction of the Bard at work.*

and objects, were comparatively dim, and of no interest in themselves, and which began to interest only when they were reflected in the mirror of his mind. Hamlet beheld external things in the same way that a man of vivid imagination, who shuts his eyes, sees what has previously made an impression on his organs.

The point that the poet-critic was making was that Hamlet lives as much in his mind, in his thoughts, and in his words as he does in his actions. And it was appropriate that the poet who wrote "Kubla Khan," a verse about a make-believe pleasure dome that exceeds all boundaries of the imagination, should consider Hamlet in this light. *Hamlet* is a play of the mind, a false creation, a grand illusion that reveals the inner workings of a protagonist's soul. It is about emotional and psychological exposure. It is less about the pursuit of outward truth than it is about the revelation of one's own weaknesses—less about truth than about the process that appears to point towards the truth. In the character of Hamlet, Samuel Taylor Coleridge, one of the great English Romantic poets, saw himself in all his uncertainty and soulful, restless probing.

As Coleridge perceived it, Hamlet lived in "his own disordered fancy . . . conjured up by the spirit of his father." In other words, Hamlet's whole modus operandi is in his mind. And Hamlet, who defines himself as a "dull and muddy-mettled rascal," is the first to admit it:

O, what a rogue and peasant slave am I!
Is it not monstrous that this player here,
But in a fiction, in a dream of passion,
Could force his soul so to his own conceit
That from her working all his visage wanned;
Tears in his eyes, distraction in his aspect,

A broken voice, and his whole function suiting
With forms to his conceit? And all for nothing.

Hamlet knows that his inner world, a world he continually shares with the audience through his soliloquies, is where the real dramatic action is taking place. He thinks his way through the labyrinthine twists and turns of that world, and by the end of the play is no more certain of his situation than when he began. (Laurence Olivier opened his film version of *Hamlet* with a Chorus declaring that "this is a story about a man who cannot make up his mind.")

Hamlet lives in unreasonable times. His uncle is a Machiavel who has murdered his father and married his mother. His home is haunted by a marauding ghost that cannot take off his armour and seems minuteman ready to do heroic battle in the afterlife, even though he was caught sleeping on the job. Hamlet feigns madness, but those around him—his mother, who ignores the reality of the situation, and Ophelia, who has her dreams of bliss shattered by the vise-like pressures of the dark regime—do go mad. As one of the inhabitants of Elsinore declares, "Something is rotten in the state of Denmark."

Elsinore is a site of displacement, a decaying ruin where inaction reigns. Claudius has displaced Hamlet's father as king, and Hamlet has been displaced from his birthright by his uncle. He is a *spoudaios* who has been reduced to the role of a *phaulos* and is in need of some other means of relating to himself.

The worst that can be said of *Hamlet* is that it's about four and a half hours long, if the director chooses to present the unabridged text of the play. But in those four and a half hours, Shakespeare offers a commentary on the very nature of tragedy. *Hamlet* is, in essence, a tragedy about tragedies. At the heart of the drama is an individual engaged in one of the greatest epistemological wrestling matches in literature. Hamlet not only studies an idea but wants to know how

The acclaimed nineteenth-century actor Edwin Booth, here portraying the character of Hamlet, one of his most famous roles. Booth's brother, John Wilkes Booth, was responsible for running amok in Ford's Theatre in April 1865 and assassinating Abraham Lincoln.

he knows it, and he constantly deconstructs the reality around him both as a matter of play and as a matter of introspection. In his most famous speech, Hamlet muses on the nature of his own existence:

> To be, or not to be—that is the question:
> Whether 'tis nobler in the mind to suffer
> The slings and arrows of outrageous fortune,
> Or take arms against a sea of troubles
> And by opposing end them. To die, to sleep—
> No more—and by a sleep to say we end
> The heart-ache, and the thousand natural shocks
> That flesh is heir to. 'Tis a consummation
> Devoutly to be wished. To die, to sleep—
> To sleep—perchance to dream: ay, there's the rub,
> For in that sleep of death what dreams may come
> When we have shuffled off this mortal coil,
> Must give us pause. There's the respect
> That makes calamity of so long life.

The language or diction of Hamlet's speech—his actual choice of words—is the most puzzling aspect. He raises the question of "outrageous fortune," the challenge and heartbreak of "the thousand natural shocks / That flesh is heir to," and examines the nightmare of a reality beyond the commonplace of the here and now, the vision of "what dreams may come" in the world of disaster and death. He uses the word "suffer" because he sees himself as a victim, someone on the receiving end of misfortune. And he blames his own foibles and weaknesses for what is happening to him. Shakespeare is defining through Hamlet the tragic hero, the type of character who unwittingly finds himself on a collision course with a catastrophe he often cannot see. The tragic hero in literature can be likened to a pilot who is trying to fly an aircraft through a thick fog.

The tragic hero, by Shakespeare's definition, is someone who bears

. . . the whips and scorns of time,
Th' oppressor's wrong, the proud man's contumely
The pangs of despised love, the law's delay,
The insolence of office, and the spurns
That patient merit of th' unworthy takes,
When he himself might his quietus make
With a bare bodkin? Who would the fardels bear,
To grunt and sweat under a weary life,
But that the dread of something after death,
The undiscovered country, from whose bourn
No traveller returns, puzzles the will,
And makes us rather bear those ills we have
Than fly to others that we know not of?

Hamlet recognizes that he is a tragic hero who has found himself misplaced in a non-tragic universe—a Christian world of grace and redemption, where suicide and resignation are options only if one wishes to be punished in the afterlife. Like Job in the Old Testament, Hamlet knows he cannot simply curse God and die. There is no option but to suffer. And his suffering occurs in his mind.

What Hamlet realizes—just as Shakespeare himself did when he struggled with plays like *King Lear* and *Othello*—is that tragedy is a paradox in the Judeo-Christian universe. The tragic event should never happen because the whole universe is geared towards acceptance, salvation, and redemption. Tragedy offers none of these. In the classical universe, there was no divine grace—there was only fortune. And fortune—whether the whims of the gods, the capriciousness of coincidence, or the jagged path of destiny—was highly circumstantial and very rarely favourable. In the classical universe, a protagonist expected to be a victim because heaven was a disordered and dysfunctional realm, and the consequences of living under the yoke of a heaven without

Cordelia stands over her sleeping father, King Lear, in this depiction of a nineteenth-century production of Shakespeare's play.

grace, mercy, or compassionate justice were borne by those on earth. As the Chorus in Sophocles' *Antigone* laments, "For mortals to greatly live is greatly to suffer." Such was the nature of the classical universe.

Shakespeare is faced with a serious problem. He wants to present his audience with the structures and ingredients of classical tragedy, but those same audience members live in the non-tragic Judeo-Christian universe, where the presence of a benevolent God prevents the dismal and obsolete finality of tragedy from taking hold. Looming over Shakespeare's shoulder is *The Consolation of Philosophy* by Boethius. The late Roman philosopher argued that the universe was not a tragic place, and that a loving and protective God oversaw everything. That God dispensed grace, and would ensure that no one met with the dreadful finality of tragedy as long as he worked with the laws of nature and morality. To Boethius, "All fortune, whether pleasant or adverse . . . is good."

But tragedy, in the Sophoclean sense, turns on the presence of misfortune, the "sea of troubles" that Hamlet speaks of. To "take arms" against such challenges, the tragic hero must have a kind of faith, a determination to make order of the chaos. Boethius appears to be a type of Pollyanna, an eternal optimist whose beliefs fly in the face of the circumstances that, to Aristotle, make tragedy possible. He argues,

> Often it happens that supreme power is given to good men so
> that the exuberance of wickedness may be checked. Others
> receive a mixture of good and bad fortune according to their
> quality of mind. Providence stings some people to avoid
> giving them happiness for too long, and others she allows to
> be vexed by hard fortune to strengthen their virtues of mind
> by the use and exercise of patience.

Boethius seems to be saying that what does not kill us can make us stronger. This is of little compensation to the philosophical Hamlet, who returns from a German education in Christian Renaissance philosophy to find himself fatherless, dispossessed of his birthright, and in mortal fear of his own uncle, Claudius. What preoccupies his mind is the fear of suffering and the struggle to come to terms with the problems of living in a foul universe where calamities can occur. Boethius's book *The Consolation of Philosophy* again appears to be percolating beneath the surface of Hamlet's mind:

> Some people are excessively afraid of suffering for which
> they have the endurance; others are full of scorn for suffering
> they cannot in fact bear. Both kinds she [Fortune] brings to
> self-discovery through hardship. Some men at the price of a
> glorious death have won fame that generations will venerate;
> some indomitable in the face of punishment have given others
> an example that evil cannot defeat virtue. There is no doubt
> that it is right that these things happen, that they are planned
> and that they are suited to those to whom they actually happen.

The idea that tragedy is tailored to an individual does not sit well with the Danish prince, and he laments the great uncertainty he struggles with as he faces the paradox of tragedy within the Judeo-Christian context of providential reassurance:

Thus conscience does make cowards of us all,
And thus the native hue of resolution
Is sicklied o'er with the pale cast of thought,
And enterprises of great pitch and moment
With this regard their currents turn awry
And lose the name of action.

As a drama, *Hamlet* is all thought and very little action. It's about a character who is trying to solve the problems of evil in a world where providence is supposed to be the operative principle. Hamlet uses his head, but very little else.

Shakespeare, in what almost seems an act of mercy, finishes the play with a duel that leaves four of the principals dead on the stage. It is a messy end, dramatically speaking, for one of the greatest tragedies in the English language. Shakespeare, however, would not have seen his play as an awkward drama. With Aristotle's *Poetics* likely open in front of him, the Bard decided to redefine tragedy and the tragic hero by examining the tragic recipe and deciding if there were elements he could do without. "Tragedy," Aristotle states in the *Poetics,* "is a representation of an action that is worth serious attention, complete in itself, and of some amplitude; in language enriched by a variety of artistic devices appropriate to the several parts of the play; presented in the form of action, not narration; by means of pity, fear and bringing about the purgation of such emotions." He goes on to note that tragedy has six constituent elements: plot, character, thought, diction, spectacle, and song. *Hamlet* is rich in character; heavy on thought; revealing, if not illuminating, in diction; and short on plot, spectacle, and song.

As Aristotle saw it, a person who showed up at the theatre to watch a tragedy knew that something dreadful was going to happen. Against despair, that same person would wait out the play in the hope that things would not end badly for the protagonist. Shakespeare, however, believed that no theatre-goer should sit through a play merely to see what happens; the other elements of the drama were, in his mind, just as important as a good story. Still, to Elizabethan audiences, *Hamlet* must have been a supreme letdown. They were expecting blood, guts, gore, and action. Instead, Shakespeare staged the first murder of the play, that of Polonius, behind a tapestry. The death of Ophelia happens offstage, and the audience hears about it only second-hand. Even Hamlet's battles with the pirates in the English Channel are recounted as a traveller's tale. In fact, throughout the play, Shakespeare promises spectacle, heightens the audience's anticipation of a grand and shocking event, and then delivers a mere verbal account. But he cannot be faulted for using words rather than actions to convey information. He appears to have been working from the Sophoclean premise that horrific events—Jocasta's hanging, Oedipus's blinding—should take place offstage and be conveyed merely through description. (One of the many paradoxes in *Hamlet* is that while much of the play is language without action, the dumb show is action without language.)

The story of Hamlet was first recounted in the twelfth century in the *Historica Danica* by the chronicler Saxo Grammaticus. It described the actions of a Danish prince, Amlethus, who one night in a fit of madness slaughtered his entire family. The story entered the English imagination in the late 1500s via a French translation of Grammaticus' work by François de Belleforest. His *Histoires Tragiques* was a collection of tales that followed Aristotle's prescription for tragic heroes to the letter. In the *Poetics,* Aristotle noted that for the tragic hero, "The change in fortune will [be] . . . from prosperity to misery, and it will be due not to depravity, but to some great error either in such a man as I have described [a tragic hero] or in one better than this, but not worse." Aristotle was suggesting that the tragic hero is not necessarily insane when he commits his unspeakable action, but instead is driven to it out of a misplaced sense of good. Othello murders Desdemona to defend his own honour. Odysseus slaughters all Penelope's suitors and then hangs their mistresses to re-establish order in Ithaca. De Belleforest, too, seems to imply that the real-life Danish prince must have had some perceptible element of goodness; without that, there would be no sense in telling his story. (This was, of course, the age before tabloid journalism.) He appears to have invented the idea that the mad prince was simply taking revenge for the usurpation of his father's crown, and that the entire Danish household was somehow complicit in the overthrow of lawful order. In his mind, Hamlet's actions, no matter how bloody, were motivated by justice and a desire to re-establish order.

The first, anonymous version of *Hamlet,* dubbed the "Ur-Hamlet" by scholars and Shakespeare critics, appears to have arrived on the English stage in the 1580s, and was a tremendous hit. The Elizabethan audience's thirst for spectacle was unquenchable, and the Ur-Hamlet, according to all accounts, gave them what they came for. The Hamlet story, as a revenge cycle rather than a parable about justice or the struggle for political power, likely inspired Thomas Kyd in 1592. Kyd's play *The Spanish Tragedy,* a veiled recounting of the same story, describes the usurpation of a royal crown and the ways by which the rightful heir to the throne attempts to reinstate his birthright. The play even contains a character named Horatio, who is murdered and hanged from a tree, and a play within the play, where the truth is revealed in miniature. The play within the play concludes with a bloody battle—more gory than tragic—in which the attempted usurper, Balthazar, is murdered and his accomplice, Hieronimo (a Polonius figure), takes his own life.

With these antecedents, it's no wonder that Shakespeare's audiences thought they were in for a good blood-and-guts drama when they arrived at the theatre to watch *Hamlet.* Instead, the Bard gave them a play that delays spectacle to the point of exasperation. Even more intriguing, he gave them a protagonist who is a study in ambivalence. Just when the audience believes Hamlet is a seeker of justice, someone out to serve the interests of his murdered father, he mistreats Ophelia and murders Polonius. It's as if Shakespeare was caught between his desire to portray a protagonist with good qualities and the desire to depict just how a thinking Renaissance man would react if the world around him came undone.

In *Hamlet,* Shakespeare appears to be struggling with Aristotle's definition of the tragic hero and with the constraints of dramatic theory (still the cornerstone, in Shakespeare's time, of a successful drama). Aristotle wrote in the *Poetics* that to be believable enough to engage the audience in the action of the play, a tragic hero must possess four basic qualities: he had to be appropriate, lifelike, consistent, and good. To be "appropriate," he had to be true to what the audience expected of him. "Lifelike" meant that the audience members had to be able to see something of themselves—even the briefest hints of familiarity—in the hero. To be "consistent," he had to behave according to the traits of his personality and could not suddenly act in a way that would seem out of character. But Aristotle's chief concern had to do with the hero's "goodness." Goodness was perceived as the necessary ingredient in nobility—the core element that separated a *spoudaios* from a *phaulos,* and eventually a hero from an anti-hero.

As Aristotle perceived it, goodness was not merely a matter of moral virtue, but a sense of verbal elegance and a refinement of judgment and mind. Hamlet, until his mistreatment of Ophelia, appears to be a good character, a philosophical figure whose reasoning raises great, universal questions about the nature of life and truth. When he tells Ophelia to "get thee to a nunnery"—slang for a brothel—she is shocked that Hamlet has fallen so far from grace:

O, what a noble mind is here o'erthrown!
The courtier's, soldier's, scholar's, eye, tongue, sword,

Th' expectancy and rose of the fair state,

The glass of fashion and the mould of form,

Th' observed of all observers, quite quite down!

For Ophelia, Hamlet is no longer the model courtier, the poet of the mind and the textbook example of decorous, courtly behaviour who would have made Baldesarre Castiglione (author of the Renaissance text *The Book of the Courtier*) proud. This, in effect, is the first tragic fall for Hamlet, and the shock of it is borne by Ophelia, who can only look at her hero in dismay and reflect on how the change in his personality will impact her status as an eligible young woman. She exclaims "O, woe is me / T' have seen what I have seen, see what I see!" The moment is a surprise for the audience as well. Hamlet's wrath, while induced by the stress he is under, seems misplaced.

The hero, to hold the audience's attention and win their sympathy, had to be a thinking man who could philosophize his way through the "slings and arrows of outrageous fortune." In Chapter 15 of the *Poetics,* Aristotle states:

> First and foremost, the characters should be good. Now
> character will be displayed, as I have pointed out, if some
> preference is revealed in speech or action, and if it is a
> preference for what is good the character will be good.
> There can be goodness in every class of person; for instance,
> a woman or a slave may be good, though one is possibly an
> inferior being and the other in general an insignificant one.

To say that all characters in a play have some redeeming quality pleads for a leap of understanding among most audience members. The world that drama reflects simply is not built that way. What Aristotle is asking for is closer to what modern audiences would consider an "open hearing" for each character. Shakespeare, however, builds this feature into the character of Claudius, who is struggling to pray when

Hamlet attempts to assassinate him. In soliloquy, he confesses his sin of murder not to God but to the audience. Claudius' admission of guilt mitigates the evil in his character to some degree. But however hard he attempts to pray, he is haunted by his own emptiness:

> But, O, what form of prayer
> Can serve my return? "Forgive me my foul murder"?
> That cannot be, since I am still possessed
> Of those effects for which I did the murder,
> My crown, mine own ambition, and my queen.
> May one be pardoned and retain th' offense?
> In the corrupted currents of this world
> Offense's gilded hand may shove by justice,
> And oft 'tis seen the wicked prize itself
> Buys out the law . . .
> There is no shuffling; there the action lies
> In his true nature, and we ourselves compelled,
> Even to the teeth and forehead of our faults,
> To give in evidence. What then? What rests?
> Try what repentance can. What can it not?
> Yet what can it when one cannot repent?
> O wretched state! O bosom black as death!

In a world of "corrupted currents," where appearances are the foundation of power, what is seen can be deceiving at the best of times, and goodness is only an illusion. Hamlet, believing that Claudius' soul will go to heaven if he is killed while communicating with God, backs off from murdering his uncle at that point. But the irony is that what appears to be prayer is not prayer itself, and Hamlet misses his opportunity for a swift vengeance.

The second major assertion Aristotle makes is that the tragic hero must possess traits that are appropriate to his character. Aristotle is rather cryptic about this matter, and suggests that what is "appropriate" is a matter of gender. "A character may possess manly qualities," he writes, "but it is not appropriate that a female character should be given manliness or cleverness." The premise behind Aristotle's argument is that audiences anticipate that characters will behave according to their expectations. The tragic hero is worthy of an audience's attention because he is dignified, restrained, and philosophical about events, even in the face of tremendous disaster. He is expected to keep his head when all about him are losing theirs—except during that moment of calamity, when the shock of the revealed truth is too much for any human being to bear. In *Oedipus the King,* from Sophocles' *Theban Plays* (the model on which Aristotle bases his assertions), Oedipus declares that he is a "child of Fortune" as he struggles with the revelation of his birth and identity. Despite learning that he has murdered his father and married his mother, he assumes a dignified responsibility for his situation, saying, "Born thus, I ask to be no other man / Than that I am, and *will know who I am.*" Then he quietly leaves the stage and blinds himself so he can no longer look upon a world so full of illusions and lies. His intellectual blindness is transformed into a physical blindness, and paradoxically, he at last sees the truth of himself.

Oedipus lives in a universe that is essentially contradictory: what he sees is not the truth, and what he cannot see is the reality behind events. The Chorus laments this state of illusion and disillusion:

All the generations of mortal man add up to nothing!
Show me the man whose happiness was anything more
    than illusion
Followed by disillusion. . . .

What is dignified about Oedipus is that he had the presence of mind not to blind himself in front of the audience and the Chorus, and lower the dramatic action to the level of cheap sensationalism. Indeed, his suffering is enlarged rather than diminished because it is set offstage, in the realm of the imagination. The idea that presentation has its limits is as old as the Greek stage, and suggests that the work the audience does with the action is far more important than anything a direct depiction can offer.

Shakespeare does not directly address the issue of appropriateness in these terms in *Hamlet* (though he does confront it in many of his comedies, where women often disguise themselves as men). Instead, the idea of appropriateness becomes clear through Hamlet's behaviour. A tragic hero is expected to take action even if that action fails. But even Hamlet doubts his position as a tragic, highborn character, projecting himself into the role of someone far beneath his station and his dramatic responsibilities:

> O, what a rogue and peasant slave am I!
> Is it not monstrous that this player here,
> But in a fiction, in a dream of passion,
> Could force his soul so to his own conceit
> That from her working all his visage wanned;
> Tears in his eyes, distraction in his aspect,
> A broken voice, and his whole function suiting
> With forms to his conceit? And all for nothing,
> For Hecuba!
> What's Hecuba to him or he to Hecuba,
> That he should weep for her? What would he do
> Had he the motive and the cue for passion
> That I have? He would drown the stage with tears
> And cleave the general ear with horrid speech,
> Make mad the guilty and appall the free,
> Confound the ignorant, and amaze indeed
> The very faculties of eyes and ears.
> Yet I,
> A dull and muddy-mettled rascal, peak
> Like John-a-dreams, unpregnant of my cause,
> And can say nothing. No, not for a king,

Upon whose property and most dear life
A damned defeat was made. Am I a coward?
Who calls me villain? breaks my pate across?
Plucks off my beard and blows it in my face?
Tweaks me by the nose? gives me the lie i' th' throat
As deep as to the lungs? Who does me this?

Hamlet cannot bring himself to recognize that he is master of his own destiny, at least to some small degree. Instead, he chooses to debate himself into the position of a victim because it is the only position open to a tragic protagonist. Shakespeare seems to suggest that victimization is an appropriate position for all tragic heroes because they respond to events through thought. Hamlet debates action, recoiling from precipitous moments when a single act, such as the killing of Claudius at prayer, would change the meaning of the play and also his world. The fact that action is replaced by consideration and plot superseded by thought suggests that Shakespeare knew he could play with definitions and limits, just as he was playing with and reinventing the six elements of tragedy. In Shakespeare's time, a prince was, by the rules of politics, someone who could and should control his own destiny, so the Bard places Hamlet in a position where he was unable to do so. This is a situation that confronts many of Shakespeare's tragic heroes. King Lear, for example, throws his power away for the sake of flattery, and as a result, his entire play is set in a negative universe, both dynamically and linguistically.

Shakespeare recognizes that calamity—what Aristotle terms "reversal," where the character's world becomes the opposite of what he expects—is a means of portraying appropriate behaviour in an inappropriate environment. In a Shakespearean tragedy—like *Coriolanus*, for example—the quick route to catastrophe is to live up to the expectations of being oneself. The universe of *Hamlet* is disordered and operating in an inappropriate manner, and in that context, appropriate behaviour becomes the blazon of absurdity. The only thing in *Hamlet* that is true to life is death. In Act V, Scene i, as Hamlet and Horatio watch the gravedigger, the Clown, work on what will be Ophelia's final resting place, the prince muses on the universal "appropriateness" of death—the one thing in Elsinore that can be said to live up to its billing. He asks,

> Why may not imagination trace the noble dust of Alexander till a
> find it stopping a bunghole? . . . Alexander died, Alexander
> was buried, Alexander returneth to dust; the dust is earth;
> of earth we make loam; and why of that loam whereto he was
> converted might they not stop a beer barrel?
> Imperious Caesar, dead and turned to clay,
> Might stop a hole to keep the wind away.
> O, that that earth which kept the world in awe
> Should patch a wall t' expel the winter's flaw!

At the root of this absurdity proposition, which ends with a mocking ditty about the frailty of all power, is the idea of wisdom. There are echoes in this speech of Ecclesiastes 3: "To everything there is a season, and a time to every purpose under the heaven." The Bible suggests that there is an accepted structure to the universe that a human being cannot escape, and the motto "live with it" is the only appropriate course of action. The acceptance of the way things are (the fundamental principle behind wisdom), and the finality that comes with such an outlook, can be reassuring in the Judeo-Christian universe, which is run by a loving God. But in the context of a Pagan Classical universe, acceptance borders on resignation and defeat. What is noble about Hamlet is that his mind, his sole source of dramatic energy, refuses to accept things as they are; the tragedy is that he does not change the things he can, and he does not possess the wisdom to know the difference. The result is that appropriateness is translated into an absurd, purgatorial existence. The protagonist lives in hope of something better, but he cannot define what that might be or how he will get there.

In *Hamlet,* Shakespeare takes this concept of absurdity in earnest. Things do *not* make sense. A ghost appears on the battlements of the castle and presents the digressional information needed to move the plot forward. He explains, for instance, that the royal lineage passes from brother to brother, rather than from father to son. The more things fail to make sense, the more Hamlet attempts to explain them, like a student who has not studied for his exam and tries to fake the answers. Life, in this instance, *is* the test. Aristotle, rationalist observer that he was, would likely have cast a disparaging eye on the more inexplicable aspects of *Hamlet.* The presence of the absurd is not Shakespeare's homage to Aristotle but a nod to Roman tragedy, particularly as practised by the philosopher and playwright Seneca. Senecan tragedy, as opposed to Aristotelian or Sophoclean tragedy, leaves nothing to the imagination. In his rendering of the Oedipus story, for example, Seneca kept the blood and violence onstage, and his audiences loved it. Put simply, Senecan tragedy is the tragedy of revenge, where a father must avenge his son or a son his father. It usually includes supernatural forces, ghosts whose appearance is beyond the limits of reason. The fact that Hamlet believes the apparition that appears on the battlements of Elsinore should, by logic, cast the whole play under suspicion. But the presence of the supernatural sets the tone for Hamlet's ruminations on the nature of existence, and places the play in a purgatorial world between life and death. *Hamlet* and its protagonist teeter between Sophoclean and Senecan tragedy.

Shakespeare had to have been swayed by Kyd's *Spanish Tragedy,* with its brash sense of Aristotelian spectacle, and he constantly worked against turning *Hamlet* into a gore show. There is a sense in the play that Shakespeare is attempting to serve two masters at once. On the one hand, he's trying to meet his audience's demands for spectacle. On the other, he wants to create an aesthetic commentary on the work of Aristotle, who defined the conditions for making literature important and lasting. Should he play to the groundlings or the gallery? Shakespeare found his answer in Seneca's play *Octavia,* a work that had appeared in English translation in 1581. *Octavia* was a very odd play for Seneca to write. It is an exposé of court life in the palace of Nero—a first-hand account from Seneca, Nero's tutor and adviser—that offers a glimpse of the madness that possessed the corrupted *spoudaios* of Rome's imperial family. Octavia, the first wife of the emperor, realizes that her time in the court is limited. Nero has found a new lover and wishes to marry her. A divorce would be scandalous, so the emperor tries to terrify his wife into renouncing her matrimonial claim by murdering those around her. As Octavia laments the mysterious death of her brother, his ghost appears to her in a dream:

> When sleep has come to soothe my weary limbs
> And close these ever-weeping eyes, my brother's
> Spirit in woeful form has come before me.
> Sometimes his helpless hands aim angry blows
> With smoking torches at his brother's face;
> Sometimes he flees in panic to my chamber,
> And while I cling to him, the enemy
> Comes on, to thrust his sword through both our sides.
> Terror and dread then shake me from my sleep . . . .

Next, she is visited by the apparition of Nero's mother, Agrippina, whom he put to sea in a leaky boat and then, when that failed, had executed by the blade. Agrippina warns Octavia that she too will become a victim of the mad emperor. What Shakespeare gleaned from *Octavia* is that madness, ghosts, violence, and above all, suffering are the odd ingredients that school characters like Hamlet in their quest for the truth and their pursuit of survival. But Shakespeare decided to transform *Hamlet* from a play of the stage into a play of the mind. The presence of supernatural forces only serves to make the drama more of a psychological experience. Shakespeare, in a twist of horror, makes his audience afraid of the depths of the human mind, the dark recesses that are home to the wild imaginings that can take place atop a foggy tower of a Danish castle. *Hamlet* exists within a dream-like miasma. The audience knows that the play is set not in a specific place but in that netherworld of strange possibilities where anything can happen, a place as close to the murky world of the imagination as Shakespeare can approximate.

What Seneca contributes to Shakespeare's idea of tragedy and the tragic hero is the element of the gothic, that collision of life and death that unsettles the inhabitants of both realms. For Seneca, the world is and always shall be a plain inhabited by both the living and the dead; the two can seldom reconcile their uneasiness with each other. Therefore, what is "appropriate" to the tragic realm can seem completely alien to audience members who are rooted in logical reality. Part of the engagement of tragedy lies in the playwright's ability to create a drama of distraction, where the truth becomes buried in sensational events and spectacles. Hamlet realizes that he is caught up in a drama of distraction and spends most of the play pursuing the truth in the only way he knows how, through philosophy; yet he too pays attention to the wrong thing.

Paying attention to the wrong thing, in tragedy, is a type of *hubris*, arrogant or excessive pride in oneself and one's place in the world, which, according to Sophocles and Shakespeare, is a form of blindness. In the Pagan Classical world, the gods punish those who become so self-absorbed that they forget who they are: mortal beings with mortal lives and a mortal ability to suffer. *Hubris* has also been described as overconfidence, a false sense of security that leads a protagonist to turn aside from the action and to cease to pay attention to his situation. Classical tragedy suggests that there is no ease in the universe. The world, to those who temporarily blind themselves by dropping their guard, is a "darkling plain," a place of hopelessness where a minor oversight can blow up in a character's face and trigger a catastrophe.

That catastrophe leads to suffering that's witnessed by the audience. Suffering is something we want to avoid, yet for the tragic hero—and his audience—it is the pathway to understanding, the pain everyone pays as the price of gain. Saint Augustine, in his *Confessions,* realized that we gawk at things that seem horrible and catastrophic because we are transfixed by the absurdity of the situation. The fact that we cannot turn away, he noted, elicits an outpouring of emotion, especially if the situation that gives rise to the catharsis is an illusion. Saint Augustine remembered that as a young man, he was fascinated with theatre, and especially with tragedies and tragic heroes, "because the plays reflected my own unhappy plight and were tinder to my fire." He wondered why it was that men "enjoyed feeling sad at the sight of tragedy and suffering on the stage, although they would be most unhappy if they had to endure the same fate themselves."

Augustine felt that there was absolutely no justification for the delirium of emotion triggered by tragedy. "The more a man is subject to such suffering himself," he argued, "the more easily he is moved by it in the theatre." He felt that an audience ought to be called upon to offer assistance to the sufferer—although that, perhaps, is Augustine demonstrating his natural sense of saintliness. He feared that sorrow and tears were enjoyable, and that even when we felt pity when confronting unfortunate characters, we still could not see beyond our sense of awe at their suffering. What tragic heroes taught him, he realized, was that pity was something to be welcomed, and that spectacle and misfortune are empty experiences if they do not evoke from us a sense of compassion and a desire to help. For Augustine, tragedy was a learning experience and the tragic hero was the teacher:

> But now I feel more pity for a man who is happy in his sins than for one who has to endure the ordeal of forgoing some harmful pleasure or being deprived of some enjoyment which was really an affliction. . . . Sorrow may therefore be commendable but never desirable.

*Richard Burbage,
Shakespeare's boss
and the first actor to
play Hamlet on the
English stage.*

Goodness and appropriateness are not enough to justify a piti-
able spectacle, however, or excuse the inhuman treatment to which
most tragic heroes are subjected. Aristotle's third assertion about the
tragic hero was that he had to be lifelike in his qualities. A figure like
Hamlet or Oedipus appears on stage and has to contend with both
the expectations of the audience and the demand that he represent
the human condition. Aristotle noted that being lifelike "is not the
same thing as making [characters] good, or appropriate in the sense
of the world." His take on the tragic hero is that he should be believable because there are elements in him that can be easily recognized
and identified with by the audience. The impact of tragedy stems
from its ability to evoke a *catharsis*, "a spontaneous outpouring of
powerful emotions" as a result of the downfall of the hero. Audience
members, in recognizing something of themselves in Hamlet, identify with the character, or at least suspend their disbelief to the point
where their awareness of themselves becomes subsumed in the experience of the play. This sense of audience participation is essential to
the play because the action evokes from each beholder a powerful

response of pity, or "There but for the grace of God go I." As the protagonist's fortunes falter and his world falls apart, those watching are left with dismay and despair. To Aristotle, they have become friends of or even accomplices with the character, and they want him to succeed in spite of it all. In the *Poetics,* he wrote:

> Let us now consider what kinds of incident are to be
> regarded as fearful or pitiable. Deeds that fit this description
> must of course involve people who are either friends to
> one another, or enemies, or neither. Now if a man injures
> his enemy, there is nothing pitiable either in his act or in
> his intention, except in so far as suffering is inflicted; nor
> is there if they are indifferent to each other. But when
> sufferings involve those who are near and dear to one
> another, when for example brother kills brother, son father,
> mother son, or son mother, or if such a deed is contemplated,
> or something else of the kind is actually done, then we have
> a situation of the kind to be aimed at.

At the heart of tragedy, Aristotle suggests, there is a kind of familial intimacy, a dysfunctionality of the highest order, wherein audience members can see the failings in their own relationships and recognize problems they have had to work through in their own lives, albeit usually on a much smaller scale.

The contemporary view of literature is that it should not be read or viewed didactically, but what resides at the root of the link of identification between audience and character is the idea that tragedy has something to teach us about ourselves. Hamlet's flaw is that he thinks too much, and that he believes everything in his world has to be explored through reason. His adherence to logic tells him that information received from spirits atop battlements is not reliable, yet the veracity of the ghost's message leads Hamlet to feel that he must take action. He is a character whose Renaissance mind is almost

MR BARRY SULLIVAN AS HAMLET.

HAMLET. "Slanders, sir: for the satirical rogue says here, that old
men have grey beards; that their faces are wrinkled; their
eyes purging thick amber and plum tree gum; and that they
have a plentiful lack of wit, together with most weak hams.
All of which, sir, though I most powerfully and potent-
ly believe, yet I hold it not honesty to have it thus
set down; for you yourself, sir, should be as
old as I am, if, like a crab you could go
backward." *HAMLET.*
Act 2, Sc 2.

The famous nineteenth-century actor Barry Sullivan, in his portrayal of Hamlet.

Baconian in its need for verifiable data. When his mother remarks on his black apparel, Hamlet retorts viciously:

> 'Tis not alone my inky cloak, good mother,
> Nor customary suits of solemn black,
> Nor windy suspiration of forced breath,
> No, nor the fruitful river in the eye,
> Nor the dejected havior of the visage,
> Together with all forms, moods, shapes of grief,
> That can denote me truly. These indeed seem,
> For they are actions that a man might play,
> But I have that within which passeth show—
> These but the trappings and the suits of woe.

Hamlet is torn between what he knows and what he suspects, and his great weakness is that he cannot decide whether to take action or keep thinking. Just as a man cannot serve two masters, as we are reminded in the New Testament, a character cannot serve two worlds. Hamlet, tragically, becomes a victim of circumstances that he cannot control with either thought or action.

The tragic flaw in a character is called the *hamartia,* a Greek word that means "fault" or "guilt." *Hamartia* is the tragic hero's fatal error, a mistake that leads to his destruction and downfall. And everyone makes mistakes. That's human nature. As a type of drama and as an art, tragedy attempts to comment on life by, as Hamlet put it, "holding . . . a mirror up to nature." The idea that a *spoudaios* can be just as flawed as a *phaulos* is present in Shakespeare's thinking throughout *Hamlet;* it's also present in Aristotle's thinking, whether he admits it or not. The play is aimed at the common man; it's a form of instruction, a lesson for the audience in how to handle life's rougher moments. In Sophocles' *Antigone,* one of the plays on which Aristotle based his observations about tragedy, the Messenger, the bearer of bad news, tries to contextualize the suffering of great people from the perspective of a lowly, no-name character:

> What is the life of man? A thing not fixed
> For good or evil, fashioned for praise or blame.
> Chance raises a man to the heights, chance casts him down,
> And none can foretell what will be from what is.

But for Shakespeare, like all tragedians, the problem lies in suggesting that something survives the pitched battle that is life. The question is, what remains?

Shakespeare seemed to imply that higher virtue is what outlasts the folly of law and fortune. In Ophelia's last broken-hearted scene, she appears singing a song about St. Valentine, the martyr of love:

> Tomorrow is Saint Valentine's day.
> All in the morning betime,
> And I a maid at your window,
> To be your Valentine.
> Then up he rose and donned his clo'es
> And dupped the chamber door,
> Let in the maid, that out a maid
> Never departed more.

Even in the throes of madness, Ophelia is still transfixed by the idea of love, as shattered as it is. And she is not alone in suffering for the higher principle of love. Ophelia's antecedent is Antigone, a tragic character who puts love and justice ahead of all other considerations.

In her argument with her nemesis, Creon, who condemns Oedipus' daughter for having done justice to the dead by burying her treasonous brother, Antigone states that she serves a higher power. She signs her own death warrant by declaring, "My way is to share my love, not share my hate," a statement that echoes through the ages as a rallying cry for *Eros* in the face of *Thanatos*. The poet Philip Larkin expresses the same sentiment in "An Arundel Tomb," a description of a medieval church monument in Chichester Cathedral. Instead of crafting an elegiac tomb piece, Larkin turns the tables, suggesting that there is an element in our humanity that can cheat death. He concludes his poem with the wonderful line "What will survive of us is love." Creon, by contrast, tells Antigone to "go and share" her "love among the dead." She dies a martyr's death, like St. Valentine. Even Seneca suggests that something survives the purge of life that is tragedy. In attempting to persuade Nero to spare the life of Octavia and keep her as his wife, he argues, "Only the virtues of the mind and heart / Are everlasting, indestructible. / The flower of beauty withers day by day."

Tragedians have always struggled to hold on to something in life. As Adam falls from the Garden of Eden—the moment of mankind's collective tragedy—God reminds him that "dust thou art and unto dust thou shalt return." Tragedy, it would seem, is everywhere. What is important about the tragic hero, however, is that he constantly strives to find some solution to the human predicament. What's more, he rises to face his fate with dignity, even though he may not comprehend his suffering or what anyone will gain from witnessing it. But we watch tragedy to learn how to find our own courage, even when the odds are completely stacked against us.

That brings us to the fourth quality that Aristotle looked for in tragic heroes: consistency. He wrote, "Even if a person who is being represented is inconsistent, and this trait is the basis of his character, he must nevertheless be portrayed as consistently inconsistent." Aristotle argues in the *Poetics* that a character must remain true to himself, and that what he stands for sets him on a path of behaviour from which he cannot deviate. The problem with Shakespeare's protagonist is that he dons an attitude that is inconsistent with his philosophical makeup. His madness is not only troubling to other characters in the play, but also disturbing to the audience—which is yet another element of distraction. Hamlet believes that he can hide behind a mask of madness, using it as a shield for his fury just as his historical forebear, Prince Amlethus of pre-medieval Denmark, did.

In the case of the great hero of antiquity, Hercules, madness overwhelms the hero and reduces his chances for happiness. In his play *Herakles,* the classical Greek playwright Euripides presents the story of the madness of the son of Zeus. Returning from the completion of his twelve labours to a doting wife and lovely children, the satisfied hero lets down his guard and quickly becomes the victim of his nemesis, the goddess Hera, for whom he is mockingly named. (The name Herakles literally means "the glory of Hera" in ancient Greek.) To spite the hero for having accomplished his twelve impossible tasks, Hera sends the furies to drive him into a state of uncontrollable rage. He murders his family before he comes to his senses. Theseus, the same figure who slew the Minotaur in the labyrinth, consoles Herakles, reminding him that grief, a form of living death, was something that they shared when Herakles rescued Theseus from the underworld. Herakles asks, "When you were down in the underworld, how high was your courage?" Theseus responds, "I was completely crushed. Less than the meanest soul." The tragic hero, because he falls from a great height, suffers more than the average individual, but the end result is the same for everyone, regardless of station, strength, or stamina. What keeps a true tragic hero ahead of mere mortals, even in the underworld, is his nobility, the one feature of his soul that even death cannot crush. Dignity, it would seem, is imperishable. It is the hallmark of a significant human being.

Herakles realizes in his moment of despair that he is human. He laments, "A god is self-contained. Perfect. Needing nothing. He's his own atmosphere. And his own world." Theseus, however, contends that even the gods suffer, and the semi-divine Herakles is proof of that. The recompense in tragedy—if there is any recompense, and not merely despair and hopelessness at the end of a long, drawn-out travail—is that regardless of the amount of his suffering, the protagonist

Raccolta Maffei

A seventeenth-century engraving depicting Hercules, as drawn from
an antique Roman statue.

reaches the same end as everyone else. Death makes no distinctions. And yet, the point of tragedy is not to make everyone feel empty—although that is accomplished as part of the process of *catharsis*—but to suggest a universality to human dignity. In everyone, there is the courage not merely to die but to live life in the mind or heart or in action, and to express ideas and emotions as suffering is confronted. What emerges from the diction, the thought, and the character in tragedy is a better understanding of how we can approach inevitability and not be cheated by it into a state of fear. Fear, it would seem from Hamlet and Oedipus and Herakles, is what robs us of life. To say that you will not be afraid is to conquer the presence of death in life until it cannot be vanquished any longer.

The truly great tragic heroes of literature, Oedipus, Hamlet, and Antigone, possess an incredible tenacity of mind that they attempt to fuse with their character, despite moments when they appear to give in to despair, madness, and chaos. What they learn is that they hurt only themselves when they lash out against forces much greater than they are. Oedipus blinds himself, and Hamlet ousts himself from the court at Elsinore through his bad behaviour.

The twentieth-century Russian poet Anna Akhmatova turned to Shakespeare's *Hamlet* as a source of inspiration for her own poetry during the 1930s, when it appeared that state-sanctioned terror would crush not only those around her but also her dignity. Akhmatova's son and husband both fell victim to the Stalinist purges that haunted Soviet society like an absurdist nightmare. Her response, a triptych of poems that she worked on even when she herself was a victim of the regime, became a testament to courage and paved the way for her to write her magnum opus, a long, meditative poem titled "Requiem." Her other famous piece, "Poem without a Hero," is structured much like T. S. Eliot's "The Waste Land." It is a collage of voices from the past, a highly intertextual narrative about the search for answers to the challenges and tragedies of her age. The world that "Poem without a Hero" presents is a bleak place of uninhabited echoes and absences, a place much like that in the final scene of Shakespeare's *King Lear,* where the only characters left standing are a madman, a weak husband, and an aging counsellor. In the first part of the poem, "The Year Nineteen Thirteen," Akhmatova recalls the false splendour of czarist St. Petersburg before the First World War. Like Scrooge visited by ghosts on Christmas Eve, she sees a parade of shades, an underworld of dead souls similar to that which Homer presents in the *Odyssey.* One of the shades is an anonymous hero, a figure who vanishes from the remainder of the poem as Akhmatova's society spirals into darkness and chaos:

> The hero's on stage! Ah
> Yes, here he comes, displacing
> The tall one without fail and
> Of holy vengeance he sings.
> But why have you all fled, as
> Though to a communal wedding,
> Leaving me in the gloom
> Face to face with a frame's blackness
> Out of which starts that hour
> Which became most bitter drama
> Never sufficiently wept.

In looking back on her life and the terrible century in which she lived, Akhmatova realizes that events eradicated the hero from her imagination. No one did anything to prevent history from unfolding in the most catastrophic way. What she determined to do was to speak out against her misfortune by writing about it. She set about proclaiming and defending herself in a world where she would have to be her own hero. Her stance, like Job's, was to refuse tragedy as an option, and in doing so, she dignified her own humanity and the humanity of those who perished in the Stalinist purges and who might perish in the future. After almost a quarter century of composition, "Poem without a Hero" finally appeared in print in 1962, and by the end of her life, Akhmatova was being accorded great honours by the same nation that had once attempted to destroy her. For Akhmatova, fear was not something she could give in to. It would have got in the way of her poetry.

The tragic hero, as T. S. Eliot points out in his poem "The Love Song of J. Alfred Prufrock," is tragic only as long as he resigns himself to his fate and to his fear. Using *Hamlet*'s theme of indecision as a pointer for his own argument, Prufrock debates the merits of action, whether merely sexual or determinedly intellectual. Published on the cusp of the First World War, "The Love Song of J. Alfred Prufrock" sounded a note of uncertainty, though no one at the time (Eliot included) knew just what it meant. The suggestion, however, is that the world is shaped by action—by the fusion of thought, character, and diction with plot—not merely to create spectacle, but to "take arms against a sea of troubles, and by opposing, end them." Prufrock, who declares that he is "not Prince Hamlet, nor was meant to be," considers himself a bit player in life and wonders:

It is impossible to say just what I mean!
But as if a magic lantern threw the nerves in patterns
   on a screen:
Would it have been worth while
If one, settling a pillow or throwing off a shawl,
And turning toward the window, should say:
   "That's not it at all,
   That's not what I meant, at all."

Eliot never provides his reader with answers to any of these rhetorical questions. The purpose of the tragic hero, it would seem, is to show us that we all have to work out life's problems for ourselves, finding the courage to ask "To be or not to be" questions and answer them, in the name of life, to the best of our abilities.

4 THROUGH A GLASS DARKLY
The Infernal Hero

The flamboyant English Romantic poet George Gordon, Lord Byron, was something of a show-off. On May 3, 1810, he decided to take on the risky challenge of swimming the Hellespont, the strait that separates Europe from Asia. Not only would he be able to say that he had accomplished a great feat of athletic stamina, but he would also add his name to the catalogue of the great lovers of history. And what was more, he would write a poem to celebrate the great lengths a person would go to indulge his passions.

Born with a clubbed foot, the Achilles heel of his striking persona, Byron never felt as at home on land as he did in the water. He was almost as well known as a marathon swimmer as he was a poet. Indeed, he was among the first poets to have a personal trainer, the noted pugilist Gentleman George Jackson. Byron, however, was never one to swim alone; on his frequent dips in the Thames, he was always accompanied by his faithful Newfoundland dog, Boatswain. For his 1810 crossing of the treacherous Hellespont, from Sestos in Asia to Abydos on the European side, he chose the company of a

The English Romantic poet George Gordon, more widely known as Lord Byron, from a print made during his lifetime.

young British army lieutenant by the name of Ekenhead. Though it was only a mile or so from one side to the other, Byron noted that the swim would seem more like four miles because of the treacherous current that rushed eagerly from the Black Sea towards the Mediterranean. In one grand gesture, he believed, he would bridge continents and cultures, as well as history and mythology.

Byron was re-enacting Leander's nightly ritual to reach his beloved Hero. Unlike Leander, however, Byron chose to swim by daylight so that the gods who had extinguished Hero's signal fire would not enter the picture and imperil him any more than was necessary for the stunt. Unfortunately, he miscalculated, and he and Ekenhead almost met the same fate as the tragic lover of ancient times. Ekenhead suffered a severe cramp. Byron, who was yards ahead, turned back to save the English officer, but in so doing, he exhausted himself. The two were eventually pulled from the water by a passing fisherman, who must have been surprised to find two Englishmen flailing about in the Hellespont.

Not to be outdone by a mere gush of water, Byron set about recording the adventure in a poem, "Written After Swimming from Sestos to Abydos." There, he not only drew upon the legend of Hero and Leander—which poets like Christopher Marlowe had celebrated as a kind of lover's *nekusis,* a harrowing swim through the waters of death—but also portrayed himself as "a degenerate modern wretch" in quest of glory:

But since he crossed the rapid tide,
According to the doubtful story,
To woo—and—Lord knows what beside,
And swam for Love, as I for Glory;

'Twere hard to say who fared the best:
Sad mortals! thus the gods still plague you!

He lost his labour, I my jest;
For he was drowned, and I've the ague.

Byron understood that his athletic exploits were purely for glory, and had nothing to do with proving whether a real Leander had actually crossed the Hellespont. Glory aggrandizes a hero. It enlarges his sense of himself and represents the ego drive behind his actions. Byron's poetics were solid, but we also get the sense that he was one of the first-rate self-promoters of the literary world. He marketed both his poems and his persona.

Ego is what gets the better of one of Byron's most famous literary creations, Don Juan. The rogue lover who pushes his sinfulness and outlandish behaviour beyond bounds even Ovid would never have crossed first appeared as a literary character in seventeenth-century Spain, in a story by the playwright Gabriel Tellez. By the time Byron began his mock epic, in 1818 in Venice, Don Juan was already a stock bad boy of the stage and the opera house, appearing, most notably, in Mozart's *Don Giovanni*. Byron, always willing to be roguishly tongue-in-cheek, announces at the opening of the first canto of his poem:

I want a hero: an uncommon want,
When every year and month sends forth a new one,
Till, after cloying the gazettes with cant,
The age discovers he is not the true one;
Of such as these I should not care to vaunt,
I'll therefore take our ancient friend Don Juan—
We all have seen him, in the pantomime,
Sent to the devil somewhat ere his time.

He then offers a catalogue of heroes—from General Wolfe, the conqueror of Quebec, to the fallen admiral of Trafalgar, Lord Nelson,

The Death of Wolfe, *an engraving based on the painting by Benjamin West. None of the other figures shown, aside from possibly the Indian, was present at the time of Wolfe's passing at the Battle of Quebec. The people depicted in the picture paid by subscription to have themselves included.*

and the leaders of the French Revolution—declaring each man, in turn, not "fit for my poem." What Don Juan has that the others lack is a kind of heroic sex appeal, a dark streak that fascinates. Beneath the poem's satirical attitude to heroes who get carried away by their personal desires resides a deeper, more mysterious character who dares to break taboos and push through social barriers, all in the name of slaking his ego-driven sense of self-satisfaction and pointing an accusing finger at the mores of an inhibited society. Don Juan is a pseudonym for the libido.

In the seventeenth canto, Byron admits that Don Juan's interior landscape is a battleground between good and evil—an eschatological no man's land—and evil is winning out. Don Juan describes himself as a series of surface appearances masking a very different emotional and psychological reality; he's a Pandora's box of mixed emotions, a potential berserker waiting to be unleashed:

Temperate I am—yet never had a temper;
Modest I am—yet with some slight assurance;
Changeable too—yet somehow "Idem semper:"
Patient—but not enamour'd of endurance;
Cheerful—but, sometimes, rather apt to whimper:
Mild—but at times a sort of "Hercules furens:"
So that I almost think that the same skin
For one without—has two or three within.

The reference to *"Hercules furens"* is taken from Euripides' play *Herakles,* the story of how the son of Zeus is driven into murderous madness by the Furies. Byron is aware that *Hercules furens* is a catchword for a personality that is propelled by dark forces it cannot control—forces that unleash a terrible buried rage. Don Juan knows he is complex, and it is this complexity that Byron admires in his character. Byron realized that Don Juan was not merely a Romantic character, chafing against the boundaries of the social norms he inherited from the past, or even a metaphor for the poet himself, but a deeper study in the range and depths of the heroic personality. At the root of this personality is an ego determined to serve only itself. Some would argue that Byron was a product of his age—an age that discovered the might of individualism. But with liberty comes responsibility, and Byron was all too aware that an unchecked personality rich with possibilities could be as darkly destructive as it could creative.

In what was almost a commentary on the Romantic age, an age that championed the intellectual investigation of revolution, invention, and unbridled freedom, Byron wondered just where such explorations in possibility would lead. In the fourteenth canto, he lets his reader know that his protagonist is strange—stranger than truth—and that in examining the actions and ideas of this dark hero, the reader must look beyond what he or she knows. The dark hero is the avenue to the unfamiliar:

'Tis strange,—but true; for Truth is always strange—
Stranger than fiction: if it could be told,
How much would novels gain by the exchange!
How differently the World would men behold!
How oft would Vice and Virtue places change!
The new world would be nothing to the old,
If some Columbus of the moral seas
Would show mankind their souls' antipodes.

In this canto, Byron evokes an anthology of tempters from works of the past, including the rogue navigator Odysseus, from Canto XXIV of Dante's *Inferno,* who dares to break the taboo of living death in life by sailing to the threshold of Mount Purgatory, the gateway to paradise, at the farthest reaches of the world. But Byron has something else in mind. Perhaps, he suggests, the world lies within a person as well, and in that inner geography reside places and ideas and experiences that we should not visit. To go or not go: that is the question. The resulting debate is a battle between virtue and vice, and ultimately good and evil.

For his age, Don Juan was a new type of hero, the dark hero. Dark heroes like him are reflections not of the actual world but of the inner world, the id and the ego that lie beneath the veneer of societal commonalties such as law, morals, religion, and even art. They are upstarts who fascinate readers because they challenge convention and live lives as mysterious and disturbingly resonant as a deep well that blocks out all reflections of the familiar world.

The potentially volatile nature of the dark hero is part of the appeal. Charlotte Brontë appears to have been fascinated by the Byronic personality. She built it into her novel *Jane Eyre* in the dark hero and demi-protagonist of Mr. Rochester. When Jane first encounters him, her mind is dwelling on the Gothic fantasy of the mythical Gytrash, a half-man, half-beast that roams the countryside and, like the Sphinx, tears people apart with either its claws or its questions.

Her initial observations of Rochester, her employer and future husband, could just as easily have been written about Lord Byron, by Byron himself:

> He had a dark face, with stern features and a heavy brow;
> his eyes and gathered eyebrows looked ireful and thwarted
> just now; he was past youth, but had not reached middle age:
> perhaps he might be thirty-five. I felt no fear of him, and
> but little shyness. Had he been a handsome, heroic-looking
> young gentleman, I should not have dared to stand thus
> questioning him against his will, and offering my services
> unasked. I had hardly ever seen a handsome youth: never
> in my life spoken to one. I had a theoretical reverence and
> homage for beauty, elegance, gallantry, fascination; but
> had I met those qualities incarnate in masculine shape, I
> should have known instinctively that they neither had nor
> could have sympathy with anything in me, and should have
> shunned them as one would fire, lightning, or anything else
> that is bright but antipathetic.

Jane Eyre is a study in the dynamics of attraction. For Jane, Rochester is a mystery because he possesses those two or three skins within the appearance he displays to the world. On the surface, he is an aloof master, a nobleman whose past and present are both cloaked in secrecy. The more secretive he is, the more Jane becomes attracted to him. Rochester himself realizes that he is a mystery wrapped in a riddle, and he even tells his governess, "To live for me, Jane, is to stand on the crater-crust which may crack and spue fire any day." Brontë wants her readers to see Rochester as a volcanic personality, full of fire and brimstone. Jane looks upon him and sees the Byronic possibility that something strange, full of passion and uncontrolled desire, will suddenly well up beyond the control of manners, social codes, or even beliefs. She reads Rochester's tectonic nature as if it is a mystery she needs to solve, and the more impenetrable it becomes, the more she is drawn to him:

> And as for the vague something—was it a sinister or a sorrowful, a designing or a desponding expression?—that opened upon a careful observer, now and then, in his eye, and closed again before one could fathom the strange depth partially disclosed; that something which used to make me fear and shrink, as if I had been wandering amongst volcanic-looking hills, and had suddenly felt the ground quiver and seen it gape: that something, I, at intervals, beheld still; and with throbbing heart, but not with palsied nerves.

When the earth does eventually move for both Jane and Rochester, the results are catastrophic. Rochester's first wife, a madwoman locked in the attic, burns down the ancestral manor, and Rochester is left blind as a result. The oft-jilted Jane, who has discovered her true identity as the heiress of a wine merchant, returns to her former employer and becomes both his eyes and his wife. Rochester realizes that he has been a scoundrel—hiding the details of his life from Jane, and even dressing up as an old gypsy woman to tell her fortune—and that he has also played the dark hero to her imagination-driven heroine. Having lost his physical vision, he has acquired a new kind of clarity that allows him to strip away illusions, the disguises of both lies and costume that he used to toy with Jane's emotions. With a note of remorse for having gone to the extremes of the Byronic personality, he defines himself as someone who has literally been blasted by divine punishment. He's a figure who has stood outside the norms of society, challenging the laws and conventions of morality and ethics, and lost:

> "Jane! you think me, I daresay, an irreligious dog: but my heart swells with gratitude to the beneficent God of this earth just now. He sees not as man sees, but far clearer: judges not as

man judges, but far more wisely. I did wrong: I would have sullied my innocent flower—breathed guilt on its purity: the Omnipotent snatched that from me. I, in my stiff-necked rebellion, almost cursed the dispensation: instead of bending to the decree, I defied it. Divine justice pursued its course; disasters came thick on me: I was forced to pass through the valley of the shadow of death. *His* chastisements are mighty; and one smote me which has humbled me for ever. You know I was proud of my strength: but what is it now, when I must give it over to foreign guidance, as a child does its weakness?"

What lies at the heart of Rochester's confession is his realization of the power he held for her as a dark hero. And Jane, who is only human, accepts him as the poster boy for the mysterious veil behind which resides her own unspoken sexuality.

The dark hero is someone who breaks the taboos of sexuality and social constraints in the hormone-driven image of a James Dean. But the idea of the rebellious outsider—the rebel with or without a cause—has much older roots in the Western tradition. Traditionally, poetic justice was the operative principle in literature: the good were rewarded and the bad were punished. The only exceptions were characters called *nemeses,* who acted from both a sense of justice and a sense of revenge. A *nemesis,* usually a goddess, was an agent of divine punishment. Like Hera harassing Hercules, she would set upon the hero at his moment of triumph, often to counter his *hubris.* No matter how bad the consequences for the protagonist, there was always the sense that he had it coming, that he had become too big for his britches and needed to be humbled. There is a cold, business-like quality to the *nemesis.* He or she is there simply to present a contrary position to the hero's. He should not take his or her presence personally.

With the shift in the Western imagination that came with the arrival of the Judeo-Christian system of beliefs, the idea of *nemesis,* where retribution was merely part of doing business with life, became

Lord Nelson, as his own age saw him—a commander and leader, a focal figure who surrounded himself with displays of his own glory.

transformed. In the Judeo-Christian imaginative universe, God was responsible for retribution, and He would deal with that in the after-life (because mercy and justice were the operative principles of the universe). Punishment in this life became replaced in the grand cosmological scheme by the idea of hell. Divine law was something that would catch up with a character later. The Judeo-Christian God, as Job 38 tells us, has better things to do than to become wrought up in human anxieties and human miseries. He has a universe to run.

The problem of the disappearance of *nemesis* was not lost on philosophers like Boethius. In *The Consolation of Philosophy*—which is an attempt to understand the relationship, and the difference, between good and bad fortune, to understand why bad things happen to good people—the imprisoned Roman thinker arrived at the idea that there are those who reject the laws of God and nature. In confronting the question of the presence of evil in the universe, Boethius accidentally invented the contemporary notion of the antagonist as an evil-doer:

But the greatest cause of my sadness is really this—the fact that in spite of a good helmsman to guide the world, evil can still exist and even pass unpunished. This fact alone you must surely think of considerable wonder. But there is something even more bewildering. When wickedness rules and flourishes, not only does virtue go unrewarded, it is even trodden underfoot by the wicked and punished in place of crime. That this can happen in the realm of an omniscient and omnipotent God who wills only good, is beyond perplexity and complaint.

Boethius knew whereof he spoke. He had lost all his property and been imprisoned and tortured without knowing why. In attempting to explain the absurdity of his situation, he argued that misfortune is largely a matter of how you perceive events. Boethius is like the father of modern spin-doctoring. Look on the bright side, he says, and even the darkest clouds will have silver linings.

Dame Philosophy, with whom Boethius is having his prison conversation, assures him that "sin never goes unpunished or virtue unrewarded, and that what happens to the good is always happy and that what happens to the bad is always misfortune." The wickedness of others, Dame Philosophy asserts, "can never wrest the glory from the good." Glory, she argues, is something you borrow, a temporary pride in yourself that may feel and look good at the time but has no lasting value. This was the kind of glory that Byron was aware of when he saw the transient fame of Danton, Nelson, and Bonaparte. The bad can wrest good fortune from the good, but their triumph is only temporary. Being good was a reward in itself, and we need not look beyond that goodness for any further reward because earthly rewards were fleeting. Goodness, as a virtue in itself, would improve and strengthen an individual. But even in that scenario, it only paved the way to something beyond this world. In Arthurian romance, a knight is measured by his ability to overcome himself, to find himself by losing himself. Alfred, Lord Tennyson, in "The Holy Grail" of

Idylls of the King, borrows a passage from Matthew 10:39—"He that findeth his life shall lose it: and he that loseth his life for my sake shall find it"—and uses it as the inscription on the magical chair, the Siege Perilous, on which only Sir Galahad may sit. To Victorian readers, this must have been a perplexing compensation. The idea behind the Siege Perilous, and behind Boethius' argument, is that any ego stands in the way of spiritual achievement, and that true worth can be measured only in the abstract. Boethius states, in *The Consolation of Philosophy,* that "you cannot think of anyone as human whom you see transformed by wickedness. You could say that someone who robs with violence and burns with greed is like a wolf."

Dante takes Boethius at his word, filling a portion of his hell with those who have committed the sins of the wolf, ravenous crimes against humanity solely for the sake of material gain. As Dante passes through hell in the *Inferno,* he cannot help being fascinated by the people he encounters, and he stops and chats with them in an attempt to acquire important lessons about the nature of the human condition. Dante's fascination with evil gave modern readers their taste for characters who commit wrongs and then revel in their mistakes by making them the focus of a story. Those whose souls reside in hell are trapped in their personal narratives. They see nothing beyond their own egos or the desires that led to their eternal condemnation. Their wants overcome their ability to perceive themselves in relation to the larger picture of God and eternity. The question at the heart of Dante's *Inferno,* and ultimately of *The Consolation of Philosophy,* is why the damned place so much importance on the ends they seek that they exclude all other possibilities, including legality and morality. Boethius never completely answers the problem of envy—that in seeing the bad triumph, the good feel somehow cheated, especially in material terms. The troubling question of just what could be done to even the score with those acting against a suffering protagonist was never fully resolved in Judeo-Christian literature until a materialistic way of looking at the universe, the Renaissance, reinvigorated a

Dante stopping to chat with some of the damned in hell, from Canto IV of Gustav Doré's nineteenth-century rendering of the Inferno.

fascination with the successful antagonist who triumphs over good in the temporal world. As dismaying as it may seem, evil was given a place in literature, and readers ate it up with a mix of fascination and revulsion.

In 1512, in one of the hallmark texts of the Renaissance, the Florentine Niccolò Machiavelli argued that this strange fascination with wrongdoing was, in purely material terms, a normal trait of human nature. If you had to do something ugly to satisfy your greed, perhaps that impetus could be built into the regular systems of human government and society. Wrongdoing, he wrote in *The Prince,* could be worked with and turned, ultimately, towards the greater end of the common good:

> The wish to acquire more is admittedly a very natural and
> common thing; and when men succeed in this they are always

praised rather than condemned. But when they lack the ability to do so and yet want to acquire more at all costs, they deserve condemnation for their mistakes.

For Machiavelli, the goal—the end that justified the means—was the unification of Italy, the expression of a spirit of nationalism that would eventually evolve itself into a kind of higher nobility. But in his mind, this lofty goal justified almost any means of getting there. He argued that violence and treachery were necessary, and that individuals were expendable—assertions that ran counter to all that had been expressed by Christian morality since the time of Boethius.

There was one major problem with Machiavelli's little book: in the early sixteenth century, it was read not as a clinical study of the dirty realities of politics—the business of doing business, if you will—but as a statement of moral corruption. Florentines and other European readers looked upon *The Prince* as the kind of book they should not read, and therefore *had* to read. The word "Machiavel," meaning someone who is "treacherous, driven by greed and evil motivations, and determined to succeed in his ambition regardless of the costs to others," entered the language. As a type of literary character, the Machiavel twists circumstances to his own advantage, whatever the cost to those around him. He is an immoral character, someone without compunction or scruples. He usurps the virtuous characters in a drama or narrative, focusing the writer's and the reader's attention on the success or failure of his own ventures. With the arrival of the Machiavel, evil was now capable of stealing the starring role. The devil, ever lurking in the shadows, was suddenly front and centre, flaunting his vices and displaying human failings on a grotesque scale. The Machiavel showed audiences the darkness in their own human natures. Perhaps the only solution, his presence suggested, was to work with human failings to turn them towards some acceptable outcome. The antagonist could become the protagonist, and those who in a most virtuous age would have turned away, repelled by the drama of the success of evil, watched in shock and awe. What Machiavelli was suggesting was that evil was not outside the structure and order of nature, but a part of it. *The Prince* created its own aura by explaining just how the darker side of life and politics functioned.

Among the first to jump into the fray of condemnation for the Florentine political tract was a London under-sheriff who was intent on climbing the ranks of English political society. In a book that was written before 1520 but would not be published until 1557, the law officer condemned those who used bad means for good ends. His target was Richard III, the last Plantagenet ruler of England, whose death in 1485 at the Battle of Bosworth Field had ended the War of the Roses. The London law officer perceived himself as an apologist for the Tudor regime of Henry VII, who had a rather questionable claim to the crown. To secure the authority of the new regime, the *ancien regime* had to be trashed, and the rising young Londoner turned to Machiavelli for his definition of evil.

In his *Historie of the pitiful life and unfortunate death of Edward the fifth and the then the Duke of York his brother,* a work that would later become known as *The History of King Richard III,* the ambitious law officer recast history to make the past seem worth forgetting. The Londoner's name was Thomas More, and he did succeed in his political ambitions, becoming Lord Chancellor of England in 1529. Henry VIII must have liked what More had to say about the man his father had overthrown at Bosworth Field. He awarded him Richard III's old palace, Crosby Hall, which More promptly moved from Holborn, in the centre of London, down the Thames, to be next door to the king's palace at Chelsea.

It would take more than four hundred years for Richard III to recover from More's portrayal of him in his *History.* More lavished on Richard attributes of the unnatural, the deformed, and the darkly villainous. (Whether he had his facts right is still a matter of debate among historians.) What emerges is a portrait of a man who resided outside the laws of God and nature:

Richard III, from an early eighteenth-century engraving. Note that in this image, based on an actual court painting of Richard, he bears none of the hallmarks of the Machiavel, as Thomas More depicted him.

Richard, the third son, of whom we now entreat, was in wit and courage equal with either of them, in body and prowess far under them both; little of stature, ill-featured of limbs, crookbacked, his left shoulder much higher than his right, hard-favored of visage, and such as is in states called warly [i.e., in great men called warlike], in other men otherwise; he was malicious, wrathful, envious, and, from afore his birth, ever froward. It is for truth reported that the Duchess his mother had so much ado in her travail that she could not be delivered of him uncut, and that he came into the world with the feet forward, as men be borne outward, and (as the fame runneth) also not untoothed; whether men of hatred report above the truth, or else that nature changed her course in his beginning, which in the course of his life many things unnaturally committed. None evil captain was he in the war, as to which his disposition was more meetly than for peace. Sundry victories had he, and sometimes overthrows, but never in default, as for his own person, either of hardiness or politic order; free was he called of dispense, and somewhat above his power liberal, with large gifts he got him unsteadfast friendship, for which has was fain to pill and spoil in other places and got him steadfast hatred. He was close and secret, a deep dissimuler, lowly of countenance, arrogant of heart, outwardly companiable where he inwardly hated, not letting to kiss whom he thought to kill; dispiteous and cruel, not for evil will alway, but ofter for ambition, and either for the surety or increase of his estate.

In other words, according to More, Richard was a nasty-looking thief who bought his friendships and whose prime motivation was greed. Thirty-five years after More's *History of King Richard III* was published, a young playwright in London would turn to it to create one of the most evil characters ever presented in drama.

In Act V, Scene iii, of William Shakespeare's *Tragedy of Richard III,* the Duke of Richmond, later to become Henry VII, speaks to his troops about the nature of their opponent:

> Richard except, those whom we fight against
> Had rather have us win than him they follow.
> For what is he they follow? Truly, gentlemen,
> A bloody tyrant and a homicide;
> One raised in blood and one in blood established;
> One that made means to come by what he hath,
> And slaughtered those that were the means to help him;
> A base foul stone, made precious by the foil
> Of England's chair, where he is falsely set;

One that hath ever been God's enemy.
Then if you fight against God's enemy,
God will in justice ward you as his soldiers;
If you do sweat to put a tyrant down,
You sleep in peace, the tyrant being slain;
If you do fight against your country's foes,
Your country's fat shall pay your pains the hire;
If you do fight in safeguard of your wives,
Your wives shall welcome home the conquerors;
If you do free your children from the sword,
Your children's children quits it in your age.

Richmond suggests that when confronted by the immorality of a tyrant monster, there is no immorality in killing him, an argument Dietrich Bonhoeffer expressed to justify his role in the attempted assassination of Hitler. *Sic semper tyrannus.* Live by the sword, die by the sword is his view, and it's a view that is as real and brutally clear as the motives of his opponent. Richmond's lieutenant, Blunt, is equally aware that the Tudor forces on the eve of Bosworth Field are up against a Machiavel. Blunt observes that Richard "hath no friends but what are friends for fear," a direct allusion to Machiavelli's assertion that it is "better to be feared than loved." Despite the depths of depravity to which he sinks—murdering his brothers and his nephews, attempting to marry his niece when his sister-in-law rejects him—Richard is thoroughly vilified by those who rise to oppose his boundless greed and unchecked drives. Richmond points out to Blunt that the country under Richard is "Bruised underneath the yoke of tyranny"; it is like a vineyard trampled by a boar—the symbol for Richard's House of York—that "Swills your warm blood like wash, and makes his trough / In your emboweled bosoms." The fact that Richard is compared to a boar—not just here but again in a speech by the condemned yes-man, Hastings, in Act III, Scene ii—

suggests that the presence of a Machiavel protagonist in the drama is a metaphorical turning of the tables:

> To fly the boar before the boar pursues
> Were to incense the boar to follow us
> And make pursuit where he did mean no chase.

The hunted has become the hunter. The universe of *Richard III* is one of inversion, not merely perversion, where life, morality, and justice are supplanted by their opposites because the kingdom has become a place of misrule.

Shakespeare, oddly, titles the play *The Tragedy of Richard III,* which suggests that at the heart of the play there is a flawed protagonist with a *hamartia* or strategic blindness that leads to his downfall. But Richard not only *has* a tragic flaw, he *is* a tragic flaw—a walking, talking bundle of self-delusion that runs rampant over the landscape of an entire country. What drives Richard is his unbridled ego. In a scene that Shakespeare borrows straight from Senecan tragedy, Richard confronts the accusers within his own conscience. He tries to talk his way out of the unwelcome realization that he does possess some scruples and will have to pay for his crimes:

> What do I fear? Myself? There's none else by.
> Richard loves Richard: that is, I am I.
> Is there a murderer here? No. Yes, I am.
> Then fly. What, from myself? Great reason why!
> Lest I revenge. What, myself upon myself?
> Alack, I love myself. Wherefore? For any good
> That I myself have done unto myself?
> O no! Alas, I rather hate myself
> For hateful deeds committed by myself.
> I am a villain.

Richard's pangs of conscience appear too late in the play to rescue those who have fallen in his way. The tragedy, Shakespeare seems to imply, is borne not by the protagonist, but by those who, accidentally or intentionally, have found themselves within the king's orbit. The fact that Richard fears himself and realizes what he has done is of little consequence. By the end of the play, no one is cheering for Richard, and his downfall is a matter of course that the entire audience expects:

> There is no creature loves me;
> And if I die, no soul will pity me.
> Nay, wherefore should they, since that I myself
> Find in myself no pity to myself?

Perhaps the only justice in the play, other than Richmond's triumph over the dark Machiavel, is that Richard realizes he is a self-contained universe, where his inner fantasies are entertained to the point of exhaustion. Shakespeare seems to be saying that human beings have their limits, and that to try to go beyond those limitations is to confront the inner absence of the unchecked self—one's own ego and the black hole of the id that lies beneath it like a hungry Minotaur.

As Shakespeare wrote *Richard III,* he likely had in mind another play that had been performed around 1588, though it was not published until 1604. The play was by Shakespeare's rival and sometime dramatic role model, the mysterious dark hero of English Renaissance drama, Christopher Marlowe. The university-educated Marlowe was fascinated by the struggles that occurred within a character. He puzzled over eschatology, the branch of theology concerned with what the Greeks called *eskhatos,* or last things—that is, the soul of man in judgment. The good soul, as Marlowe was well aware, went to heaven for its reward, and the bad went to hell. Punishment was inevitable for the unrepentant sinner. But, Marlowe asked, what if an individual could delay his punishment long enough to achieve the sin of playing God on earth?

The answer to that question was his play *Doctor Faustus*. Marlowe drew on the legend of a Polish astrologer who, during the 1480s and 1490s, gained a reputation throughout Europe as a charlatan for his exaggerated claims to have mysterious powers. His equally mysterious murder was ascribed to the devil, and the legend evolved that the astrologer, Faust, had made a pact with the chief infernal, selling his soul in exchange for knowledge and power. The humanists, in the tradition of Thomas More, realized that although knowledge was infinite, there were limits set upon the reach of man—and for a good reason. The Humanists, who viewed the Faust legend as a parable of unbridled energy, saw in the Polish magician a warning for how man's ideas could outstrip his sense of moral and intellectual responsibility. In other words, they perceived Faust as a walking Pandora's box, a challenge to the maxim that "man's reach should exceed his grasp." Faust attempts to leap from life into the driver's seat of divinity, and in doing so, he sells himself short, trading an eternity of bliss for a few fleeting years of seductive marvel and wonder. The scant facts of the actual Faust's life were assembled in a book called the *Volksbuch,* which was published in English shortly before Marlowe composed his *Tragical History of Doctor Faustus.*

Marlowe's protagonist is a dramatic example of Boethius' assertion that evil is the conscious rejection of natural and divine laws. The Renaissance line of thought argued that knowledge could open a new world for mankind. Faustus, a university professor who has learned almost all there is to learn, thirsts after more. Like Shakespeare's Richard III, he is insatiable in his greed for ideas, wealth, fame, and status. He is overcome not merely by his intellectual curiosity, but also by his lust to see just how much he can grab for himself within the confines of his mortality, "to practice more than heavenly power permits." In lines that will echo in the pages of Mary Shelley's

Frankenstein, Faustus muses to himself about the potential for achieving power over life and death, but he never realizes that life is both physical existence and spiritual survival:

> The end of physic is our body's health.
> Why, Faustus, hast thou not attained that end?
> Is not thy common talk sound aphorisms?
> Are not thy bills hung up as monuments,
> Whereby whole cities have escaped the plague
> And thousand desp'rate maladies been cured?
> Yet art thou still but Faustus, and a man.
> Wouldst thou make man to live eternally,
> Or, being dead, raise them to life again.

Healing the sick through the power of science, effecting social justice through knowledge, and achieving celebrity status for good works—these are not enough for the hungry heart. His imagination is a limitless dominion that stretches before him, tempting him, and he becomes a victim of his own desire for possibilities:

> But his dominion that exceeds in this,
> Stretcheth as far as doth the mind of man:
> A sound magician is a demi-god.
> Here, tire my brains to get a deity.

There resides at the core of Faustus a revolutionary spirit that re-emerges in Romanticism in the late eighteenth century, partially because of the impact *Doctor Faustus* had on literary consciousness. William Blake's declaration that an individual must create his own system or be imprisoned by another man's resonates throughout Marlowe's treatment of the Faust legend. The restless seeking after more is summed up in the doctrine of *Che sera, sera,* or "What will be, will be." Inevitability? Is this what is driving mankind? Is each individual touched by just enough desire to attain something more to push beyond himself? And if so, what is lost in the process? Marlowe suggests that an individual who is blinded to everything but his own desires loses the peace of mind that comes from recognizing what Boethius called the true home for mankind: heaven. This is what Jesus, in the Gospel of Matthew, says resides in each of us. Marlowe is suggesting, indirectly, that the heroic lies in the recognition of the self. Lose that recognition, and the individual not only fails to attain heroic status but also becomes a victim of his own ambitions, triumphing over nothing. And he loses the inner peace that is the appropriate and available avenue to something greater than himself. Faustus is willing to push the envelope and break the rules of God and nature because he wants to see just how far he can go with his game of chance, no matter how self-deluding that game may be. To set one's own rules, seemingly an act of intellectual maturity, is actually a trap, an addiction to uncertainty, rather than a trust in a certain but seemingly intangible thing. Faustus has the heart of a gambler.

For a while, the gamble pays off for Marlowe's protagonist. Faustus rises to the heights of a *spoudaios,* a man celebrated by his society for his amazing contributions to science and knowledge. It seems he can reach no higher; yet each achievement makes him lust after more. His lofty status is undermined by several scenes involving clowns, the low-born *phaulos* who know better than to tempt divinity. Faustus even undergoes a type of *nekusis* when his spiritual dealer, the fiend Mephistopheles, introduces him to the Seven Deadly Sins—Pride, Covetousness, Envy, Wrath, Gluttony, Sloth, and Lechery—just so Faustus can say he met them. What is troubling, and would have spelled tragedy for Renaissance audiences, is that all Faustus encounters are shades, ephemeral visions that are not of the real world but of the mind. When he encounters Helen of Troy, in one of the most famous speeches from English Renaissance drama, all Faustus sees is what his own mind already contained, the image born in literature. Like Don Quixote, he confuses the textual experience with reality—the very thing St. Augustine warned against. It comes down to being a poor reader—a dupe who fails in the process of critical discernment. Tragedy, Marlowe suggests, arises from being caught up, reflexively, in a system of your own creation. Still, what Faustus encounters is, according to Marlowe, marvellous, even though the learned scholar of Wittenburg could have got the same results simply from reading the *Iliad*:

> Was this the face that launched a thousand ships
> And burnt the topless towers of Ilium?
> Sweet Helen, make me immortal with a kiss.
> Her lips suck forth my soul: See where it flies!
> Come, Helen, come, give me my soul again.
> Here I will dwell, for heaven in these lips,
> And all is dross that is not Helena.

Faustus has Helen conjured because he wants to gaze on the epitome of human beauty, the kind of beauty that a dedicated knight or an armoured hero is willing to die for. The great tragedy in *Doctor Faustus* is that the individual is limited by his knowledge: a person wants only what he knows. What Faustus knows is what his learning has taught him, and the grave suggestion underscoring the play is that knowledge is finite. Heaven, on the other hand—the very thing Faustus is prepared to trade off for the gratification of his earthly imagination—is infinite. The pity lies in the fact that Faustus cannot grasp the true value of value. In the end, the learned doctor is a prisoner of both his knowledge and his imagination.

In some ways, Marlowe appears to offer a critique of materialism, especially as it applies to religion. Faustus is tempted only by things that he can know, not by "evidence of things not seen." He begins the play as an earnest traveller in the world of knowledge and imagination, as someone who desires to reach God; yet when he realizes that God resides in the intangible, he opts instead for the dangerous role of playing God in the realm of the tangible for a meagre twenty-four years. The more he is reminded that's he's simply a man, the more he attempts to exceed his limitations and to "practice more than heavenly power permits."

What resides at the root of this drive is the heroic impetus for more, the desire to outstrip oneself or to increase one's stature. And it is this razor's edge that Faustus walks throughout Marlowe's play until he can go no further. His personal demon, Mephistopheles, reminds him of just how far he himself fell with the other rebel angels when their desire to overreach themselves failed miserably:

> Why, this is hell, nor am I out of it.
> Think'st thou that I, who saw the face of God
> And tasted the eternal joys of heaven,
> Am not tormented with ten thousand hells
> In being deprived of everlasting bliss?
> O Faustus, leave these frivolous demands,
> Which strike terror to my fainting soul!

But Faustus rushes in where even fallen angels fear to tread. When the time comes for him to pay the bill for exceeding his own mortality, he sees himself as lower than the animals whose souls, according to the doctrine of metempsychosis, or the transmigration of souls, are allowed to return to the earth. For Marlowe's protagonist, the realization that an eternity in damnation awaits him is terrifying. He faces a sentence without respite for having traded life in the higher reality he always desired for a handful of illusions:

> Let Faustus live in hell a thousand years,
> A hundred thousand, and at last be saved.
> O, no end is limited to damned souls.

Why wert thou not a creature wanting soul?
Or why is this immortal that thou hast?
Ah, Pythagoras' *metempsychosis*, were that true,
This soul should fly from me and I be changed
Unto some brutish beast.
All beasts are happy, for, when they die,
Their souls are soon dissolved in elements,
But mine must live still to be plagued in hell.
Curst be the parents that engendered me!
No, Faustus, curse thyself. Curse Lucifer,
That hath deprived thee of the joys of heaven.

Faustus, like his artistic descendants, Don Juan and Don Giovanni, is carried off to hell to pay for his crimes. In the end, he does find a home for his soul, but he would have had a better one had he simply been humble and acknowledged his own limitations. The point Marlowe is making is quite clear: as much as we may want to trade up in matters of spiritual and intellectual attainment, we will still have to confront, and endure, the limitations of what and who we are. *Che sera, sera.* The infernal hero, in this respect, is someone who fools himself into thinking that he has the wisdom to know the difference between what he can change and what he must simply tolerate. The heroic is a matter of recognizing where you fit in, and doing the best you can within that particular context. To deny that context and its limitations is to make an exile of yourself within yourself.

This idea of the troubled hero, the questing questioner, as a type of wanderer is the subject of one of the greatest works of the Romantic period, Johann Wolfgang von Goethe's *Faust, Part I.* Inspired by Marlowe, and perhaps troubled by the questions the English Renaissance dramatist had raised in his play, Goethe first attempted a version of the Faust story between 1771 and 1775. He abandoned the work, only to resume it early in the next century and publish the first part of his poetic drama in 1808. What made the 1808 version work for Goethe was that the ideology of his time, the very tenor of Romantic idealism, had finally caught up with the story he was attempting to tell. Goethe's Faust is a spiritual exile in the tradition of Marlowe's Faustus, but he's a very different type of being who is questing after understanding to obtain a kind of limitless knowledge of divinity. Goethe asks why God does what He does, and how we as human beings can comprehend it.

Goethe's work is haunted by the Book of Job. In what amounts to a dialogue between *Eros* and *Thanatos* (to put the matter in Freudian terms), the play opens with a conversation between God and Mephistopheles. And it is Mephistopheles, the spirit of temptation, who appears as a "subtil serpent" to tempt mankind into knowledge and to explain the restlessness at the core of the human spirit:

> The fool is nourished on no earthly food,
> And his own ferment's driven him so far
> That he himself can almost see his folly.
> From heaven he demands the fairest star,
> From earth its wildest ecstasy,
> And all that's near and all that's far
> Leaves his deep-shaken breast unsatisfied.

Goethe's Faust has, in the words of Tennyson, a "hungry heart" that yearns after knowledge and eternal truths, and is unsatisfied by all that it has already learned. During a discussion with Mephistopheles in Scene IV, Faust explains just how ravenous his desire for knowledge is:

> In any dress I shall still feel the torment
> Of this earth's narrow life. I am too old just to play,
> Too young to keep living without wishes.
> What more can the world give? You must do without,
> Must do without! That is the eternal song

That, our whole life long, keeps ringing

In every ear, that each hour keeps hoarsely singing.

Faust acts against God because he sees Him as a barrier between humanity and heaven, an obstacle in the way of man's access to divine knowledge. Man is in perpetual exile from his original state of being (a Boethian idea); he is separated from his original, divine sense of understanding, his true home.

But Goethe's Faust does not go easily into the midst of the old antagonist. Mephistopheles allows him to experience the possibilities that lie within his reach if only he is willing to be tempted by the promises of obtaining divine knowledge. What then transpires is an eschatological struggle between good and evil, with Faust bearing witness to the sufferings of mankind that divine knowledge might alleviate. The battle is played out not only within Faust's soul and mind, but within the world. The problem is that any struggle carries the possibility of collateral damage. That collateral damage here is borne by Gretchen, the innocent object of Faust's attentions, the Beatrice to his Dante. Gretchen kills her mother and her baby while under Mephistopheles' powers, and then becomes a wandering fugitive at the mercy of the powers of evil and the forces of justice. The demon tortures the young maiden by sending her world out of control; this is also meant to tempt Faust, who mistakenly attempts to purchase from her a love that is already his. It is Gretchen who bears the weight of tragedy in Goethe's work; she becomes a metaphor for a humanity that is struggling to return to its original state and yet is thwarted by the same powers of darkness that brought about man's first fall from grace. In Gretchen, Goethe plays out the history of time, and Faust is torn between what he desires for the betterment of mankind and what he desires on a simple human level. What Faust hungers after is a lost kingdom where the soul and intellect were one. Scene XXIII opens with his monologue on the nature of Gretchen's exile and torment:

Goethe, the author of the Romantic rendering of the Faust story, in which mankind's aspirations towards enlightenment are spiritual rather than merely material.

In misery! In despair! For so long pitifully wandering over the earth, and now a prisoner! A criminal shut up in a dungeon, in awful torment—that lovely ill-fated being! To have come to this! To this!—Treacherous, vile spirit, to have hidden it from me!

Beneath the Sturm und Drang of Faust's torment and Gretchen's suffering is the sense that human beings are just the scapegoats in a much larger conflict between good and evil, the outcome of which is beyond their capabilities to understand.

Through Gretchen's miseries, Goethe reminds his readers that there are two sides—good and evil—to the universal struggle for existence, and that often an individual can end up on the dark side and become an outcast. The wanderer, the outcast who finds himself in a state of prolonged or eternal exile for crimes of passion or momentary lapses of sanity, is a recurring motif in literature. Like Cain—who is "cursed from the earth" for slaying his brother, Abel—wanderer figures are damned to suffer a punishment greater than they can bear. As fugitives or vagabonds, they pass through nature with a "mark" or some other protective device upon themselves, tormented by their own longevity and their segregation from the normal circumstances of life and community. In his "Rime of the Ancient Mariner," Samuel Taylor Coleridge portrays a luckless wandering sailor who decides to kill an albatross that is following his ship:

"God save thee, ancient Mariner!
From the fiends, that plague thee thus!—
Why look'st thou so?"—With my cross-bow
I shot the Albatross. . . .

And I had done a hellish thing,
And it would work 'em woe:
For all averred, I had killed the bird

Gustav Doré's nineteenth-century rendering of Coleridge's Ancient Mariner. In the hooded, bearded character, we see the grizzled visage of one who has endured long hardship.

That made the breeze to blow.
Ah wretch! said they, the bird to slay,
That made the breeze to blow!

Having taken the wind out of his own sails through his thoughtless act of seagoing venery, the Ancient Mariner watches helplessly as his crew perishes and his ship drifts through the icy polar wastes. He then suffers the fate of having to share his horrific story with those he encounters. He even interrupts a wedding with his grief-stricken bulletin, the bird hanging about his neck as a constant reminder, like the mark of Cain, of the curse he must carry with him. As his story progresses, the reader is told that the Mariner is

Alone, alone, all, all, alone,
Alone on a wide wide sea!

And never a saint took pity on
My soul in agony.

Like many wanderers, the Mariner can find no sympathy for
his predicament, and it is his loneliness, not just his curse, that
evokes pity in most readers. The wanderer motif reappears in Mary
Shelley's *Frankenstein,* where Victor Frankenstein is pursued across
the northern expanses by his Daemon for having played God and
then abandoned the project. In similar stories, such as Charles
Maturin's gothic thriller *Melmoth the Wanderer,* a cursed figure is
given everlasting life, and he takes out his aggressions on those
whose happiness he cannot share. Classical mythology offers its
equivalent in the stories of Sibyl and Tithonus, two figures who
are given eternal life but not eternal youth. Sibyl is compensated by
the gods with the gift of prophecy, and is hung in a basket in the
temple, where, as T. S. Eliot points out in "The Waste Land," she
wishes to die. Tithonus, on the other hand, becomes a grasshopper.
An anonymous Anglo-Saxon poet saw the importance of belonging
and community, and wrote about the consequences of losing one's
place in society in a poem titled "The Wanderer." There, he used
the word for "grasshopper" to explain the predicament of a vassal
who has lost his liege lord. For the Anglo-Saxon wanderer, the
world is a cold, cruel, pitiless place that not only lacks the amenities
of home, but also is without context.

Being without context—not knowing your place in the grand
order of things—is in itself a form of severe punishment. In Genesis,
Cain goes out into the Land of Nod to dwell there until the end of
time; for other wanderers, the world becomes a metaphorical Nod,
a no-place, a living purgatory with only a flicker of redemption and
hope. Wanderers are trapped in timeless prisons that paradoxically
permit them considerable freedom of movement and remind them
that the ultimate boundless existence is actually a grim situation. In

absolute freedom there is no freedom at all. In this sense, there is no context and no structure, and the world becomes antithetical to both nature and divinity.

The greatest literary depiction of a place without context is John Milton's vision of hell in *Paradise Lost*. As Milton notes in Book I, the rebel angels fall out of heaven into the fiery lake of hell, a place completely devoid of organization, landscape, or landmark. Its only context is that it is not heaven:

> The dismal Situation waste and wild,
> A Dungeon horrible, on all sides round
> As one great Furnace flam'd, yet from those flames
> No light, but rather darkness visible
> Serv'd only to discover sights of woe,
> Regions of sorrow, doleful shades, where peace
> And rest can never dwell, hope never comes
> That comes to all; but torture without end
> Still urges, and a fiery Deluge, fed
> With ever-burning Sulphur unconsum'd:
> Such place Eternal Justice had prepar'd
> For those rebellious, here their Prison ordained
> In utter darkness, and their portion set
> As far remov'd from God and light of Heav'n
> As from the Center thrice to th'utmost Pole.

Like Dante's, Milton's hell is a place of raw emotions, a landscape of unresolved tensions and questions. It is "the vast and boundless deep," a limitless, disorganized mass of material. What makes it into a place at all is the will of the character who has been viewed by many readers as the contestant protagonist of *Paradise Lost:* the chief rebel angel, Satan.

Many commentators, George Bernard Shaw among them, have argued that Milton's Satan is too fascinating a character to be relegated

Milton's Satan from Paradise Lost *in an early eighteenth-century English engraving. Satan is depicted here as the leader rallying his fallen rebel angels following their defeat in the war in heaven.*

to secondary status. But Milton, the puritan Christian, certainly had no intention of giving Satan equal billing with God. When the rebel angels fall from heaven and find themselves flattened and exhausted on the fiery lake of the adamantine depths, the first thing Satan does is to rally his troops. What drives Satan is a need for possession, and he asserts his ownership over his own New World as if he's a conquistador arriving on the shores of an undiscovered island. Possession in this sense is not merely an acceptance of a place, but the desire to assert the ego over it, to make the place a reflection of the character's psychology. Hell is as much within the raging Satan as it is around him.

Milton realizes how much pathos he has evoked with Satan's recognition that he has lost heaven. It is the same sort of pathos that will be evoked in Book XII, when Adam and Eve, hand in hand, make their way out of Eden and into the cold, cruel world. To compensate, the blind puritan poet offers a form of correction by having Satan declare that hell is a type of mind game, and that he is determined to win the battle with God through the power of will:

The mind is its own place, and in itself
Can make a Heav'n of Hell, a Hell of Heav'n.
What matter where, if I be still the same,
And what I should be, all but less than hee
Whom Thunder hath made greater? Here at least
We shall be free; th' Almighty hath not built
Here for his envy, will not drive us hence:
Here we may reign secure, and in my choice
To reign is worth ambition though in Hell:
Better to reign in Hell, than serve in Heav'n.

Essentially, Satan is attempting to "spin" his situation to persuade himself that he has not landed in the worst possible place in the cosmos. In an act of pathetic optimism, he tries to look on the bright side of his hopeless situation. But what lies beneath Satan's rhetoric is a wilfulness to turn any situation to his advantage, one of the key traits of the infernal hero.

Satan's wilfulness is what Milton hyperbolizes to show just how self-destructive and futile an angry focus can be to a leader:

What though the field be lost?
All is not lost; the unconquerable Will,
And study of revenge, immortal hate,
And courage never to submit or yield:
And what is else not to be overcome?
The Glory never shall his wrath or might
Exort from me.

In this speech to his disheartened troops, the chief rebel echoes the final words of Shakespeare's dark hero of the Scottish highlands, Macbeth, who declares to Macduff that he "will not yield" shortly before the avenging laird hacks off his head. Macbeth—who wins his throne in perfect Machiavellian fashion, by killing Duncan and slaughtering anyone else who gets in his way—remains defiant even though he knows that his string of fortune has come to an end. This defiance, even in the face of physical evidence—"though Burham Wood be come to Dunsinane, and thou opposed being of no woman born"—is both fascinating and pathetic. It is the voice of the child who declares that he will hold his breath until he gets his way and it is the cry of the failing figure grasping for straws that are no longer there. What is cunning and devious about Milton's Satan, however, is that he knows he still has energy left to regroup. In declaring that he still exists even though he has fallen from heaven, he suggests that rebelliousness is at the core of his being and will not be satisfied as long as he is able to fuel his love of hatred. Satan proposes a scorched-earth policy against God; he wants "to wage by force or guile eternal War" that is ultimately "irreconcilable to our grand Foe." He uses the vocabulary of a revolutionary bent on liberty or death, and it is not surprising that revolutionaries since Milton's time have turned to the fallen Satan and his diction of defiance to express their rhetoric. As a literary construct, Satan is Milton's metaphor for pure will; he's like the personification of a temper tantrum that's as methodical and plotted as a chess game. This defiant resistance to order will, in later centuries, fire the expressions of dark heroes such as Byron and the Romantic imaginings of poets such as Percy Bysshe Shelley and Charles Baudelaire. Enraged will is a form of denial, wherein the individual heads off on his own course into unknown territory with unconsidered consequences.

Milton's portrayal of the infernal chieftain suggests that Satan's sense of pride, his *hubris,* is what has blinded him to the realities of his enemy. During the debate in the parliament of hell prior to the raising of the infernal city of Pandemonium, one of the fallen angels, Moloch, suggests that a suicidal frontal assault would be the best way to attack God and breach the gates of heaven. But since a single blow from God had knocked all the rebels from the celestial seat, it is eventually agreed by the scorched multitudes that they had severely underestimated the power of the infinite. Milton suggests that pride,

A nineteenth-century engraving depicting Macbeth driven to madness and his ultimate downfall by his wife, Lady Macbeth.

Satan's *hubris,* is a form of blindness—not physical blindness or even second-sighted prophetic blindness—and that a character like Satan sees more of himself than he does of his enemy. This narrowness of vision is a flaw. The true hero of *Paradise Lost,* God, has infinite vision and can see beyond his own drives and limitations. The hero, in Milton's view, is Argus-eyed, a character who can see not only the moment but also the alpha and the omega, the beginning and the end of things. The point of providence, as the reader learns in Books XI and XII, is that there is a much larger plan to the universe than can be comprehended by a single point of view. Those who are truly heroic—who take responsibility for their actions and possess foresight—are the ultimate victors.

Again, Milton tests his reader's ability to discern the difference between storybook heroism and moral heroism. Storybook heroism is easy: all a character has to do is to follow a pattern established in other stories through to its resolution. Milton obliges by sending Satan on a heroic voyage to earth in Book II. At the conclusion of the parliament of the fallen, the rebel angels concur with Satan, who decides that the best way to attack God is to attack his new creations, mankind and the world. When no volunteers can be found to travel through the void of chaos up to the little pendant of the world that God has suspended by a golden chain from heaven, Satan decides to do the deed himself. After passing through the gates of hell, he stands on the precipice of the underworld and stares into the great abyss of chaos before him:

> Into this wild Abyss the wary fiend
> Stood on the brink of Hell and look'd a while,
> Pondering his Voyage: for no narrow frith
> He had to cross. Nor was his ear less peal'd
> With noises loud and ruinous (to compare
> Great things with small) than when Bellona storms,
> With all her battering Engines bent to raze
> Some Capital City; or less than if this frame
> Of heav'n were falling, and these elements
> In mutiny had from her Axle torn
> The steadfast Earth.

Satan undertakes a *nekusis* in reverse, a harrowing of chaos. What drives him is his will to destroy God's creations and to fight God on whatever front He may present. There is an element in this description of something far more treacherous than the "wine-dark sea" of the *Odyssey;* yet chaos presents Satan with the puzzle that he must solve if he is to effect his action.

The link between Homer's mesmerizing waves and the abysmal ocean of uncreated and unorganized matter was not lost on Milton, who presents Satan as a wandering voyager who makes a pact with chaos in order to traverse it:

John Milton, the author
of Paradise Lost.

Chaos and ancient Night, I come no Spy,
With purpose to explore or to disturb
The secrets of your Realm, but by constraint
Wand'ring this darksome Desert, as my way
Lies through your spacious Empire up to light,
Alone, and without guide, half lost, I seek
What readiest path leads where your gloomy bounds
Confine with Heav'n.

Here is the source for Coleridge's Ancient Mariner, Maturin's wandering Melmoth, and a host of displaced characters who find themselves drifting alone towards their destinations—solitary voyagers who are battered by external forces. Satan's voyage, of course, is a damnable act: it serves no purpose other than to trigger the forces of *Thanatos* in what, at that point, is a perfect, deathless, and timeless world. Milton concludes Book II by comparing Satan's voyage to that of Ulysses, a character from the pages of classical literature who can be read in two different ways. To the Greeks, Odysseus was a cunning survivor, a metaphor for an individual who stands up to the capricious nature of the universe and uses everything he has at his disposal to return to his home, but not before learning about the world and himself in the process. To the Romans, Ulysses was the sacker of the holy citadel of Troy, a rogue and a liar who was willing to sacrifice honour and heroic credentials to save his own skin. Hero or villain, Odysseus/Ulysses is the universal metaphor for a wandering voyager who is willing to pit himself against the forces of the universe to achieve his purpose. Milton's allusion to Ulysses, however, comes not from Homer but from a later author's reinvention of Odysseus/Ulysses as a counsellor of fraud and a con artist. In Canto XXIV of the *Inferno,* the Florentine exile, Dante, and his guide and master, Virgil, stumble across Ulysses in the circle of hell to which deceivers are consigned. Taking Dante's words almost verbatim, Milton draws a crucial comparison between Ulysses and Satan in order to evoke some sympathy for his die-hard antagonist:

> Or when Ulysses on the Larboard shunn'd
> Charbydis, and by th' other whirlpool steer'd.
> So he with difficulty and labour hard
> Mov'd on, with difficulty and labour hee;
> But hee once past, soon after when man fell,
> Strange alteration!

Satan's heroic voyage to earth often raises the natural empathy a reader is inclined to feel for the underdog, the outsider, the loser who is trying to even the score. In doing this, Milton created a matrix into which later outsiders, exiles, wanderers, dark heroes, and infernal characters would be cast. The question is why.

In his study of Milton's poem, *A Preface to Paradise Lost,* the English literary critic and theological writer C. S. Lewis suggests that Satan was really an instrument of God's will—a pawn in the larger plan for divinity's endgame. There is a dialectic structure at work in the universe, so the argument goes. The infernal hero holds up to the reader a mirror of the darker self, with the aspects of personality that, if left unchecked, can bring about horrific consequences. But he is not just a reminder of what a person should not be. He points to the alternative path, the path of goodness. This may seem a simplistic argument to a contemporary reader, who's more familiar with the shades of grey that are the stock in trade of the modern writer. But in a morally determinate universe, where characters and readers alike are forced to take sides in order to avoid being "tepid," the infernal serves as a touchstone against which good can be measured. The infernal hero presents us an image of ourselves as if we are looking, in the words of St. Paul, "through a glass darkly." That image is not necessarily a reflection but more a question of what we wish to make of ourselves and whether we wish to be part of the order of things or outside of it.

C. S. Lewis argues that if God is almighty, He has foresight of everything that will happen. Mankind's fall is essential to the relationship between God and man because man, for all his suffering and his battles to persevere in the name of good, justice, courage, and love, will learn from the experience and grow closer to God in the process. Man will fall, but in falling he will begin a quest that will help him define goodness by coming to understand the nature of evil. He will be able to work with the raw materials of virtue to build a better world. The hero will be someone who will trust in himself, and in his ability to confront chaos and transform it through the power of generosity and selfless creativity into something where order and structure prevail. The hero will rise above himself and perceive higher, if intangible, principles at work in the world and in his purpose.

5   ABOVE AND BEYOND
The Hero Saint

S hortly before guards at Auschwitz were to select ten men to be punished for the escape of an inmate, a Polish priest spoke to his fellow prisoners. "They will never kill our souls," he vowed. "We prisoners are different from our persecutors. They cannot kill our dignity." When one of the ten chosen men cried out that he was a family man with children, the priest immediately stepped forward. "I am old and I am sick," the cleric told his captors. "I want to take his place." The ten men were locked in a starvation cell for three weeks; one by one, they died. When the cell was opened again, only the priest and two others remained. The Nazis then injected the remaining prisoners with carbolic acid.

The priest in this story was Father Maximilian Kolbe, a Polish Franciscan journalist, utopian thinker, and anti-Nazi activist who had been seized during the 1939 invasion of his homeland. Kolbe was a personal hero of a post-war Polish cardinal, Karol Josef Wojtyla, who saw him as an exemplum of sacrifice and a symbol of resistance to oppression. Cardinal Wojtyla set in motion the events that would

The questing saint, St. George, depicted here in the archetypal battle between good and evil, as he slays the dragon and saves the maiden. This storybook situation crosses chivalry with saintly virtues and makes St. George into an active or "cherubic" saint.

eventually transform Kolbe into a saint. Seven years after Kolbe was canonized, in 1978, the Polish cardinal became Pope John Paul II, and he modelled his pontificate, in many ways, on the ideals he had learned from his hero.

Saints are heroes whose actions are not confined to the physical world, and whose ideals speak to the spiritual aspects of our beings. They are figures whose struggles are waged on two fronts, the temporal and the extemporal, and they function as links between divinity and reality. For many saints, there is no barrier between the two. The idea of sainthood is universal to the human condition, and saints can be found in most of the world's religions. At the core of sainthood is the idea that these people are champions of life, combatants against *Thanatos* whose actions both express and sustain the values of civilization. They are virtuous persons of great real or affected holiness. The word "saint" in the English language comes from the Latin *sanctus,* meaning "holy," which itself derives from *sancire,* meaning "to consecrate" or "to dedicate something to a divine purpose." The Latin word *sanctus* carried with it the notion of something or someone set apart from common reality. In Greek, the term for "anything holy or sacred" was *hagios,* which gives us our modern-day word for the study of saints, "hagiography."

One of the best illustrations of the nature of a holy life is Jacobus de Voragine's story of the disciple and apostle St. Thomas, in the medieval bestseller *The Golden Legend.* St. Thomas turned the sayings of Jesus into a work known as the Thomas Gospels, which became one of the primary texts of Gnosticism, an early version of Christian faith. Following the Crucifixion, St. Thomas made his way to India, where he began to preach the Gospel. In the beautiful, exotic setting of India's western coast, Thomas converted thousands to Christianity, becoming, in the early years of the faith, one of the most successful professors of the ideas of Jesus. Specifically, Thomas preached the "Twelve Virtues," a pattern for leading a moral, not just Christian, life. The message caught on like wildfire.

The virtues, according to de Voragine's story, consisted of the following points:

> The first is believing in God who is one being yet three
> persons in one. . . . The second degree of virtue is receiving
> baptism; the third, abstaining from fornication; the fourth,
> avoidance of greed; the fifth, the control of gluttony; the
> sixth is living a life of penitence; the seventh, persevering in
> good works; the eighth, the practice of liberal hospitality; the
> ninth, seeking out and actively doing the will of God; the
> tenth, seeking out what is not God's will and avoiding it; the
> eleventh, practicing charity towards friends and enemies alike,
> and the twelfth, being scrupulous in observing all these things.

Thomas's message amounts to wise advice for how an individual should avoid leading a complicated life. Of particular note is the eighth virtue, the offering of hospitality, which is one of the key messages of Homer's *Odyssey*. This virtue suggests that generosity of both place and spirit is essential to the nature of the saint, who is a hero of giving. Thomas's Twelve Virtues tell us that the spirit of saintliness, the way in which an individual could lead a holy and pure existence, unfettered by self-created problems of earthly reality, was in place as early as a decade after Christ's Crucifixion. The idea underlying sainthood is that an individual assumes a mantle of moral responsibility and spiritual culpability, but only if he or she is willing to do so. Saints are willing participants in the challenge to perform exemplary actions, to answer a call that encourages them to amplify their inherent talents. As such, sainthood is the moral maximization of one's own good nature, and historically, it comes in many forms, suited to several different personalities.

In all, there are four different categories of saints. Mythic saints are those, like St. George, whose narratives bear a startling resemblance to myths from the classical catalogue. There is no historical evidence that such figures ever existed, and their life histories often have a fairy-tale quality that borders on the fantastic. In many cases, their stories were co-opted from existing mythologies when nations converted to Christianity. For example, St. Michael, a slayer of dragons, reminds us of traditional mythological heroes like Theseus or Hercules. Michael appears on earth wielding a phallic sword, and his conquest is not just of a dragon but of old earth- and seasonal-related beliefs. In fact, his name is often associated with ancient sites where the pagan earth mother goddess was worshipped. Place names all over England and France—from Glastonbury Tor, which is crowned by a tower dedicated to the archangel, to St. Michael's Mount in Cornwall and Mont St. Michel in Normandy—bear witness to the connection between Michael sites and pre-Christian pagan activity. Such sites are usually hills, where the feminine earth principle and the masculine sky come into closest contact.

The second category is for legendary saints, characters who exemplified the struggle between two religious mindsets during the transition from the pagan to the Christian world. St. Ursula—whose story may have inspired the Crusades—was the daughter of an English chieftain who had converted to Christianity. Betrothed to a pagan prince in order to cement a political alliance, Ursula found herself in a rather serious predicament. Her father, according to the *Golden Legend,* "thought it would be improper of him to hand over a girl who was such a devout Christian to a worshipper of idols," but he was absolutely terrified of "the savage reprisals the pagan king might exact" if he did not. Ursula came up with a brilliant solution. She would marry the pagan prince on the condition that he finance a pilgrimage to the Holy Land. The prince readily agreed. He was flabbergasted, however, when his bride announced that she would be accompanied on her journey by eleven thousand young English virgins. Not willing to be tricked by a Christian princess, the pagan prince put up enough money for ships to transport the army of young women across the continent. From there, however, things

In a very melodramatic rendering, complete with hungry lions, early Christian martyrs await their fate at the hands of sports-mad Romans.

started to go badly. The prince, fearing that his treasury would be bled dry by the crusade, conspired with officials in Rome, who themselves feared that a tide of young, beautiful women in the city of St. Peter would wreak havoc on local morals. The concerned parties decided that they would solve all their problems by encouraging the Huns, who were quickly approaching Rome, to attack the army of young women. As Ursula and her legion of maidens were encamped beside the Rhine, at the site of present-day Cologne, the Huns descended on them and slaughtered every one. The last to die was a young woman named Cordelia, the likely namesake of the character in Geoffrey of Monmouth's *History of the Kings of Britain,* which was the source for Shakespeare's play *King Lear.* The legend of St. Ursula stands as a parable for the struggle between personal purity and bureaucratic authority.

A few legendary saints, like St. Nicholas, for example, have morphed into stock characters of Western culture—generating billions of dollars as icons of modern holidays to boot. According to his legend, Nicholas, heir to a large fortune, decided to give away all his worldly goods prior to becoming a priest. He heard of a man with three daughters who could not afford expensive dowries and was facing the prospect of selling them into prostitution to survive. Nicholas chose the three girls as the candidates for his charity. The night before the first daughter was to be sent to the brothel, Nicholas threw a bag of gold over the family's garden fence. The eldest daughter found the bag of money and was rescued from a life of sin. When the second daughter was about to enter the house of ill-repute, Nicholas tossed her present in through her bedroom window; according to some versions of the legend, it landed in her stocking. The father of the young women felt ashamed that someone knew his plight, however, and he shut up his house to avoid being the recipient of charity. But Nicholas was not to be thwarted. The night before the third daughter was to make her way to the brothel, he tossed his last bag of gold down the chimney with a shot whose accuracy would impress any contemporary basketball fan.

Although there is no evidence that Nicholas ever existed, the proximity of his annual feast day, December 6, to the start of the advent season was a key element in his evolution into Father Christmas, Père Noël, Father Frost, and Santa Claus. As a figure who represents charity, St. Nicholas has become the ubiquitous annual hero for millions of children around the world. His progression from a faceless but bearded cleric of the early Christian church into the "jolly old elf" of Clement Moore's "'Twas the Night Before Christmas" was helped immeasurably by the marketing department of the Coca-Cola Company. Bedecked in Coca–Cola's signature red and white colours, which have become emblematic of Christmas, Santa Claus makes his way down chimneys each Christmas Eve to deliver gifts—usurping even the three eastern "kings" who followed a star to Bethlehem.

St. Nicholas's evolution has been the most dramatic of that of any figure in the canon of holy personages, with the possible exception of St. Valentine, whose own acts of Christian generosity and kindness are now associated with an annual festival of love, lingerie, and chocolate. Unlike Nicholas, Valentine almost certainly did exist.

Indeed, there may have been three Valentines, two shadowy priests and one rebellious bishop from the small Italian city of Terni. It is this latter figure who is most often associated with the contemporary St. Valentine. When Emperor Claudius II decided that marriage was bad for army morale and abolished it, the bishop Valentine continued to perform marriages in secret. Eventually arrested and imprisoned, he developed a close relationship with the jailer's blind daughter, and in a miraculous act, he even restored her vision. When he was being led away to his execution, he is supposed to have passed her a letter in which he said, "Remember your Valentine."

Many saints have their origins in pagan legends and traditions that were easily adapted to illustrate Christian ideas and messages. Valentine appears to be the Christianized expression of the annual feast of Lupercalia, which honoured the *lupa* (a she-wolf or prostitute) that suckled Rome's founder, Romulus, and his twin brother, Remus. In what was essentially a classical Mother's Day celebration, this festival marked the importance of purification and fertility, the harbingers of a merry springtime.

The credit for the evolution of an obscure bishop into an icon of mating, matrimony, and procreation goes to the medieval English poet Geoffrey Chaucer. In a court poem composed for the feast of St. Valentine in February 1383, Chaucer parodied the conventions of courtly love and the Italian, continental idea (espoused by such sonneteers as Dante) that love was something that could be openly debated. The conventions of courtly love—namely, the way men were supposed to treat women—had been described in the mid-thirteenth century in *The Art of Courtly Love,* a book by Andreas Capellanus. The tradition dated back to Ovid, but it was Capellanus who transformed the ritual of mating into a game where the men had to play by the women's rules. The practice of courtly love transformed the way men had to treat women, and emphasized the necessity of manners and decorous behaviour. Chaucer built his poem around the old English folk belief that the middle of February, the time of St. Valentine's feast, was the seasonal moment when birds pair up and begin building their nests. As the goddess Nature chairs a parliament on love, the birds conclude that it is worth the effort:

And when they'd finished all that argument,
The goddess gave a mate to every bird
In full accord, and on their ways they went.
O Lord! with what delight and bliss they stirred!
For each with wings and arching neck then spurred
His partner in the deed of loving creature,
Thanking the while the noble goddess Nature.

But first, as was their custom year by year,
Some birds were picked to sing a sweet farewell,
A roundel as a parting song to cheer
And honour Nature and to please her well.
The tune was made in France, I truly tell;
The English words are such as you may find
In these next stanzas, which are in my mind:

"Now welcome, summer, with your sunshine soft!
The winter weather you have put to flight,
And driven off the season of black night.

Saint Valentine, who is so high aloft,
The little birds sing thus for your delight:
The winter weather you have put to flight,
And driven off the season of black night.

They have good cause for gladness oft and oft,
Since each one freshly has his partner bright;
They sing in bliss when they awake to light.
Now welcome, summer, with your sunshine soft!

The winter weather you have put to flight,
And driven off the season of black night!"

Chaucer's roundel (a poem with repeated lines known as *repetons*) is a celebration of the rebirth and circularity of life. In the Middle Ages, just as now, the return of light and life to the world, noticeable by the middle of February, is cause for considerable celebration. With a few strokes of his pen, Chaucer transformed an obscure saint into a deity personifying love and procreation. Modern marketing took the transformation several steps further, linking the bishop of Terni with the classical figure of Cupid. In one of the strangest figurative evolutions in Western culture and literature, St. Valentine has become a faceless figure whose feast day is now associated with a putto, a small, diapered, winged sprite who serves as a stand-in for Cupid, the god of love.

The problem with both mythic and legendary saints is that their stories are so fanciful that the saints themselves tend to become more and more remote from the principles for which they originally stood. Over the past several decades, the Catholic Church has moved to downplay, if not expunge, these murky, mythic, and often playful figures from the canon of saints in favour of individuals whose works are concrete and have a direct bearing on contemporary beliefs. These individuals belong to our third category, the historical saint.

Historical saints are men and women whose lives and works are verifiable, and who helped transform a society from a pagan to a Christian one. In Canada, the Mohawk saint, Kateri Tekakwitha, is venerated for her role in bringing Christianity to her people, albeit at a terrible cost. Tekakwitha was persecuted throughout her life, first for her baptism and then for her vow of chastity, both so at odds with Mohawk culture. As saints often do, she stands as a figure caught between two worlds. Ostracized by her tribal society, she embraces a new religion, but seeks to increase her holiness by torturing herself in penance for perceived sins. Tekakwitha plays a crucial role in

Leonard Cohen's 1966 novel, *Beautiful Losers,* in which a psychologically wounded Montreal man attempts to ease his own suffering by invoking her as his patron. (In one of the strange turns in the relationship between literature and cultural fact, passages from Cohen's novel, including a series of poems that the narrator writes about the young woman, were read into the records at Tekakwitha's beatification process in 1980. This was a rare moment in cultural history when literature assisted in the creation of a saint.) In one passage, the nameless narrator of Cohen's novel attempts to reconcile himself to his adopted patron, a woman who herself was tortured by her own demons:

> I have been writing these true happenings for some time now. Am I getting any closer to Kateri Tekakwitha? The sky is forever foreign. I do not think I will tarry with the stars. I do not think I will ever have a garland. I do not think ghosts will whisper erotic messages in my warm hair. . . . How do I get close to a dead saint?

The sufferings of Kateri Tekakwitha have become a metaphor for the experience of indigenous peoples throughout the world. She also represents what can happen to an individual who is caught between what she is and what she aspires to become. Historical saints, many of them martyrs or self-scourging sufferers, now have a place in almost every culture. St. Andrew Kim, Korea's first Catholic priest, became the patron saint of his country following his martyrdom in the 1840s. St. Martin de Porres became the patron saint of both Peru and social justice for his work among the poor and starving of colonial Lima. These figures place real people, real dilemmas, and real challenges at the core of sainthood. This transforms them into heroic metaphors for how the problems of the world can be answered through acts of faith. Faith, it would seem, is the bridge between the other world and the temporal world, and if saints are to continue to be a vital force in spiritual matters, they must remain relevant.

Maximilian Kolbe represents the fourth type and a new breed of saint, the contemporary saint. These men and women are exemplars for how modern Christians should conduct their lives. What is startling about Kolbe's life is that he spent most of it as a modern storyteller. He was born into an impoverished family of weavers in 1894, and by 1910 he had decided to become a Franciscan monk. He studied in Rome until he was diagnosed with tuberculosis in 1919, when he returned to his native Poland. There, Kolbe founded a small magazine for the Catholics of Cracow. By 1927, the magazine had become so popular that it had a worldwide circulation of over one million. The staff of his magazine eventually grew to 762 friars, and those men helped Kolbe establish of one of Europe's first media centres—a complex that eventually included a radio station, a publishing house, a college, and an airfield. Kolbe saw his work as a vehicle for spreading his beliefs and for countering the forces of evil in the world. He was an outspoken critic of the Nazis, and when they invaded Poland on September 1, 1939, Kolbe's City of the Immaculate, as his media centre was called, was seized and converted into a refugee camp and later a concentration camp. Kolbe was sent to Auschwitz, where he met his end, as we learned at the beginning of this chapter.

As heroes, martyrs present a paradox. On the one hand, the martyr triumphs over evil by maintaining his beliefs in the face of death. On the other hand, however, the result of the suffering is the death of the individual, which should make the saint a tragic figure. Yet saints are triumphant, not tragic. The pervading concepts of sainthood have addressed this issue, not only in the Christian tradition but also in the Islamic system. To die for your beliefs is considered a good thing, and the peril of death is offset by the reward of eternal life. Throughout the present-day Middle East, children collect trading cards featuring the faces and vital statistics of suicide bombers who have blown themselves up for their cause. Like the Christian martyr saints, these suicide bombers are venerated for their strength of conviction, even though other cultures abhor their actions. Most moderate Islamic commentators have pointed out that martyrdom is annulled if the process does injury to others, but that has done nothing to staunch the flow. The obvious difference between a suicide bomber and someone like St. Pelagia, St. George, or St. Sebastian is that the Christian saints took no active part in their own deaths. In the Christian tradition, and that of almost every religion, that would have represented the sin of suicide.

According to de Voragine, the years 238 and 287 A.D. were particularly hard on Christians, and the persecutions produced a bumper crop of martyrs, including St. Ursula and her band of eleven thousand virgins, and St. Sebastian. The long and painful death of St. Sebastian, as de Voragine recounts it, is a metaphor for his refusal to submit to earthly authority:

> Diocletian then had him tied to a tree in the middle of an open field, and told his archers to use him for target practice. They hit him with so many arrows that he looked like a hedgehog, and they left him there for dead. But within a few days he recovered and was standing on the steps of the palace, and reproaching the two emperors for the terrible things they were doing to the Christians. "Is this not Sebastian," they exclaimed, "whom we had shot to death?"

In the end, Sebastian's tormenters are forced to resort to beheading—a metaphorical separation of soul and mind from body. A beheading liberates the faithful soul, transporting it to the realm of incorporeal, eternal bliss, thus thwarting the intentions of the executioner.

To the early Christians, dying for one's faith was seen as an act of heroic courage that others ought to emulate. By the nineteenth century, however, martyrdom was being viewed as a sign of weakness by those who professed a "survival of the fittest" philosophy. Friedrich Nietzsche was one who perceived the saint as a figure of weakness. Writing about saints in 1902 in *The Varieties of Religious*

The Last Communion of St. Jerome *by Domenichino is a seventeenth-century depiction of an unnamed saint. There is a profound sense of the individual surrendering himself to a higher order—in this case, a final Eucharist. Note the lion of St. Mark seated at the saint's right hand.*

Experience, the philosopher William James (brother to the novelist Henry James) cited the German philosopher's distaste for holy heroes. To Nietzsche, the saint was the lowest form of life on the food chain because of his passive stance. He "represents little but sneakingness and slavishness," James said, explaining Nietzsche's position. "He is the sophisticated invalid, the degenerate *par excellence,* the man of insufficient vitality. His prevalence would put the human type in danger." James himself saw in the saint a higher form of individualism that was worthy of veneration. Such personalities, he thought, were able to transcend the jungle madness that often makes up reality. The saint was a very different character from the strong man, but one no less useful to either society or the imagination. His gift, as James saw it, was the ability to communicate divine principles to mortal audiences. "The saint is therefore abstractly a higher type of man than the 'strong man,' because he is adapted to the highest society conceivable," James wrote, "whether that society ever be concretely possible or not. The strong man would immediately tend by his presence to make that society deteriorate." James is alluding to the conflict between barbarism and transcendent human values that was played out in Auschwitz between Kolbe and his captors. What seems important, in James's view, is that saints live without compromising the dignity that sustains them, even in the face of death. The saint is heroic because he stands up for what he believes in.

Saints represent in the Christian era what was called *apotheosis* in the classical era: the elevation of a human being to a semi-divine status. Because they know both heaven and earth, they are looked to as intercessors, as spokespersons for the human condition. Like the classical deities, many answer prayers for specific ailments or situations and perform acts of correction for things that have gone wrong. For eye problems, for example, prayers are offered to St. Lucy, who was blinded before her martyrdom. For toothaches, prayers are offered to St. Catherine, who suffered through the unanaesthetized extraction of her teeth before her death. Saints are said to be able to cure ailments because it is believed that various parts of the body or certain actions or occupations correspond to the saint's life or his or her martyrdom. When cures are evoked, a person is supposed to be reminded not just of the malady itself but of the sufferer whose character offers a solution to the problem at hand. In other words, saints represent the process of problem-solving.

Saints also act as champions for mortal existence as it is perceived from the other world. They do this because they possess a trait known as heroic virtue, which Pope Benedict XIV defined as the ability "to perform virtuous actions with uncommon promptitude, ease and pleasure from supernatural motives and without human reasoning." In other words, heroic virtue is the inclination to do good without giving the matter a second thought. Those who possess this quality make a habit of repeating their actions, as if there is an invisible force motivating them. This pattern of good acts is eventually noticed by someone and recorded in the form of a story, so that the life of the saint becomes not simply a series of good deeds, but a narrative of exemplary behaviour. Essentially, saints are individuals who tell stories through actions, not just words. They draw attention to the intent behind their actions by the way they live. When a saint is honoured or worshipped, the reverence paid to him is different from that paid to God. In worshipping God, a believer offers *latria,* or strict adoration, but to a saint, that same believer offers *dulia,* or humble reverence. The lives of the saints are presented in literature as *exempla,* stories aimed at encouraging others to live according to beliefs that are deemed right. The hope behind every saint's life is that the reader will learn something and be a better person for it.

In writing about the "Value of Saintliness" in *The Varieties of Religious Experience,* William James tried to define just what it was that made a saint a saint. He wrote,

The saintly character is the character for which spiritual emotions are the habitual centre of the personal energy; and there is a certain composite photograph of universal saintliness, the same in all religions, of which the features can easily be traced.

For James, all saints, regardless of their religious background, shared four key attributes. The first of these was what he described as "a feeling of being in a wider life than that of this world's selfish little interests." The saint was someone who could rise above the world because he had learned how to live beyond the grasp of need, greed, desire, and want. This ability to transcend the world translated into an understanding that embraced "abstract moral ideals; civic or patriotic utopias; or inner visions of holiness or right." Each saint also possessed "a willing self-surrender" to the control of an ideal power (chiefly God), as well as a love of humanity that superseded a love of the self. Saints, according to James's second attribute, checked their egos at the door of life.

James's saint was someone who could experience "immense elation and freedom" by allowing the confines of selfhood to "melt down." This ecstatic sense of losing oneself in a larger experience, the third attribute, is echoed in Tennyson's "The Holy Grail" in *Idylls of the King,* where the saintly knight, Sir Galahad, is willing to sit in the chair known as the Siege Perilous, which spells death to all but the pure and the good. He is the only knight able to sit there—the only one capable of overcoming his own ego. Galahad survives his seat in the magical chair and undertakes a successful quest for the Holy Grail because he is willing to lose himself in order to save himself. Tennyson tries to explain this paradox of saintliness when he writes:

In our great hall there stood a vacant chair,
Fashioned by Merlin ere he past away,

In this engraving from Gustav Doré's series for Tennyson's Idylls of the King, *the fellowship of the Grail quest is celebrated by the Knights of the Round Table prior to their scattering in search of the elusive prize.*

And carven with strange figures; and in and out
The figures, like a serpent, ran a scroll
Of letters in a tongue no man could read.
And Merlin called it "The Siege Perilous,"
Perilous for good and ill; "for there," he said,
"No man could sit but he should lose himself."
And once by misadvertence Merlin sat
In his own chair, and so was lost; but he,
Galahad, when he heard of Merlin's doom,
Cried, "If I lose myself, I save myself!"

Tennyson's lines paraphrase Luke 17:33 and a similar passage in Matthew: "Whosoever shall seek life shall lose it; and whosoever shall lose his life shall preserve it." This paradox is crucial to the nature of sainthood. Not only does the saint dedicate himself to higher principles, but he also dedicates himself to the compassionate service of others.

The fourth attribute of saintliness, James explains, is "a shifting of the emotional centre towards loving and harmonious affections, towards 'yes, yes' and away from 'no' where the claims of the non-ego are concerned." To embrace the positive, an individual had to build into his character four virtues: asceticism, strength of soul, purity, and charity. Asceticism, James suggested, entailed surrender of ego and self-consciousness to an all-consuming divinity that focuses the saint's attention outside or beyond himself. To achieve strength of soul, a saint would first have to let go of fears and anxieties. For a pure life, James noted, the saint would have to practise a kind of disciplined focus, to "deepen [his] spiritual consistency and keep unspotted from the world." And charity would come when he had learned to rise above his own emotions. "The saint," James wrote, "loves his enemies, and treats loathsome beggars as brothers." By any measure, being a saint is a tall order for a human being. And becoming a saint is no easy matter.

Canonization is a twenty-step process that resembles a jury trial. First, candidates are subjected to an inquiry under the direction of a postular-general. Witnesses testify to the reputation of the individual and the sanctity of his or her miracles. Next, a document—the transcript of the inquiry, in effect—is assembled and presented to a group of cardinals known as the Congregation of Rites. The Congregation of Rites has given the language one of its most famous clichés, "the devil's advocate." The devil's advocate is an individual appointed to argue against the would-be saint's case. In a courtroom-style drama, the Congregation of Rites hears the petition of the candidate and then re-examines all the evidence, from documents and testimonials to evaluations of the miracles. In the final stages, the candidate saint is examined for the presence in his or her life of heroic virtue. If all this evidence stands up to scrutiny, the Congregation of Rites passes on the recommendation for canonization to the pope, who then declares the individual worthy of veneration.

The question of how one becomes a saint, even in the secular sense, is explored by Graham Greene in his novel *The End of the Affair*. Greene, who converted to Roman Catholicism in 1926 to better understand what was going on in the mind of his fiancée of the time, spent the greater part of his literary career grappling with the great questions of the spirit. In works like *Brighton Rock, The Power and the Glory,* and *The End of the Affair,* Greene explored how individuals lived with the amalgamation of flesh and spirit when the spiritual aspect took command of their destiny. In *The End of the Affair,* a novel set in London during and after the Second World War, Greene told the story of a hack writer, Maurice Bendrix, and his relationship with a couple, Henry and Sarah. Bendrix has an affair with Sarah, an event that leads to her return to Roman Catholicism and Bendrix's disaffection from God. When she believes her lover has been killed by a bomb during the Blitz, Sarah makes a pact with God. Greene uses this pact to explore the nature of sainthood on a small scale in the modern world, following Sarah as she acquires the attributes of saintliness. Bendrix tries to console himself as he loses his lover to God (and eventually to tuberculosis) by telling himself that "unlike the rest of us," Sarah "was unhaunted by guilt." Sarah lives in that unique state of freedom that comes from a denial of the needs of the self:

> The moment only mattered. Eternity is said not to be an extension of time but an absence of time, and sometimes it seemed to me that her abandonment touched that strange mathematical point of endlessness, a point with no width, occupying no space. What did time matter—all the past and the other men she may from time to time (there is that word again) have known, or all the future in which she might be making the same statement with the same sense of truth? When I replied that I loved her too in that way, I was the liar, not she, for I never lose the consciousness of time: to me the present is never here: it is always last year or next week.

The great irony at work in Greene's novel is that for all his disdain for God, Maurice Bendrix is the one who pens Sarah's *acta sanctori*, her record of holiness. Bendrix even records the requisite three miracles. The first is the gift of life that is given to him when he lies bleeding at the door of his flat during the bombing raid. The second miracle is Sarah's attempted redemption of Bendrix when he thinks he hears her voice on Oxford Street:

> "Don't worry," she said. "Something always turns up. Don't
> worry," and suddenly I didn't worry. Oxford Street extended
> its boundaries into a great grey misty field, my feet were
> bare, and I was walking in the dew, alone, and stumbling in a
> shallow rut I woke, still hearing, "Don't worry," like a whisper
> lodged in the ear, a summer sound belonging to childhood.

The third miracle takes place when a childhood drawing of Sarah's makes its way into the hands of the son of a private detective who has been following Bendrix to determine Sarah's infidelity to Henry. As the boy, Lance Parkis, lies gravely ill with appendicitis, Sarah appears to him as a vision and he is miraculously cured. With the *acta sanctori* and the three miracles in hand, Sarah qualifies for a type of sainthood, even if Bendrix and Henry are the only ones who venerate her memory.

The presence of the miraculous in a saint's life is one of the key ingredients of sainthood. The miraculous suggests that the saint has the power to transform reality, to make right things that are wrong. The presence of the miraculous also strongly points to the idea that the world is still in possession of the forces of divinity and has not been completely given over to concrete, logical reality. Miracles and poetry come from the same source—the leap from the concrete to the abstract through the power of metaphor. Both demand that concrete logic be abandoned in favour of metaphorical logic, the identification of one image with another (even though reason says that a love cannot possibly be like a "red, red rose," and that a moon cannot be "a ghostly galleon tossed upon cloudy seas"). What is at work in metaphorical logic is a leap of faith.

For Greene, the great transforming power that propels the actions of a saint is love. When Bendrix takes stock of what he has been reporting throughout the novel, he is struck by the fact that love always seems to overcome the baser emotions, especially when it comes to his relationship with a modern saint:

> When I began to write our story down, I thought I was
> writing a record of hate, but somehow the hate has got
> mislaid and all I know is that in spite of her mistakes and her
> unreliability, she was better than most. It's just as well that one
> of us should believe in her: she never did in herself.

For Bendrix, misery and unhappiness are the markers for life, and he clings tenaciously to them, all the time sourly blaming God for what he is witnessing:

> The sense of unhappiness is so much easier to convey than that
> of happiness. In misery we seem aware of our own existence,
> even though it may be in the form of a monstrous egotism:
> this pain of mine is individual, this nerve that winces belongs
> to me and to no other. But happiness annihilates us: we lose
> our identity. The words of human love have been used by the
> saints to describe their vision of God, and so, I suppose, we
> might use the terms of prayer, meditation, contemplation to
> explain the intensity of the love we feel for a woman. We
> too surrender memory, intellect, intelligence, and we too
> experience the deprivation, the *noche oscura,* and sometimes as
> a reward a kind of peace.

Bendrix perceives himself as a kind of an anti-martyr, someone who suffers in opposition to God. He's the mirror image of Sarah, who embraces the suffering of her own death as an act of dedication to God. In her farewell letter to Bendrix, Sarah declares that she has become totally consumed by belief:

> I believe there's a God—I believe the whole bag of tricks, there's nothing I don't believe, they could subdivide the Trinity into a dozen parts and I'd believe. They could dig up records that proved Christ had been invented by Pilate to get himself promoted and I'd believe just the same. I've caught belief like a disease. I've fallen into belief like I fell in love. I've never loved before as I love you, and I've never believed in anything before as I believe now. I'm sure. I've never been sure before about anything.

Ultimately, what resides at the core of saintliness is the desire to emulate the divine. The medieval theologian Thomas à Kempis wrote a manual, called *On the Imitation of Christ,* for how one should conduct a holy life. He wrote of the need for emulation, where the saint heroically re-enacts the life and sufferings of Christ, for himself, for others, and for God. Kempis realized that there could be an element of egotism, pride of faith, involved in leading a holy life. Certainly, that is the warning sounded by commentators who have observed the self-destructive behaviour of people like Kateri Tekakwitha. In *On the Imitation of Christ,* Kempis warned of the perils of making holiness a goal for purely personal reasons:

> Seldom is anyone so spiritual as to strip himself entirely of self-love. Who can point out anyone who is truly poor in spirit and entirely detached from creatures? His rare worth exceeds all on earth. If a man gave away all that he possessed, yet it is

nothing. And if he did hard penance, still it is little. And if he attained all knowledge, he is still far from his goal. And if he had great virtue and most ardent devotion, he still lacks much, and especially the one thing needful to him. And what is this? That he forsake himself and all else, and completely deny himself, retaining no trace of self-love. And when he has done all that he ought to do, let him feel that has done nothing.

For Kempis, the holy life demanded that an individual should, by virtue of his holiness or even his demeanour, set himself apart from the world, even though he might be closely connected with worldly activities. Some early hermit saints understood this paradox and purposely made themselves into outsiders, withdrawing from society for a life of contemplation and prayer that emulated Christ's time in the desert. Emulation, however, need not be self-conscious or even an act of will. It can be a matter of circumstance.

In his novel *Light in August,* William Faulkner tells the story of Joe Christmas, an outsider who has often been called one of the most tragic figures in American literature. Christmas rejects love and ends his life pursued, castrated, and murdered—rejected by society. Christmas's very name suggests that Faulkner designed his character to be Christ-like. His birth is a moment surrounded by mystery, yet it's lower than even that of Christ, watched over only by God, an old, racist doctor, and a group of witnesses:

From that very first night, when He had chose His own Son's sacred anniversary to set it a-working on, He set old Doc Hines standing in the dark just behind the corner where he could see the doorstep and the accomplishment of the Lord's will, and he saw that young doctor coming in lechery and fornication stop and stoop down and raise the Lord's abomination and tote it into the house. . . ."We'll name him Christmas," and another one said, "What Christmas. Christmas what," and God said to old Doc Hines, "Tell them," and they all looked at old Doc Hines with the reek of pollution on them, hollering, "Why, it's Uncle Doc. Look what Santa Claus brought us and left on the doorstep, Uncle Doc," and old Doc Hines said, "His name is Joseph," and they quit laughing and they looked at old Doc Hines and the Jezebel said, "How do you know?" and old Doc Hines said, "The Lord says so," and they laughed again, hollering, "It is so in the Book: Christmas, the son of Joe. Joe, the son of Joe. Joe Christmas," they said, "To Joe Christmas," and they tried to make old Doc Hines drink too, to the Lord's abomination, but he struck aside the cup.

Evil things are predicted for Joe Christmas, who's a kind of anti-saint. He is a character who is fated to suffer from the moment of his birth. Like Kateri Tekakwitha, Christmas finds himself caught between two worlds—in his case, the two races of the southern United States. He is a thief who is waiting for redemption, but he's never permitted the opportunity for it by the society in which he lives. He spends fifteen years wandering after fleeing from his adoptive father, McEachern, just as Christ wandered in the desert. Like Christ in the garden at Gethsemane, Joe undergoes a kind of agony in his cabin on the Friday morning before he commits the murder of Joanna Burden, a reclusive white woman who lives in the remnants of an old plantation manor. As a boy learning the catechism, Joe Christmas is severely beaten by his adoptive father, McEachern, for laying the Bible on the floor of the stable where he sleeps. When McEachern confronts him and declares that the floor of the stable is no place for the word of God, Christmas rejoins that the floor of a stable was where the word of God made flesh was born.

Although Joe Christmas is far from being a saint, his life still reads as a hagiography. The point Faulkner was attempting to make was that emulation need not be sanctified, and that holiness can fall on the shoulders of anyone. The structure of the miraculous, Faulkner appears to be saying, is present in the world whether we recognize it or not, and even the lowest *phaulos* is capable of being raised up and dignified when he is touched by divinity.

That anyone can be touched by divinity is the point that the Venerable Bede made in his *A History of the English Church and People*. Written in 731 A.D., the book chronicles the history of England's conversion to Christianity and introduces the saints who affected the proselytization. In the midst of his narrative, Bede breaks off to tell the story of the miraculous birth of English poetry. In the abbey of Whitby lived a stablehand named Caedmon who was filthy, illiterate, and the butt of jokes among the monks of the community. The regular after-dinner entertainment in the abbey's refectory involved passing around a cup of honey wine known as mead. Each person was expected to have a drink of the potent beverage and then sing a song, make up a bawdy rhyme, or recite a favourite passage from Latin literature. One night the cup was passed to Caedmon. Embarrassed, he declared that he did not know how to sing and ran away to the stables to be with the swine and cattle that he tended. He threw himself down in a dung heap and bewailed his ignorance. Bede recounts what happened next:

There when the time came he settled down to sleep.
Suddenly in a dream he saw a man standing beside him
who called him by name. "Caedmon," he said, "sing me a
song." "I don't know how to sing," he replied. "It is because
I cannot sing that I left the feast and came here." The man
who addressed him then said: "But you shall sing to me."
"What could I sing about?" he replied. "Sing about the
Creation of all things," the other answered. And Caedmon
immediately began to sing verses in praise of God the
Creator that he had never heard before.

What came out of Caedmon's mouth that evening, to the astonishment of the monks at Whitby Abbey, was the beginning of a whole series of extended poems setting the entire Bible into Old English verse. The only parts of Caedmon's great, miraculous opus that remain are the first words that came out of his mouth, as recorded by Bede:

Nu scylun hergan   hefaenricaes Uard,
Medudaes maecti   end His modgidanc,
uerc Uuldurfadur,   sue He uundra gihuaes,
eci Dryctin,   or astelidae.
He aerist scop   aelda barnum
heben til hrofe,   haleg Scepen.
Tha middungeard   moncynnaes Uard,
eci Dryctin,   aefter tiadae
firum foldu   Frea allmectig.

These words seem strange and unusual to all but Old English scholars who study the roots of our language. Yet within Caedmon's words are echoes of Modern English: *uundra* for "wonders"; *hefaenricaes* for "kingdom of heaven"; and *Frea allmectig* for "Father Almighty." When translated into Modern English, Caedmon's invocation to God to assist him with the telling of a great story seems simple and almost childlike in its directness and sincerity:

Now must we praise the Guardian of heaven,
The power and conception of the Lord,
And all his works, as He, eternal Lord
Father of all glory, started every wonder.
First He created heaven as a roof,
The holy Maker, for the sons of men.
Then the eternal Keeper of mankind
Furnished the earth below, the land for men,
Almighty God and everlasting Lord.

At the heart of the Caedmon story is the idea that praise of God and the celebration of the wonders of the universe can give birth to holiness. Caedmon sees himself as simply a conduit for divine information, just as epic poets like Homer saw themselves as channels for information that was too big for human minds and tongues to handle. What writers have always known is that the path to understanding life and the universe must ultimately pass through the process of storytelling, where the voice of the imagination can have its say in the service of all that is good and life-affirming.

At the root of Christian sainthood is the prime source for the story of Christianity, the four Gospels that open the New Testament, and it can be said that all Christian saints' stories are essentially paraphrases of these texts. The individuals who are believed to have written the original texts, Matthew, Mark, Luke, and John, tell the story of the life of Jesus from four unique perspectives. The word "gospel" comes from the Old English words *god* and *spel,* which in Modern English mean "good news," "good spelling," or "good speaking." These are the essential stories, at least as Christian culture views them, by which one should live. They bring a humanity, a human presence, and a human face to the increasingly remote and strict divinity of the Old Testament.

The Gospels were selected as "essential texts" for practicing Christians by the Council of Nicaea, held in 325 A.D. (Among the texts that did not make the cut was the Gospel of Thomas, a collection of the sayings of Jesus. But some sayings—essentially those that were not metaphorically or philosophically too obscure to be understood by the average reader—did pass editorial muster and can be found repeated in the texts of the four existing Gospels.) The phraseology and even the details of the life and sayings of Jesus shift slightly from Gospel to Gospel, as if the four authors were engaged in a very subtle game of broken telephone. By the time a reader arrives at the Gospel of John, there is a strong sense of familiarity with the text. Some commentators have suggested that some of the texts, chiefly Matthew and Mark, were originally transmitted orally and only recorded at a later date. (If this is the case, there is a very strong argument to be made that the Gospels are an oral epic, like *Beowulf* or the *Odyssey,* because of the way that statements and events get repeated with slight variations, and that they are the product of the same kind of literary production that went into Homer's works.) Luke 1:1–3 even suggests that his Gospel is simply a compendium of what others have already said:

> For as much as many have taken in hand to set forth in order a declaration of those things which are most surely believed among us,

> Even as they delivered them unto us, which from the beginning were eye-witnesses, and ministers of the word;

> It seemed good to me also, having had perfect understanding of all things from the very first, to write unto thee in order.

The opening of Luke echoes the invocations that are found in the first lines of many classical epics; indeed, the story being told is as epic as literature can be.

These books amount to a metafictional approach to the life of Christ. They tell the same story in an almost postmodern way—from various angles, approaches, and points of view—much like William Faulkner's *As I Lay Dying* or John Fowles's *The French Lieutenant's Woman.* By the time a reader finishes Matthew, he or she has a basic awareness of the life of Jesus, his acts, and his beliefs. Why, then, are there four stories, all about the same information? The answer may lie in the fact that each Gospel reflects a different style of narrative.

Matthew is a novelist, and his narrative takes an epic approach to Christ's life and lineage. The reader knows right from the start that Jesus is no ordinary figure: he has a pedigree equal to that of just about any epic hero. We see with the earliest Western epics,

The Epic of Gilgamesh and the *Iliad,* that heroes are the products of their bloodlines. Matthew is essentially epigrammatic, a strong narrative writer who loves aphorisms, memorable turns of phrase, and repeatable quotes. Some of the most familiar phrases in the English language—"man shall not live by bread alone," "let not thy left hand know what thy right hand doeth," "there shall be weeping and gnashing of teeth"—originated in Matthew. His Gospel also contains the Protestant version of the Lord's Prayer (the Catholic version can be found in Luke 11:2–4) and offers the only explanation of what purpose the Gospels serve. And it is Matthew who says that the gospellers are conduits for divine information ("It is not ye that speak, but the Spirit of your Father which speaketh in you").

There are two theories about who Matthew was. Some believe he may have been one of the apostles, and early biblical commentators certainly thought that the author of the Gospel and the apostle were one in the same. Others think that the Gospel of Matthew was written by a Greek-speaking Jew who lived in Syria and composed the text well after the death of the apostle Matthew. Whatever the case, Matthew's Gospel shows the connection between the individual life of Jesus and his ideas. It is a philosophical novel in which the protagonist, like Birkin in D. H. Lawrence's *Women in Love* or a Sophoclean-type figure, shares his sense of "thought" (as Aristotle termed it in his six constituent elements of tragedy).

There is a drama to Matthew's Gospel that is missing from Mark's. If Matthew is the novelist, Mark is the reporter, the journalist. His narrative is straightforward and, as many commentators have noted, very unliterary. His style is almost Hemingway-esque in its terseness and lack of metaphorical language. The historical Mark, it is believed, slipped himself into the narrative as the young man who follows Christ after his arrest in Gethsemane. Judging by the style of writing, Mark may also have been an eyewitness to Jesus' Crucifixion. He takes a war correspondent's approach to his material, as if only the facts matter. Later in his life, Mark served Peter as an interpreter,

*An eighteenth-century
French engraving depicting
St. Matthew announcing
the message of the Gospel.*

someone who had to get his ideas right as a matter of life and death.
After assisting Peter, Mark is said to have travelled with St. Paul to
Cyprus, but he eventually left the team of evangelists to return to
Jerusalem. Shortly before his martyrdom, Paul is said to have urged
Timothy to bring Mark to Rome, where the Gospel of Mark was
likely written. It is uncertain whether Mark was martyred or not.
His legend suggests that he died in Egypt, where he was serving as
the bishop of Alexandria. The story Mark tells presents itself as a
record in order to highlight the key point he makes in his text: that
Jesus was a model of leadership.

Luke, who tells a very different kind of story, was a physician
by trade. His Gospel has a clinical flavour, as if he's dissecting and
analyzing events just as a modern biographer does in presenting the
life of a contemporary hero. Luke, who is also said to have written

the Acts of the Apostles, experienced the evangelist's many trials and tribulations. His job must have been to defend the new ideas of Christianity in the face of Greek philosophy, Roman rhetoric, and Semitic scepticism. There is a sense throughout that Luke is about to introduce someone who will explain everything, and one of the great functions that Luke serves is to act as a bridge between the original disciples and Christianity's greatest salesman, Paul. Yet Luke is no mere preface. He reintroduces the reader to the lineage of Jesus (3:23–38), explains the nature of eternal life (10:25–37), and relates the parable of the prodigal son (15:11–32). Most important, he lays the foundations for the ideas that will animate and inspire saintliness. The origins of the cult of the Virgin Mary can be found in Luke 1:38–49. In his telling, Mary is not just a mother standing by and watching her son, but an active agent who shapes Christ's personality and shares his thinking. Luke transforms her into a heroic figure of compassion and intercession. She becomes the mortal conduit between heaven and earth, the one female human who is taken into God's inner circle. Luke also gives an account of the Transfiguration that will be repeated in John, and he explains the concept of communion (22:17–20). He even gives an account of the end of the world, predicting wars, earthquakes, famines, pestilence, and a holocaust (21:8–16). But he also says that those who possess patience in their souls will survive.

For all his clinical dispassion, however, Luke is the gospeller who offers us the link between the real and the miraculous. He's also an apologist for the Christian imagination, and he looks on the miracles of Jesus with a sense of wonder, as if his scientific mind is constantly baffled by what has been reported to him. But Luke is not shrugging. As the physician, the man of science, he connects the particular events of Jesus' life to the larger question of how faith undergoes the radical transformation from idea to belief to doctrine. Luke offers the sense of a continuum, a series of connections stretching from the preachings of John the Baptist to the first inklings of a church.

In this famous image by Renaissance artist Albrecht Dürer, St. John receives the message of the Book of Revelations while in exile on the island of Patmos. The great leap that John makes is the transformation of the literal into the conceptual.

John is the poet/philosopher of the four. He transforms the Christian message from one of actuality and physicality into a metaphorical poem of ideas and abstract concepts. His text rises above the concrete level of reality and becomes pure idea. The historical John, if the various stories are true, is one of the great heroic figures of Western history. He appears to have been in Christ's inner circle, along with Peter and James (John's brother). John, Mark tells us in his Gospel, was present at the Transfiguration, when Jesus revealed himself as a divine person to those closest to him. John was also present at the Crucifixion, and his sense of reportage gives way to his desire to reflect on the life of Christ philosophically and to see the events transformed into images rather than left as facts. The historical John, if sources such as Jacobus de Voragine's *Golden Legend* are to be accepted as fact, was taken as a prisoner to Rome to be executed. In what amounts to Christianity's great escape, John miraculously leapt over the wall of the Mamartine prison, where Peter and Paul were also being held by the Romans. Having fled his captors, John lived an incredibly long life, dying at the age of one hundred, but not before he was called before Caesar and asked to explain himself. John appears to have completely rattled the Roman authoritarian, to the point that he reversed his sentence of death on the saint and condemned John to a life of exile on the tiny island of Patmos. While living in a cave on the island, John is believed to have composed Revelations, the final book of the New Testament. It is believed that he wrote his Gospel in about 96 A.D. while residing in Ephesus, in modern-day Turkey. John was one of history's great survivors. He saw a tremendous amount during his long life and attempted to sum up that broad experience in books that would transcend fact by allowing images, or mental pictures, to stand in for millions of words. The poetic language of his Gospel serves a purpose: poetry is compact. It allows John to say a great deal in a short space, using the kind of metaphorical vision that is also active in the Song of Solomon. To read John is to acquire practice in reading the poetic language of such later visionary Christian writers as Pascal, Blake, and Milton.

The fact that John's Gospel was the last of the four books to be composed may also account for the abstractness of the language. Information is not as important to John as ideas are, and the poetic compactness of the language suggests that his account was composed as a kind of short-hand memoir after a life spent considering the events as ideas rather than mere actions. Of all the biblical writers, John is the one who lives the most in the imagination. Having witnessed the Transfiguration, he appears to want to turn all perception from the concrete to the abstract (essential to an intelligent reading of poetry). John's Gospel is the most personally aimed of the four texts. Like a poem, it is meant to be carried in the reader's mind anagogically, as a set of images rather than facts—as ideas that can be understood

In this early eighteenth-century engraving from England, based on the font at Winchester Cathedral, the life of a proselytizing saint from the Dark Ages is rendered. Note how the saint, carrying a crozier, escapes martyrdom, a plague, and undertakes a heroic voyage.

in pictures but not easily conveyed in words. Transcendence of substance is the key theme.

When viewed together, the Gospels amount to a narrative, historical, philosophical, and poetic biography of Jesus. In each, the life of the gospeller dictated how the story was told. As intellectual history, they are among the first works of their kinds; they link the individual heroic life to concepts, and as such are a history of the insoluble connection between action and spirit that is so crucial to the nature of saintliness. They go beyond the mere sub-genre of lives, although hagiographies borrow their biographical structure from Matthew and Mark. But what is even more important about Matthew, Mark, Luke, and John is that they were the first practitioners of the storytelling process that resides at the heart of saintliness. They shared what they knew and believed with others in the hope that the narratives they created would present a path for others to follow.

What remains fascinating about saints is their sense of heroic generosity, their ability to give to others, above and beyond expectations. This generosity of spirit—the idea of *caritas* that William James thought was so important to a saint, and that Maximilian Kolbe demonstrated by giving his life for that of a fellow prisoner—is sounded by Matthew in chapter 25 of his Gospel:

For I was an hungered, and ye gave me meat: I was thirsty, and ye gave me drink: I was a stranger, and ye took me in:

Naked, and ye clothed me: I was sick, and ye visited me: I was in prison, and ye came unto me.

Inasmuch as I have done it unto one of the least of these my brethren, ye have done it unto me.

It is exactly this spirit of caring and compassion that we turn to in times of grief, disaster, and suffering. It is the desire to reach out and make the world right when it appears to have gone wrong. It is the spirit that resides in every human being, whether we choose to recognize it or not: the heroic ability to converse with the divine and to pursue that sense of peace and inner tranquillity that allows the voice of the imagination to be heard.

6 THE QUEST FOR ORDER

The Epic and Romance Hero

Gilgamesh, the ancient king of Uruk, in the Tigris–Euphrates valley, lay dying more than four thousand years ago. As he faced his mortality, he wondered, in spite of all his heroic accomplishments—and according to his chronicler, there were many—just what his life had amounted to. The poet who wrote *The Epic of Gilgamesh* appears to have been encouraging the notion of heroism by creating a grand structure of praise around his protagonist, for either poetic or political reasons. The poet cannot help being enamoured of this larger-than-life figure, who seems to have accomplished more than any human being to that point in recorded history:

> I will proclaim to the world the deeds of Gilgamesh. This was
> the man to whom all things were known; this was the king
> who knew the countries of the world. He was wise and he saw
> mysteries and knew secret things, he brought us a tale of the
> days before the flood. He went on a long journey, was weary,

Homer, the author of the Iliad *and the* Odyssey. *Here the ancient bard is depicted as Demodocus, the blind, vatic storyteller with his* lurikos *or lyre over his shoulder. Homeric epics were originally sung, if even to wandering young boys. A ship, presumably Odysseus', is seen foundering in the background.*

worn-out with labour, returning he rested, he engraved on a stone the whole story.

This invocative passage suggests that the hero is not just someone of great physical prowess, but also a man who has acquired knowledge of the world and its mysteries. Gilgamesh is an expression as much of the mind as of the body. And when the hero's body breaks down, he despairs that his intellectual conquests will vanish with him. But he is wrong. By placing him at the centre of a great narrative, the storyteller sees to it that Gilgamesh's knowledge will live on.

The chronicler reminds Gilgamesh that he once tamed a wild man who challenged his power, making him a lasting friend. Together, the two men had undertaken great journeys, conquering new lands in their search for cedars for shipbuilding and urban development to increase the wealth of their nation. Gilgamesh and his friend had faced an enormous giant who guarded the cedars, a monster of nightmare proportions, and had defeated him. When the gods decided that someone had to pay for the monster's death and took the friend, the ancient king went in search of a flower of immortality to restore his companion to life, such was the depth of his love. He found the flower among the dead and was about to return to the land of the living when a serpent rose up from the dark waters he was crossing and snatched the flower away. Gilgamesh was distraught, but the ancient boatman who had ferried him across the dark waters of the unknown region was philosophic. He told the king,

There is no permanence. Do we build a house to stand forever, do we seal a contract to hold for all time? Do brothers divide an inheritance to keep for ever, does the flood-time of rivers endure? It is only the nymph of the dragon-fly who sheds her larva and sees the sun in its glory. From the days of old there is no permanence.

Gilgamesh bears the mark of great heroes by responding to impossibility and impermanence with resistance of the highest order. To surrender to inevitability is simply not part of the heroic vocabulary. Tolstoy is said to have shouted, in a tiny railwayman's cottage on the Trans-Siberian line as he lay dying in a bed too short for his enormous frame, "To seek, always to seek!" The hero is someone who not only resists inevitability but believes that he might just beat the odds and overcome it.

Despite his best efforts, however, Gilgamesh is dying, and there is nothing he can do about it. But he realizes that even the great heroes of the past have their limitations. It is small but certain comfort to him. Even the narrator laments that this is the way of the world: "The heroes, the wise men, like the new moon, have their waxing and waning." Gilgamesh sighs and feels that his life has not really amounted to anything, but the chronicler reminds him that he dared to do things that no else has done. He brought order to a world that would have been in chaos had it not been for the king's oversized ambitions.

The clay tablets on which *The Epic of Gilgamesh* was written were housed in one of the earliest recorded libraries. Ironically, the fire that was meant to destroy the library actually transformed the unstable tablets into more resilient shards of pottery. They lay beneath the sands of Iraq for centuries, until they were discovered and reassembled into the oldest complete narrative in Western literature. In contemporary literary terminology, *Gilgamesh* is an *epic*, a sustained narrative song that takes as its setting the scope of the known world and as its focus the psychological core of a moment in history. The epic poem is driven by the need to celebrate its protagonist, and to demonstrate why he is worthy of such veneration and attention. The heroes of such works endure gruelling tests. They are often pitted against the world itself, and sometimes against the forces of the divine. And while these trials punish the central figure, they do not crush him; he survives to prove that man can overcome the perils of the world. As a work of literature, the epic reaffirms a reader's need to be reassured that his surrogate in the story will, in the words of William Faulkner, "not merely endure, he will prevail." The epic usually tells the reader what it is like to confront suffering and overcome it. The central character in an epic, the epic hero, carries tremendous expectations within the narrative structure.

The epic hero is expected to be of superhuman strength, and to undertake exceedingly difficult tasks and accomplish them with the help of magical, spiritual, or intellectual powers. He fits very tightly with the *Oxford English Dictionary* definition of the hero as "a man of superhuman qualities favoured by the gods." In fact, many characters, like Gilgamesh and Achilles, are not merely favoured by the gods but directly related to them. And the gods always look after their own. But what must be remembered, as Ovid pointed out in *Metamorphoses,* is that the gods are not tragic because they cannot die. In the case of Achilles, however, whom Odysseus encounters during his journey to the underworld, the human elements in the otherwise impeccable hero are his flaw, his *hamartia*. He dies because his father, Zeus, offers him as a sacrifice to appease those gods who backed the Trojans during the war. Achilles is fated to die so that the war can be settled. In Ovid's view, to be the object of a god's attention can be fatal, but to be favoured by the gods can be a life-saving experience. It's because of Athena that Odysseus, the sacker of the holy citadel of Troy, is able to return home. He is supported and sponsored by the goddess, who also assists his son, Telemachus, in the guise of Mentor. Divine assistance literally gives us the modern word "mentor."

Often, a god or goddess will intervene in the action on behalf of the hero, saving him from a hopeless situation. Aeneas, for example, is plucked from the battlefield, and certain death, in the *Iliad* and wakes up in his bedroom with his mother, the goddess Aphrodite, standing over him. When he asks where the missing scene in his life has gone, she assures him that it was not his time to die, and that further adventures await him. He must live, she informs him, for those to whom he will be responsible in his future. The Greeks referred to this type of event in drama and epic poetry as *deus ex machina* (from the Greek words *theos ek mekhanes,* or "god in the machinery," because the actors playing the gods often descended onto the stage by ropes and pulleys). The term, in its modern sense, means an unexpected power or event that saves a seemingly hopeless situation.

Epic heroes who are more than mortal are always introduced by their authors in terms of their lineage. (In this elite club, pedigree counts for everything.) Gilgamesh, for instance, is introduced to the reader as a unique amalgam of immortality and human beauty:

> When the gods created Gilgamesh they gave him a perfect
> body. Shamash the glorious endowed him with beauty.
> Adad the god of the storm endowed him with courage, the
> great gods made his beauty perfect, surpassing all others,
> terrifying like a great wild bull. Two-thirds they made him
> god and one-third man.

Lineage is what Odysseus shouts about to the blinded Cyclops as he escapes from the one-eyed giant's cave. Lineage is what Matthew traces in the opening lines of his Gospel, where he sets the stage for the coming of the son of God and the apotheosis of all history. Matthew reminds us that Jesus' ancestry qualifies him for the role he is about to play in reshaping mankind's story:

> So all the generations from Abraham to David are fourteen
> generations; and from David until the carrying away into
> Babylon are fourteen generations; and from the carrying away
> into Babylon unto Christ are fourteen generations.

Now the birth of Jesus Christ was on this wise: When his mother Mary was espoused to Joseph, before they came together, she was found with child of the Holy Spirit.

To Matthew, Jesus is the culmination of both history and divinity, an epic hero who transcends the limitations of previous epic heroes. Dante also seemed to acknowledge the parallels between Jesus and the warriors of the past when he placed him in the Heaven of Mars, the belligerent god, in Cantos XIV, XV, and XVI of the *Paradiso.* For Matthew and Dante, Jesus is just as heroic as Achilles, and so they present his life using structures and conventions usually reserved for bronze-clad epic warriors.

Lineage defines who a hero is in terms of his ancestors, and it also determines the peculiarities of his character. Beowulf is, in many ways, the amalgamation of classical and Christian heroic conventions. His calling card to the Scyldings, the people he has come to save from the hideous Grendel, is his lineage. To prove that he is qualified for the position of pest-controller in the murky swamps of northern Europe, Beowulf asserts his pedigree:

We are men of the Geatish nation
and Hygelac's hearth-companions.
My father was well-known among men,
a noble commander named Ecgtheow;
he saw many winters before he passed away,
ancient, from the court; nearly everyone
throughout the world remembers him well.

After much courtly ado, Beowulf finally declares who he is in his own right, rather than by virtue of his heritage: "My name is Beowulf."

But the personal identity of the epic hero is not as important as his familial identity. In Homer's *Iliad,* each character presents himself for battle by first stating his lineage and tracing his bloodlines to heroes of the past. In Book VI, for example, a young warrior named Glaucus steps forward for combat. He is a descendant of the mythic hero Bellerophon, who saddled and rode the famed winged horse Pegasus into battle. Glaucus declares:

> But Hippolochus fathered me, I'm proud to say.
> He sent me off to Troy . . . .
> and I hear his urgings ringing in my ears:
> "Always be the best, my boy, the bravest,
> and hold your head up high above the others.
> Never disgrace the generation of your fathers.
> They were the bravest champions born in Corinth,
> in Lycia far and wide."
>   There you have my lineage.
> That is the blood I claim, my royal birth.

It is little wonder that both William Blake and Simone de Beauvoir called the *Iliad* the most dangerous book ever written. Not only does it depict the wholesale slaughter of a generation and the termination of the mythic households of the past, but it also serves as a statement on duty that inspires young men to exceed themselves to the point of being blind to their own weaknesses. Within a hundred lines, young Glaucus is dead. Homer cautions his reader about the waste of war earlier in the same book:

> Like the generations of leaves, the lives of mortal men.
> Now the wind scatters the old leaves across the earth,
> now the living timber bursts with the new buds
> and spring comes round again. And so with men:
> as one generation comes to life, another dies away.

Beneath this layer of wisdom is a much darker message that it is heroic to die. The tragedy of the *Iliad* appears to stem from the sense that the inheritors of the heroic traditions of the past are not the heroes themselves but later members of a less distinguished generation.

In Book I of the *Iliad,* Homer points out that the Trojan War takes place not in the age of the great heroes of myth—Theseus, Perseus, and Bellerophon—but in the age *after* these heroes. It's a time when success in venture is less likely, though the combatants may not be aware of that:

> And none of the men who walk the earth these days
> could battle with those fighters, none, but they,
> they took to heart my counsels, marked my words.

The exception, of course, is Achilles, a son of Zeus, whose physical and strategic prowess are second to none. But the reader is aware that Achilles has a weakness, his famous heel, and that it will be the undoing of him. Achilles' mother, Thetis, also realizes what is in store for her son as he embarks upon the long, costly folly that will be the Greek siege of Troy:

> O my son, my sorrow, why did I ever bear you?
> All I bore was doom. . . .
> Would to god you could linger by your ships
> without a grief in the world, without a torment!
> Doomed to a short life, you have so little time.
> And not only short, now, but filled with heartbreak too,
> more than all other men alive—doomed twice over.
> Ah to a cruel fate I bore you in our halls!

The tragic irony in this is that Achilles believes himself to be immortal, despite his mother's protestations, and he leaves for the war full of the courage to face whatever may come. It is pride that drives Achilles, and it is also pride that blinds him, as it does so many young men eager to go to war, to the realities he may face. Still, even though he has so many odds against him, the reader bets he will survive. The narrative ends before Achilles' death, leaving a strange sense of defeat and anxious anticipation. The *Iliad* ends in a miasma where both the reader and the protagonist find themselves hoping against hope, trapped in the delusion of a positive outcome.

This sense of delusion is what Cervantes mocks in his quasi-epic hero, Don Quixote of La Mancha. Cervantes suggests that his pale knight's foolishness is the result of his reading stories about others who have been equally foolish in pursuing truth, justice, and morality in their quest to set the world right:

> In short, our gentleman became so caught up in reading that he spent his nights reading from dusk till dawn and his days reading from sunrise to sunset, and so with too little sleep and too much reading his brains dried up, causing him to lose his mind. His fantasy filled with everything he had read in his books, enchantments as well as combats, battles, challenges, wounds, courtings, loves, torments, and other impossible foolishness, and he became so convinced in his imagination of the truth of all the countless grandiloquent and false inventions he read that for him no history in the world was truer.

Figures from the legends of El Cid and Hercules flutter through Don Quixote's mind and blind him to the realities of the world. Cervantes seems to be saying that epic heroes are the most powerful of all role models because they tell the reader that impossible things can and should be done. Worse yet, epic heroes encourage those who are not equipped to undertake their ventures, and the results can be horrific. Cervantes had read his Homer, especially the *Iliad,* and he was aware that there is often a great capability gap between what we believe we can accomplish and what we can actually accomplish. This capability

Aeneas relating the story of his adventures to the Carthaginian queen Dido. It is in this same tower that Dido will commit suicide as Aeneas sails away to pursue his destiny.

gap is, metaphorically speaking, the road to Tartarus, the underworld where the shades of dead heroes roam.

When a character on the battlefield before the walls of Troy perishes in the *Iliad,* the past dies with him. What makes the *Iliad* pathetic, rather than tragic, is that the reader is seeing the destruction of history. The Trojan War marks the end of the Heroic Age. The world after Troy, the world that Homer offers in the *Odyssey,* is a vacuum, a place where the individual must fight for survival because there is no greatness left. The last epic hero, Odysseus, is even willing to pass himself off as "Nobody" to avoid being eaten by a badly mannered giant.

As the centre of the universe in which his poem is cast, the epic hero must be a person who cares about the outcome of events. In Virgil's *Aeneid,* the very future of Rome rests on the shoulders of Aeneas as he shepherds his band of Trojan followers towards the "ever-retreating horizon." In *La Chanson de Roland,* the fate of France and

Christian Europe depends on whether or not Roland and his stalwart troops can defend Roncesvalles Pass. (The impact of these characters on readers cannot be underestimated. The muds of Verdun in 1916 were soaked with the literary spirit of Roland as the front-line troops fought to the last man.) But unlike their modern counterparts—who are, for the most part, nameless and faceless figures in the mass of twentieth-century history—epic heroes are individualized by virtue of their upper-class standing. The valour that such heroes display requires an incredible sense of focus and courage, attributes that in Aristotelian terms are admirable because the characters are good. The sense of responsibility that they bear would overwhelm most mortals, and because of this, epic heroes are usually cast in hyperbolized terms and their actions seem to grow in the imagination. What the epic hero represents is the idea that from among the ranks of mere mortals, there can emerge figures who are worthy of both veneration and emulation. As figures of hyperbole, gross exaggerations, they are scrutinized for both their flaws and their talents. What separates the epic hero from the tragic hero is that he wants to control his own destiny rather than be a puppet of events, and for the most part he succeeds.

An epic hero possesses a sense of certainty that seems cockily incredulous. We see this perhaps most clearly in the protagonist of the Dark Ages masterpiece *Beowulf*. What Beowulf defends is not merely Hrothgar's community hall and the gift stool from which all bounties and amenities are dispensed, but the very idea of society, the social structure that provides identity, purpose, and place for all involved in the community. A figure of imposing stature, Beowulf represents the apotheosis of what his world can offer in terms of human achievement. Presented with the crown of his kingdom after defeating both Grendel and his mother, Beowulf modestly declines. He is tempted by power, but he knows that if he gives in to that temptation, he runs the risk of diminishing himself. The hero, in *Beowulf*, is someone who is in service of society. Even the narrator steps away from his mandatory epic objectivity to warn his hero about the weakness that earthly pride can inflict upon a leader:

> Defend yourself from wickedness, dear Beowulf,
> best of men, and choose the better,
> eternal counsel; care not for pride,
> great champion! The glory of your might
> is but a little while; soon it will be
> that wickedness or the sword will shatter your strength,
> of the grip of fire, or the surging flood,
> or the cut of a sword, or the flight of a spear,
> or terrible old age—or the light of your eyes
> will fail and flicker out; in one fell swoop
> death, o warrior, will overwhelm you.

The narrator is conscious of the fact that there are any number of ways a hero can be brought down. In the end, though, Beowulf dies a heroic death while fighting a massive dragon, the last threat of an animate universe that he has set himself the task of making inanimate.

Beowulf struggles with the idea that his life has a definite path that must be followed. He believes in destiny, just as Aeneas believes that he has been "called ever onward from shore to shore" until he can re-establish his native city of Troy. But destiny can present a problem within a narrative, in that it sets a course for the story and allows no room for surprise. These narrative limitations were likely in the mind of the anonymous poet who created *Beowulf*. The operative feature of the poem is a force called *wyrd,* a word that has come down to modern English as "weird" and is closely connected to the ideas of fate and destiny. The world of *Beowulf,* generally dated to the late eighth century, the height of the Dark Ages in northern Europe, is a world in transition, caught between the mentalities of Christian providence and pagan fatalism. Within this polarized society, *wyrd* becomes a strange amalgam of both providence and Sophoclean fate.

At the conclusion of Book X, the hero stands guard in the mead hall of Heorot, waiting for the arrival of his archfiend, Grendel. Beowulf knows that events are in God's hands, but he still lives with the pagan uncertainty that casts *wyrd* as the sort of unpredictability that could lead to a tragic outcome:

> In the dark night he came
> creeping, the shadow-goer. The bowmen slept,
> who were to hold that horned hall—
> all but one. It was well-known to men
> that the demon foe could not drag them under
> the dark shadows if the Maker did not wish it;
> but he, wakeful, keeping watch for his enemy,
> awaited, enraged, the outcome of battle.

In a previous section, the poet notes that courage is what an individual can use to mitigate the force of *wyrd,* and that "*wyrd* often spares an undoomed man, when his courage endures." Survival is the combination of providence—God's plan and grace—strength, and individual determination. But the wild card is the unpredictability of events. No one can be certain of anything. The world of *Beowulf* is a miasma of both mind and boggy landscape, where things really do go bump in the night, and "*wyrd* always does as it must."

The epic hero, in this context, is someone who can harness circumstance and situation in spite of the murkiness of events. Eventually, Beowulf does relent and become the leader of his people, but only when his society is under threat from the dragon and there are no other options. When the mantle of kingship finally falls to him, he accepts it as his destiny, or his *wyrd*. Beowulf demonstrates the same reluctance that is shown by Jason in the story of the quest of the Golden Fleece in Apollonius of Rhodes' third-century B.C. travelogue and epic *The Voyage of the Argo*. In that work, the Argonauts, the heroes chosen to undertake the lengthy and risky mission of

Jason and Medea, the hero and his girl.

stealing a heap of golden wool from a city at the far end of the Black Sea, make Hercules their original choice for leader. He gratefully and humbly declines because, he insists, he is still a slave and has not yet completed his obligatory labours. Instead, he urges the Argonauts to choose Jason:

> The young men's eyes sought out the dauntless Heracles where he sat in the centre, and with one voice they called him to take command. But he, without moving from his seat, raised his right hand and said: "You must not offer me this honour. I will not accept it for myself, nor will I let another man stand up. The one who assembled this force must be its leader too."
>
> The magnanimity that Heracles had shown won their applause and they accepted his decision. Warlike Jason was delighted. He rose to his feet and addressed his eager friends.

Jason sets his men to action, just as Beowulf takes action when he is given the opportunity. The epic hero must always seize the moment by implementing a plan or spearheading a journey. Where characters such as Hamlet end tragically because they cannot take the helm of their own destinies, epic heroes always set a plan in motion, or at least understand what they must do to guarantee their progress.

It is little wonder that most epic heroes undertake tremendous voyages. The journey is, perhaps, one of the most prevalent themes in Western literature, whether that journey is Moses leading the Israelites towards Canaan or Chaucer's pilgrims wending their way towards Canterbury. The Bible itself is one large journey narrative that tells the story of mankind's passage through time, from the very beginning of the world to the establishment of a heavenly order beyond time. If the Bible is a macrocosm of the story of mankind, it is fair to say that the epic hero represents the microcosmic view of the relationship between time and experience. The epic hero's response to events, in many respects, is the human imagination's response to the need for order and security. The journey, in this sense, represents the process by which the hero goes about establishing that order.

The French symbologist J. E. Cirlot suggested that the journey, as a symbol in Western imagination, "is never merely a passage through space, but rather an expression of the urgent desire for discovery and change that underlies the actual movement and experience of travelling." The restlessness that is a trait in characters like Odysseus forms a pattern that most epic heroes follow as they pursue their adventures. The first step in this pattern is the realization that a journey must be undertaken. This stage, best described as the impetus for the task, is often the hero's answer to a challenge or a perceived need. Odysseus, for example, learns from his travels and broadens his mind. And Aeneas comes to value responsibility and homeland as he voyages. The great paradox here is that although home is the hero's absolute destination, the journey is in itself a learning process and, perhaps, a more profound accomplishment. The journey, not the arrival, is what makes the hero heroic. The twentieth-century Greek poet C. P. Cavafy, in "Ithaka," a poem that was read at the funeral of Jacqueline Kennedy Onassis, suggests that the learning process is merely a matter of reminding ourselves of what we already know:

> Keep Ithaka always in your mind.
> Arriving there is what you're destined for.
> But don't hurry the journey at all.
> Better if it lasts for years,
> so you're old by the time you reach the island,
> wealthy with all you've gained on the way,
> not expecting Ithaka to make you rich.
> Ithaka gave you the marvelous journey.
> Without her you wouldn't have set out
> She has nothing left to give you now.

Cavafy insists that life is a process, and that we must "learn and go on learning" from the experience of life itself. Cavafy's inspiration was the *Odyssey,* where Odysseus' delayed return home only sharpens his appetite for his wife, his bed, and his people. What the hero cannot have he only pines for all the more. The greatest threat that Odysseus faces is not the Cyclops or Calypso, or even Scylla and Charybdis, but the moly his men eat that makes them forget what is ultimately important to them—their homes. The process of returning home is akin to the process of education, where the learning, not the knowing, is what builds mind and character. The journey, in this sense, is the process of self-discovery. The great challenge that is thrown down before the epic hero is not to go and fetch some special object, such as Helen of Troy or a mat of Golden Fleece, but to seek to know himself in the best Greek interpretation of the idea. Most epic voyages focus not on where the hero is going, but on what will he learn about himself along the way.

The next definable stage of the epic hero's journey is the confrontation of obstacles. By this point, the hero is well aware of the purpose of his travels. Aeneas, for example, tells a colony of fellow Trojans that he has been "called ever onwards from destiny to destiny." He presses forward with his journey through paradox, pursuing a homeland that always seems to lie beyond the horizon. The pursuit, not the end result, is what preoccupies his imagination and his body.

In encountering obstacles, the hero learns the process of problem-solving. Indeed, the events of his journey act as didactic conundrums that the reader and the hero share in solving. When Odysseus must pass the Sirens' island without succumbing to their destructively enchanting song, he presents the problem to his men:

> We must beware of their song and give their flowery meadow
> a wide berth. I alone, she [Circe] suggested, might listen to
> their voices; but you must bind me hard and fast, so that I
> cannot stir from the spot where you will stand me, by the step
> of the mast, with the rope's ends lashed round the mast itself. . . .
>   Meanwhile I took a large round of wax, cut it up small
> with my sword, and kneaded the pieces with all the strength
> of my fingers. The wax soon yielded to my vigorous treatment
> and grew warm, for I had the rays of my Lord the Sun to help
> me. I took each of my men in turn and plugged their ears
> with it. They then made me a prisoner on my ship by binding
> me hand and foot, standing me up by the step of the mast and
> tying the rope's ends to the mast itself.

The rewards of listening to the Sirens' song—the experience of perilous beauty—only underscore the longing that Odysseus already feels for his home. Hearing the song, however, teaches him that he must be well equipped to confront the obstacles that challenge not only his strength and his tenacity, but also his intelligence. And the more problems he solves, the sharper his cunning when he encounters the next puzzle.

Aside from the obstacles, the epic hero's journey is troubled by delays. Anyone who has ever waited in an airport departure lounge for a flight that does not want to take off will understand the frustration and despair that temporal delays can stir up in a hero. Aeneas' time with Dido, Odysseus' eight-year delay on Calypso's island, and the Red Crosse Knight's idleness by the magical stream in Book I of Spenser's *Faerie Queene* are actually learning periods, not moments of inertia. During these learning periods, when his forward progress is impaired by either love or magic, the hero has time to assess himself, to sort what he believes is important from the dross of experience. Homer describes Odysseus' Calypso episode as period of severe introspection and soul-searching. The nymph offers Odysseus incredible sex and immortality on a deserted island—a travel brochure's most stunning enticement. But Odysseus is more troubled by what he cannot have than by what he has:

> His eyes were wet with weeping, as they always were. Life
> with its sweetness was ebbing away in the tears he shed for his
> lost home. . . . At nights, it is true, he had to sleep with her
> under the roof of the cavern, cold lover with an ardent dame.
> But the days found him sitting on the rocks or sands, torturing
> himself with tears and groans and heartache, and looking out
> with streaming eyes across the watery wilderness.

Odysseus eventually reveals to Calypso his true desire. And although he praises her and tells her that she is far more beautiful than the wife he longs for at home in Ithaka, he is determined to break off the relationship and free himself from his delay:

> Nevertheless I long to reach my home and see the happy day
> of my return. It is my never-failing wish. And what if the
> powers above do wreck me out on the wine-dark sea? I have
> a heart that is inured to suffering and I shall steel it to endure
> that too. For in my day I have had many bitter and shattering
> experiences in war and on the stormy seas. So let this new
> disaster come. It only makes one more.

*A Christian knight
battling the forces of
evil and temptation.*

The delay has fortified Odysseus for further challenges. After all,
what is one more challenge to a man who has endured so much?
"Bring it on," he seems to say.

Just when the hero thinks he has seen it all, the fourth phase of his
journey, the confrontation with death, presents itself as yet another
means of expanding mind and soul. In most epics, the hero undergoes a *nekusis,* a harrowing of the land of death. In a *nekusis,* the hero
metaphorically swims through the world of the afterlife, passing, as
it were, under water through an environment that is a metaphorical
alternative reality to the conscious world, a place without life. The
miasma of the underworld, or the waters of death, is suggestive of the
pre-birth world, where we literally float in a sea of salty water until
we are ready to enter conscious existence. In Exodus, the Israelites
cross the Red Sea with God's assistance and are reborn on the other
side as the nation of Israel. The epic hero of that story is not merely
Moses but all the children of the emerging nation, who break away

from bondage under Pharaoh. In the Christian story, Christ suffers the death of a mortal and ventures in his heavenly form down into the underworld, where he frees the souls of those who have foretold the coming of his grace and redemption.

Secular epics also have *nekusis* episodes. In Book I of Spenser's *The Faerie Queene,* the Red Crosse Knight passes through the House of Pride, a metaphorical underworld that houses the Seven Deadly Sins, among other things, and presents itself as the parody of the House of Holiness, a far less elaborate but more honest setting. Virgil reinvents Book XI of the *Odyssey* when he sends his Trojan prince to the underworld on the advice of a prophetess, the Cumaean Sibyl. To enter the land of no return, Aeneas must first pluck from its gateway a golden bough, likely a branch of mistletoe, as that plant was believed to possess magical properties. "Each time the bough is torn from its place," the Sibyl advises,

> another never fails to appear, golden like the first, and its stem grows leaves also of gold. So therefore you must lift up your eyes and seek to discern this bough, find it as it is required of you, and pluck it boldly. Then, if it is indeed you whom the Fates are calling, it will come willingly and easily; if not, by no strength will you master it, nor even hack it away with a hard blade of steel.

Mistletoe, which is a fungus rather than a plant, has no roots, and the European variety favours the top of oak trees, a symbol of divinity. When mistletoe withers, it turns a golden colour, instead of a dull brown. And because it blooms in the middle of winter, at the time of the world's lifelessness, it is perceived as a symbol of life in death. Aeneas plucks his bough so he can pass through a world of death and become golden with knowledge for having done so. The bough also symbolizes the hero's worthiness for this, his greatest test. Looking death in the eye, up close and on its own terms, is not a task for just anyone. It is the signal that the epic hero has been selected to acquire the divine knowledge that only an experience of living through death can provide.

What the epic hero gains from going down into the underworld is a complete sense of what it is in his personality that needs to be completed. When Odysseus descends to the nether regions, he learns what is happening elsewhere in his world, and what is to come for him in the future. When Aeneas disappears into the afterworld, he is reunited with his father, and the Roman themes of patriarchy, duty, and discipline are reinforced for him. As he looks on the figures of the past and the faces of the future, he comes to the maturing realization that he is answerable not only to tradition but to what is yet to be. The moment defines how he sees himself. The world is not about his momentary needs or desires, but about how he can communicate the values that have enabled him to survive to those whose existence is dependant on his faith in things to come. Aeneas stands in the middle of the stream of time, not at its wellspring, and it is this recognition that provides him with his ultimate knowledge of the self, his context.

The idea that a *nekusis* can lead to the acquisition of self-knowledge is the theme of Dante's *Divine Comedy*. In the first book of the trilogy, *Inferno*, Dante recognizes that his life's progress is barred by his vulnerability to the sins of the world. He opens his vision of hell, purgatory, and heaven with lines that speak of coming into a consciousness of his own mortal predicament:

> Midway this way of life we're bound upon,
> I woke to find myself in a dark wood,
> Where the right road was wholly lost and gone.
>
> Ay me! how hard to speak of it—that rude
> And rough and stubborn forest! the mere breath
> Of memory stirs the old fear in the blood;

It is so bitter, it goes nigh to death;
Yet there I gained such good, that, to convey
The tale, I'll write what else I found therewith.

The world, for Dante, has become a forest, a medieval symbol of confusion, darkness, and impenetrable secrets. The valley in which the forest is located is a metaphorical labyrinth, not unlike the dark passages where Theseus confronted and slew the Minotaur:

But when at last I stood beneath a steep
Hill's side, which closed that valley's wandering maze
Whose dread had pierced me to the heart-root deep,

Then I looked up, and saw the morning rays
Mantle its shoulder from that planet bright
Which guides men's feet aright on all their ways;

And this a little quieted the affright
That lurking in my bosom's lake had lain
Through the long horror of that piteous night.

As a swimmer, panting, from the main
Heaves safe to shore, then turns to face the drive
Of perilous seas, and looks, and looks again,

So while my soul yet fled, did I contrive
To turn and gaze on that dread pass once more
Whence no man yet came ever out alive.

The dread pass is the passageway to the underworld, and Dante confronts the challenge of venturing into the land of death as a swimmer would deep, uncharted waters where he could drown. The labyrinth is both psychological and cosmological. Dante has turned his

Dante being led through hell by his guide, Virgil, expressing the idea that one epic poet can teach another the ropes of the afterlife. This print from Doré's Inferno *depicts Dante and Virgil in Canto XXIII, under attack from demons.*

eyes not to the world of death as a physical place, but to the experience of dying within himself, both spiritually and imaginatively. He has wandered into the landscape of his own imagination—a landscape that has been created through his experience of the world and through his reading. It is no accident that he chances upon a guide to lead him through his worst nightmares and his gravest suspicions, the poet Virgil.

Dante turns towards the underworld and its landscape of the imagination because his way ahead on life's road has been barred by three creatures: the Lion, the Leopard, and the Wolf. Each represents a type of sin. Will he be challenged by his pride, his flesh, or his own worst nature? It is in Dante that the epic hero becomes moral champion, though the character Dante in *The Divine Comedy* is essentially just a curious and informed observer of humankind. The descent into hell is, for Dante the author and Dante the character, an opportunity to witness humanity at its most reduced level. Stripped of

Gustav Doré's rendering of Dante on the threshold of the Empyrean, beholding the splendour of the Almighty.

their pretences, the souls in hell are completely exposed. And when everything humane about them is no longer present, they become the manifestations of their sins.

This same reduction of a human being to his most absurd level occurs in the Cyclops episode of the *Odyssey,* when Odysseus saves himself by pretending to be Nobody. Dante suggests that pride is a form of consuming self-awareness, and that, in the words of the medieval English mystic Richard Rolle, "people become like what they love." The ability to abandon oneself and the preoccupations of the ego is, for Dante, the pathway to both salvation and a liberating joy. In Canto XXXI of the *Paradiso,* Dante, the pilgrim of the imaginative world, offers a prayer that seems to sum up his experience of having passed through the gamut of human experience. What he has learned is that he must unlearn everything in his mortal mind to fully comprehend and embrace the freedom of the infinite:

O thou in whom my hopes securely dwell,
And who, to bring my soul to Paradise,
Didst leave the imprint of thy steps in Hell,

Of all that I have looked on with these eyes
Thy goodness and thy power have fitted me
The holiness and grace to recognize.

Thou hadst led me, a slave, to liberty,
By every path, and using every means
Which to fulfil this task were granted thee.

Keep turned toward me thy munificence
So that my soul which thou hast remedied
May please thee when it quits the bonds of sense.

Dante ultimately realizes that his own human experience is a limitation, and that what lies beyond "the bonds of sense" may be far more marvellous than anything he can take in through the five portals of realization, his senses. Life itself is reducing. The question is, What lies beyond it?

For Boethius, one of Dante's silent guides, the answer to that question is home. The final stage in the journey of an epic hero is the return. This is the moment when the hero realizes that his journey has been a circle that has led him back to where he started and to what he always knew he had inside him. The journey, in this sense, is about release and recognition, about accessing vital knowledge that can liberate an individual both spiritually and psychologically. In *The Consolation of Philosophy,* Boethius argues that mankind's true home is God, and that the great journey of time and history began with the fall of man from his original state of grace. The way home, he declares, is to be found through wisdom. In words that likely inspired

Dante, Boethius suggests that we are always in a state of exile from our true nature and our true home:

> No wise man prefers being an exile, being poor or disgraced
> to being rich, respected and powerful, and to remaining at
> home and flourishing in his own city. For this is the way that
> wisdom is more clearly and obviously seen to be operating,
> when somehow or other the happiness of their rulers is
> communicated to the people they come into contact with,
> especially if prison and death and all the other sufferings the
> law imposes by way of punishment are reserved for the wicked
> citizens for whom they were intended. Why this is all turned
> upside down, why good men are oppressed by punishments
> reserved for crime and bad men catch rewards that belong
> to virtue, surprises me very much, and I would like to know
> from you the reason for this very unjust confusion.

Boethius is addressing himself to Dame Philosophy, his guide through what will be a heroic voyage to understand the true nature of happiness and inner peace. She informs him that she will show him "the path that will bring" him "back home."

The idea of the journey as a progression towards a state of grace resides at the core of medieval *dream-vision poems* such as William Langland's *Piers Ploughman* or Guillaume de Lorris and Jean de Meun's *Romance of the Rose*. In such poems, the hero takes on the role of a traveller through his own unconscious, a miasmal world where characters become personifications and events become allegories. As Langland notes at the opening of *Piers Ploughman,* the cosmos in a dream-vision poem is a wilderness, a place of chaos that the hero cannot navigate without profound faith:

> And I dreamt a marvellous dream: I was in a wilderness. I
> could not tell where, and looking Eastwards I saw a tower

high up against the sun, and splendidly built on top of a hill; and far beneath it was a great gulf, with a dungeon in it, surrounded by deep, dark pits, dreadful to see. But between the tower and gulf I saw a smooth plain, thronged with all kinds of people, high and low together, moving busily about their worldly affairs.

Some laboured at ploughing and sowing, with no time for pleasure, sweating to produce food for the gluttons to waste. Others spent their lives in vanity, parading themselves in a show of clothes. But many, out of love for our Lord and in the hope of Heaven, led strict lives devoted to prayer and penance—for such are the hermits and anchorites who stay in their cells, and are not forever hankering to roam about, and pamper their bodies with sensual pleasures.

Langland follows this passage with a Whitmanesque description of society as a teeming mass where each individual is driven towards his own personal goal, completely disconnected from every other person. What Langland perceives as the unifying force of mankind, however, is love, and the first book of *Piers Ploughman,* a severe work that lectures rather than delights, ends with the assertion that the path to heaven is paved with love. Love, for Langland, is what lies beneath the sense of self-forgetting that seems to come naturally to saints and responsibility-driven heroes like Aeneas: "Love is the physician of life, the power nearest to our Lord himself, and the direct way to Heaven." To achieve that love, however, the hero of the dream-vision poem, and the epic poem, must pass through the veil of the fantastic to a realm that can be read and interpreted only with cunning or charity or clear thinking.

In the medieval Arthurian narrative, *The Quest of the Holy Grail,* the knights find themselves lost alone in a thick forest. When Sir Hector and Sir Gawain, two of the less reputable members of the Round Table, meet up, they wonder why neither has seen hide nor hair of the other knights. The others, it appears, have vanished into the woodwork. The Waste Forest is a labyrinth, a place full of secrets, twists, and turns that are almost impossible to navigate. The Waste Forest, however, is also a place of tests, where characters like Sir Bors are confronted with moral and allegorical problems that they must solve before they can continue their journeys and move ahead to the next level of achievement. When Sir Bors is confronted with an image of a maiden in danger and his brother in distress, he chooses to save the maiden, believing that the chivalric obligation to the code of courtly love is the highest calling. But a hermit appears before him and tells him that his answer is wrong. The maiden, the hermit tells Bors, would have rewarded him, and Bors performed his duties out of an expectation of that reward. Although his brother would likely not have rewarded the knight, brotherly love is, according to the Gospels, the highest form of earthly dedication, and Sir Bors should have answered the call from his sibling no matter what. The answers to the questions posed in the Waste Forest lie not in logic but in moral knowledge, in the mind, heart, and soul and not in external sources. The Waste Forest is, in this respect, a metaphor for disordered thinking, for ideas without methodology. What the knights must do is find the key to unlocking the process by which they can solve the problem.

The dream vision is set in exactly the same landscape. The hero must find both the answer to the question posed and the process for moving towards that answer. In this miasmal world, the extended metaphor of each situation is meant to be a spiritual and intellectual test for the traveller. The traveller himself, the dream-vision hero, is in many ways an extension of the epic hero, in that he is a person on whom a great deal depends. But while the epic hero is supporting the survival of a people or a nation, the dream-vision hero is supporting the salvation of his own soul, and by extension enabling the salvation of others. The dream-vision poem depicts a pilgrimage, for either faith or love, within the mind of the dreamer. Such poems suggest

Bunyan's Christian knight, Christian, battling the evil giant Apollyon, the embodiment of paganism and godlessness.

that the mind of a human being is as vast and limitless as Virgil's "ever-retreating horizon," an expanse that can contain the scope of the entire universe. What lies behind poems like *Piers Ploughman* or allegorical narratives like John Bunyan's *The Pilgrim's Progress* is the idea that each individual carries with him a burden. The journey relieves the character of that burden; his path to discovery, righteousness, faith, or divine understanding is actually a set of moral instructions for the reader to follow. The dream vision carries the didacticism of tragedy and melds it with the moral imperative of the epic. A pilgrimage is not merely a pilgrim's journey, however; it's an allegory for life. The dream-vision narrative describes how we learn from life, an idea that Homer sought to include in his epic when he wrote the opening lines of the *Odyssey*. The payoff comes at the end of a dream-vision poem, when the hero either attains ethereal love—a kiss from the rose in *The Romance of the Rose*—or arrives at a holy city—the kingdom of God in Langland's and Bunyan's works.

Bunyan, who was often arrested for preaching illegally, based *The Pilgrim's Progress* on an elaborate dream he had while serving a sentence in the Bedford Gaol. In the dream, an everyman protagonist named Christian sets out on a pilgrimage that takes him through such allegorical geography as Vanity Fair, the Slough of Despond, and the Delectable Mountains—places that will seem vaguely familiar to modern readers who have encountered L. Frank Baum's *The Wizard of Oz* or heard the famous folk song "Big Rock Candy Mountain." The prize, the Celestial City, is what Boethius called "home" and what Homer referred to as "Ithaka"—a place of narrative resolution and spiritual completion.

In the poem that introduces the prose narrative, Bunyan explains that the work is a quest of the highest order:

This book it chalketh out before thine eyes
The man that seeks the everlasting prize:
It shows you whence he comes, whither he goes,
What he leaves undone, also what he does:
It also shows you how he runs, and runs,
Till he unto the Gate of Glory comes.
It shows too who sets out for life amain,
As if the lasting crown they would attain:
Here also you may see the reason why
They lose their labour, and like fools do die.
This book will make a traveller of thee,
If by its counsel thou wilt ruled be;
It will direct thee to the Holy Land,
If thou wilt its directions understand:
Yea, it will make the slothful active be,
The blind also delightful things to see.

In the Valley of the Shadow of Death, an allegorical landscape that Bunyan draws from Psalm 23:4, the persevering pilgrim, Christian, battles with an enormous, dragon-like beast named Apollyon, a metaphor for pagan wisdom as opposed to Judeo-Christian knowledge. Armed only with his faith, Christian re-enacts the struggle that St. George endured with his dragon, an epic battle that itself echoes the struggle between Theseus and the Minotaur, Gilgamesh and Humbaba, and the Red Crosse Knight and Errour in Spenser. This scenario—of a hero facing down his greatest fear, which has taken the form of a monster—lies at the heart of the epic structure and is the crowning moment in the stories of all epic heroes.

What exists at the core of all epic stories is a very simple tripartite relationship involving the hero, who must undertake a journey; the route that journey must take (a labyrinth, paradox, puzzle, or wine-dark sea for the hero to solve); and the monster, the evil that the hero must overcome to reclaim his home and his identity. What is intriguing is that the stories of epic heroes all have the same basic formula: *the hero*, *the puzzle*, and *the monster*.

In *The Divine Comedy,* the hero was Dante. His was a journey through the enigmatic puzzle of eternity, and the monster he had to overcome was sin. In the *Odyssey,* the hero was Odysseus, "the sacker of the holy citadel of Troy, king of Ithaka, son of Laertes." He must vanquish not only a host of fantastic beasts and terrors, but also the wine-dark sea itself, a metaphor for his own unconscious. His monster is not merely the sea god Poseidon, but distance, time, longing, and his own fears. And in the *Aeneid,* the hero must solve the puzzle of the "ever-retreating horizon" and the lack of a suitable homeland while doing battle with the Latins and his nemesis, Hera.

The *Aeneid* has, for many centuries, been the blueprint for this tripartite structure in literature. Virgil's work has achieved a lasting importance because it is the one epic poem that has consistently been available for writers to use as a model for their own works. It fits both the classical and Christian traditions, and expresses concepts that are shared by both. St. Augustine read it as a child. Dante had it in the forefront of his mind when he composed *The Divine Comedy,* and Milton used it as one of the major aesthetic references for the dense blank verse of *Paradise Lost*. The *Aeneid* has been accorded a special place. It was considered *the* story (other than the Bible, which was viewed as a sacred text), and was the foundation on which other authors could build their own narratives. The twelfth-century Welsh monk Geoffrey of Monmouth realized just how important the *Aeneid* was to the fledgling British consciousness when he connected his *History of the Kings of Britain* to it by claiming Trojan heritage for his countrymen. As the archetypal Roman story, the *Aeneid* became the model on which later poets built their epics and to which they believed they were adding with their own narratives. The term that the *Aeneid* has given to literature is *romance*, which literally means a story written in the Roman manner.

As an English word, "romance"—like "love" and "tragedy"—is highly abused; it can mean anything from a deep flirtation to a life-long courtship. As a literary term, however, it has come to mean a genre in which romantic love or highly imaginative, unrealistic episodes form the central theme. It also means "a medieval tale, usually in verse, of some hero of chivalry, of the kind common in Romance languages (chiefly Spanish, French and Italian)." The romance hero—like Aeneas—is a unique combination of duty, singular vision, and personal discipline. When Christian authors of the Middle Ages looked at Virgil's epic poem, they sought to paint their own realities "in the Roman manner." What they did was to Christianize Aeneas, giving him the attributes of the greatest Christian figure, Jesus, as well as his own staunchly militaristic background. The soldierly Aeneas was suddenly overlaid with the moral perfection that the authors of the Gospels record in their stories of the son of God. The result is Sir Galahad: Christian in virtue, Roman in discipline, and armed to the teeth, both literally and spiritually.

As the perfect knight, the embodiment of chivalric ideals like death before dishonour and adherence to moral and spiritual perfection, Tennyson's Galahad in *Idylls of the King* is the apotheosis

Arthur, the hero of Tennyson's Idylls of the King, *in an engraving by Gustav Doré. Here he imagines the elderly king of the Britons with his wife, Gwynevere, at the moment he learns of her unfaithfulness.*

of the romance hero. When other knights are driven mad by the vision of the Holy Grail, it beckons Galahad to follow. He makes it the focus of his journey, which is a voyage of confident discovery that becomes a quest. (A quest, for the romance hero, ends with redemption or revelation if he has passed all his tests and trials with clarity and accuracy.) To quest, in the spiritual sense, is to commit oneself to the highest form of heroism. The quest is an abandonment of the self to an anagogic and invisible goal intended to provide restoration to a nation and spiritual redemption to all. It is an invitation for others to follow the same path. It is an enticement to good behaviour.

These romance stories are what preoccupy the mind of Cervantes' Don Quixote. In his misplaced love of literature, he becomes so enamoured with his reading material that he slides into the pages of his books and takes up residence there. The effect, as Cervantes notes, is not good. Don Quixote becomes a lunatic:

The truth is that when his mind was completely gone, he had the strangest thought any lunatic in the world ever had, which was that it seemed reasonable and necessary for him, both for the sake of his honor and as a service to the nation, to become a knight errant and travel the world with his armor and his horse to seek adventures and engage in everything he had read that knights errant engaged in, righting all manner of wrongs and, by seizing the opportunity and placing himself in danger and ending those wrongs, winning eternal renown and everlasting fame.

Beneath Cervantes' humour lies an important truth about epic heroes: they work to set the world right. Of all the characters in literature, they are the ones who have chosen to exercise their heroic natures by changing what they think is wrong with the world. They see what is wrong with their environments, decipher the puzzle, and strive to vanquish those ills before they are made tragic victims by them. The epic hero is attempting to bring order to chaos.

In Homer's *Iliad,* each of the combatants steps into the fray with a sublime sense of confidence that his actions will turn the tide of a hideous and horrific situation. When that woman on the late-night news said that the firemen who entered the World Trade Center on September 11, 2001, reminded her of Greek warriors, she had in the back of her mind the image of the hoplites. She likely saw in her mind's eye the helmeted combatants of Troy or the armoured knights of Arthurian legend, latter-day Aeneases who threw themselves into the fray to salvage hope from hopelessness and to create order where there was only fear and despair. What the epic hero has given to Western literature is the idea that an individual, regardless of his or her stature or standing, should attempt to make order out of chaos. When a hero is called for, from a burning building or on the wine-dark seas, the voice behind the request is looking for someone to intervene, to overcome hopelessness, and to beat back the angry, thanatic forces of the cosmos that appear to be running out of control. Perhaps what resides at the heart of the highest definition of the hero is the notion of divinity, the idea that something greater than ourselves can create from darkness a guiding and redeeming light.

7 THE SUBSTANCE OF THINGS HOPED FOR
The Supernatural and Divine Hero

When Joe Shuster and Jerry Siegel invented a comic book hero in 1932 for a story they titled "The Reign of the Superman," their man of steel was not the champion of virtue he would become in later years but a villain, an outsider who is shunned by society because of his special powers. Shuster and Siegel based their character, Superman, on the protagonist of a science fiction novel, *Gladiator*, by Philip Wylie. Wylie had created a new type of character who could do anything, a figure without limitations and constraints. He was a hero with god-like qualities, who by virtue of his gifts was separated from the rest of mankind. But such capabilities came with a terrible burden. It was not an easy matter to be divine.

Wylie, an Englishman, set his novel in the United States. He wanted to create a hero as limitless as the American frontier and as boundless as the optimistic energy for progress, truth, justice, and the new way of life of the early twentieth-century United States. A professor, Abednego Danner, a modern-day Victor Frankenstein, finds that he's able to give powers of incredible strength to a cat. When

The Greek Olympian chief god, Zeus, seen here crowned with the laurels of victory. The irony in this scene is that Greek gods seldom enjoyed "victory." Their existence was a troubled one of continual stand-offs amongst themselves, such as Homer portrays in the Iliad.

the super-cat begins to run amok, like the Daemon in Mary Shelley's *Frankenstein* or the Golem of Prague, on which Shelley based her novel, Danner destroys the ferocious feline. But the temptation to create a superhuman being, a figure with a conscience as well as an animal physique, proves too much for the scientist. When his wife becomes pregnant, Danner intoxicates her one night and injects her fetus with his formula. His son, Hugo Danner, is born with super-human powers. But these powers are not an asset to young Danner, who grows up a lonely social outcast, constantly trying to hide his abilities from a suspicious world. No matter what he does, the pro-tagonist of Wylie's novel cannot fit into society, and he pays a price for it. Danner is both a figure of envy—who would not want to have superhuman abilities?—and a figure of pathos, because no matter how hard he tries to be a good character, his best intentions always work against him. He tries, for example, to be a star football player, but injures his opponents because he cannot control his own strength. Hugo Danner becomes the prototype for Clark Kent.

In the original version of their story, Shuster and Siegel wrote Superman as a spectre, a source of fear and terror, a character who could fly, defy physics, and stand above the law. Eventually, how-ever, good and the Aristotelian impetus to make protagonists noble overtook their desire to create a powerful dark hero. In all likeli-hood, Shuster and Siegel were not thinking of Aristotle, though the conditioning of literature seems to have got the better of them. What caused the transformation of Superman was exactly what Aristotle pointed out in *The Nicomachean Ethics* when he argued that

> Every art and every investigation, and similarly every action
> and pursuit, is considered to aim at some good. Hence the good
> has been rightly defined as "that at which all things aim."

Boethius added a corollary to this in *The Consolation of Philosophy*. He suggested that good, mankind's true home, lay in the imitation of divinity, a desire to work within the laws of God and nature because the alternative was spiritual exile, or alienation from the state of nature. The superman, however, is a paradox, in that he exists outside of nature, or as part of another nature that has become transplanted here. Shuster and Siegel realized that talents such as those Superman possessed would be wasted on evil, and that he would be a philosophical contradiction to nature, a nemesis or antagonist worth eradicating at any cost. From the reader's point of view, a figure who can fly and "leap tall buildings at a single bound" is a reassuring presence if his intentions are good. As a character who performs for goodness rather than evil, Superman is humanity's imaginative defence against the possibility of a tragic universe. The man of steel offers protection against evil through action, much as Jesus offered protection against evil through thought, moral practice, and belief. Both suggest that goodness as an active force can lead humanity into a state of happiness, the best of all possible states of existence. In *The Nicomachean Ethics,* Aristotle presents the idea that the golden mean, the concept of good behaviour and balance in life, can lead to happiness and all that happiness engenders: self-sufficiency, the ability to be your own hero.

> A self-sufficient thing, then, we take to be one which by itself makes life desirable and in no way deficient; and we believe that happiness is such a thing. What is more, we regard it as the most desirable of all things, not reckoned as one item among many; if it were so reckoned, happiness would obviously be more desirable by the addition of even the least good, because the addition makes the sum of goods greater, and the greater of two goods is always more desirable. Happiness, then, is found to be something perfect and self-sufficient, being the end to which our actions are directed.

It is no accident that Wylie, an Englishman, and Shuster, a Canadian, would choose to make their protagonists Americans. America, after all, enshrined the Aristotelian idea of happiness in its Declaration of Independence, a document of the nation's founding principles.

Superman's evolution into a guardian of truth, justice, and the American way suggests that there is a natural impetus in the human imagination to find a hero who will not only champion life, but also defend and preserve it. The sad aspect of this is that the Superman myth has devolved into a belief that any action, if deemed defendable, is an action for good. The consequences of such a misreading are unimaginable. Aristotle suggests that the highest calling for an individual who wishes to pursue an "ethical life" is politics. But even politicians should be aware that playing at superman can be dangerous, especially when the consequences to others are completely foreseeable. Even Superman has to look before he leaps. On a more positive note, superhuman figures are able to transcend the limitations of physics, mortality, and even death in order to prove, if only to the imagination, that all possibilities are within human reach. What resides at the core of the superman myth is the maxim that "man's reach should exceed his grasp," to stretch the limits of humanity a degree or two further. If Superman proves anything, it is that the average reader is capable of projecting himself into something better than himself. He flirts with an inkling of the divine, not as a Faustus but as an Einstein. The literary imagination wants us to believe that there *is* a realm where there are always answers for problems, and where every challenge, no matter how daunting, has its solution in our capacity to dream. From the Renaissance on, there has been a pervasive belief in the Western imagination that man can and will solve his problems if only he can master the "capability factor." Carlyle recognized this when he chose to write about leaders of art and politics as his heroic ideals. He didn't include men of science and invention, although they reflect Plato's suggestion that "God is always doing geometry." The capability factor is the ability not only to work with the limitations of time and nature, but to exceed them and reach for the stars.

The roots of the capability myth, so essential to the Superman legend in the American imagination, also find expression in the origins of baseball, the great American pastime. The legend had it that the game began, mysteriously, in 1839 in a small town in upstate New York as the brainchild of Abner Doubleday, whose claim to being the great American genius would soon be challenged by a telegraph operator from Menlo Park, New Jersey, Thomas Edison. Doubleday had made his mark on nineteenth-century America not only by his heroic actions at the Battle of Gettysburg, but for inventing San Francisco's cable cars and getting involved in a number of projects that put America at the forefront of civil engineering. After much deliberation, the Baseball Hall of Fame Committee decided, in 1937, that their great game could only have been the product of the mind of America's pre-Edison resident genius. Doubleday was their man, and Cooperstown, his hometown, would be the site of the National Baseball Hall of Fame and Museum. The problem, as a number of historians have since pointed out, is that when the first game was supposed to have been played in Cooperstown, in 1839, Doubleday was away at West Point, studying as an officer cadet. Eventually, the ugly truth emerged: not only had Doubleday *not* invented the game, but America's national sport may, in fact, have been invented in Canada.

What the Doubleday myth suggests is that if a hero is capable of one great gesture or heroic deed, he is often, in people's minds, capable of other important acts. Creativity begets creativity. Doubleday, the Hall of Fame committee argued, was not an unlikely candidate to have created baseball. He was a natural problem-solver, a modern-day Hercules. Of all the figures in the classical pantheon of heroes, Hercules is the one who most clearly embodies the capability factor. But with a few exceptions, he is not the protagonist of a significant work. He is most often limited to playing a glowing secondary character, as he does in Apollonius of Rhodes' *Voyage of the Argo* and in Ovid's *Metamorphoses*. Yet he also appears to have inspired the slave revolt led by the legendary Spartacus—a revolt that has been read in the modern era as a declaration of the rights of the common man. Indeed, Hercules is a strange mixture of contradictions. He is the son of Zeus and a mortal mother. When he is accused of murder, he is forced to pay for his crimes—the only member of the Olympian household to be punished according to mortal laws. He undertakes twelve labours to win his freedom, proving himself to be a figure of great intellectual capability and strength, with some divine attributes. But just when liberty is within his grasp, his happiness is dashed by the forces of his nemesis (and namesake), Hera, and he suffers the tragic fate of mortals: death. He is both a figure of godly veneration, and the archetypal overachieving human.

Hercules' twelve labours are divided between battles with monsters—an ancient form of pest control—and voyages. In this respect, he is both Theseus and Odysseus, the fumigator and the traveller. His labours are designed to test various aspects of his personality. The first two are about dealing with animals that represent puzzles. The Nemean Lion is a beast whose skin cannot be pierced by sword, arrow, or spear. When Hercules realizes that weapons are useless, he strangles the beast. He then takes on the lion's skin as a symbol of dominion over nature and god-like physical prowess. His second labour, the destruction of the Lernean Hydra, a many-headed beast that will grow new heads until the primary one is severed, tests his problem-solving abilities. If he cuts off the right head, the question is answered. If he cuts off the wrong one, two more heads will grow in its place in what is almost a metaphor for the importance of managing information and making correct choices. In solving this labour, Hercules proves himself a hero of mathematics and science, a man who works out the most direct solution to a problem with a kind of Edisonian clarity of organized thinking.

The next two labours—the capture of the Arcadian Stag and the killing of the Erymanthean Boar—are hunting expeditions. These episodes show Hercules as a hearty hunter, a figure of venery, and a sportsman of the kingly order. King David of Scotland in the

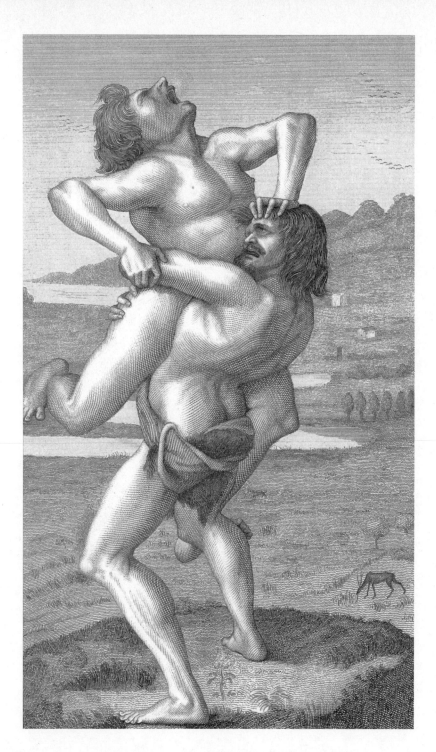

A seventeenth-century print of Hercules, wearing the lion skin,
battling the giant Antaeus by holding him aloft, out of contact with the earth.

early Middle Ages was said to have decided to locate his capital in Edinburgh after he saw a vision of a great white stag with a cross between its antlers on what is now the site of Holyrood Palace. Henry IV of France was accidentally killed while boar hunting.

Hercules' fifth labour, the cleaning of the Augean stables, proves he is a master of civil engineering. He is directed to clean a barnyard that has become so deep in filth and excrement that the entire countryside has been polluted and rendered infertile as a result. Given only hours to complete the absurd task, Hercules redirects a river that races through the stables so it will carry the pollution away downstream. The idea of the hero as someone who can alter nature and harness its incredible power for human purposes resides at the core of the modern myth of technology. This ability to transcend the physical is an important element in the idea of the hero as someone who possesses divine attributes. Time entered the world with the Fall, and it is time that mankind is trying to defeat by slowly progressing towards God. What mankind must do first, the Bible informs its readers, is order and control nature, and practise "dominion over the fish of the sea, and over the fowl of the air, and over every living thing that moveth upon the earth."

The sixth, seventh, and eighth labours deal with the policing of nature. In the sixth, Hercules rids Lake Stymphalis of a horde of carnivorous birds whose wings shoot steel darts. In the seventh, the hero captures a raging bull on the island of Crete, in a throwback to the heroic pattern set by Theseus in his vanquishing of the Minotaur. And in the eighth labour, Hercules captures a pack of ravenous, man-eating horses that have been terrorizing Thrace. In his younger days, Hercules had worked with horses under the guidance of the centaurs, and this eighth labour not only ties his adult adventures to his education among animals, but also suggests a "cowboy" attribute. As a wrangler of nature, someone who works to harness and control it, Hercules evokes American Wild West tales and men like Buffalo Bill Cody or Wild Bill Hickcock. The cowboy has become a key motif in American literature, particularly in the stories of Zane Grey, Rex Beech, and countless other authors of the American West.

The last four labours of Hercules' are voyage stories that echo themes and ideas found in works such as the *Aeneid,* the *Odyssey,* and *The Voyage of the Argo.* Hercules becomes the romance hero when he travels to the land of the Amazons, a race of warrior women, and steals the girdle of Queen Hippolyta. The girdle, like the one donned by Sir Gawain in *Sir Gawain and the Green Knight,* is said to possess magical powers and render the wearer impervious to blows. After making love to the Amazonian queen, Hercules absconds with her precious relic in a scene that parallels Aeneas' abandonment of Dido or Odysseus' departure from Calypso's island.

Hercules' second voyage takes him back to his roots as a cowboy. On this first voyage, his eighth labour, he captures the man-eating horses of Diomedes of Thrace. His second voyage is a pure act of piracy. Hercules pursues and captures the oxen of the monster Geryon and kills the giant beast in the process. Geryon appears in Dante's *Inferno* as a horrific spectre with the face of a just man, three bodies, and the dreadful stinging tail of a serpent—a depiction of a composite horror, where a variety of nightmares converge, and an allegory for deceit, usury, and con-artistry. At this point in the *Inferno,* Dante and Virgil encounter the usurers and ride on Geryon's shoulders, the con man conned, to a deeper level of hell. The monster then bounds away, "brisker than bolt from bow." Anyone who has ever held a high-interest credit card will appreciate Dante's interpretation of what Hercules did in slaying Geryon. In Dante's medieval world-view, where charging any kind of interest on loans was seen as an un-Christian affront to the laws of decency, Hercules had rid the world of a monster that would abuse mankind by trapping individuals in their own need.

Hercules' eleventh labour is about seeking a forbidden prize, the Apples of the Hesperides. The apples were guarded by a dragon that he must defeat. As Hercules searches the labyrinthine passages of the world for the secret of the garden's location, he encounters Antaeus, a giant he defeats in a wrestling match, and Prometheus, the character who broke taboos by giving fire to mankind. This labour suggests a defiance of limitations. The fact that the prize is a golden fruit, which is usually a symbol of judgment, legality, or sustenance, suggests that this labour is about how one goes beyond perceivable limits to achieve a goal.

For the last of his twelve labours, Hercules descends into hell, frees Theseus, and captures the dreaded three-headed hound, Cerberus, the guardian watchdog of Hades, thus defeating death and a monster in one visit. This last act also finds its way into Dante's *Inferno,* where the three-headed dog takes his place among the gluttons, those who sinned by indulging appetites they could not control. Dante describes the canine fiend as

> Cerberus, the cruel, misshapen monster, there
> Bays in his triple gullet and doglike growls
> Over the wallowing shades; his eyeballs glare
>
> A bloodshot crimson, and his bearded jowls
> Are greasy and black; pot-bellied, talon-heeled,
> He clutches and flays and rips and rends the souls.

This final voyage is Hercules' *nekusis,* a harrowing of the underworld that allows him to penetrate and comprehend life's bleakest mystery. Like Jesus, Hercules is able to act as a liberator, rescuing Theseus. When a later hero, Odysseus, descends into the underworld, in Book XI of the *Odyssey,* he rescues no one, even though he encounters the shade of Hercules. As a survivor of the Trojan War, Odysseus knows death in the surface world as well as anyone, but the appearance of a semi-divine hero in the underworld comes as a complete shock:

> One look was enough to tell Heracles who I was, and
> he greeted me in mournful tones. "Unhappy man!" he
> exclaimed, after reciting my titles. "So you too are working
> out some such miserable doom as I was a slave to when the
> sun shone over my head. Son of Zeus though I was, unending
> troubles came my way. For I was bound to the service of a
> master far beneath my rank, who used to set me the most
> arduous tasks. Once, being unable to think of anything more
> difficult for me to do, he sent me down here to bring away
> the Hound of Hell. And under the guiding hands of Hermes
> and bright-eyed Athene, I did succeed in capturing him and I
> dragged him out of Hades' realm."

Odysseus wishes he could stay longer in hell and converse with the great heroes of the past. But when scores of shades start to surround the sacker of the holy citadel of Troy, in a scene that could fit very nicely in a zombie movie, Odysseus' instincts prevail and he leaves the land of the dead.

For all his accomplishments, however, Hercules ends his life tragically. In *The Canterbury Tales,* Chaucer offers a litany of heroic characters from the past, and Hercules is among them:

> Thus fell the famous, mighty Hercules.
> Who then may trust the dice at Fortune's throw?
> Who joins in worldly struggles such as these
> Will be, when least prepared for it, laid low!
> Wise is the man who well has learnt to know
> Himself. Beware! When Fortune would elect
> To trick a man, she plots his overthrow
> By such a means as he would least expect.

Hercules from a seventeenth-century print where he is depicted holding the olive bough club, which he carried in combat. The club bears a strong resemblance to a baseball bat.

For Chaucer, Hercules is the archetypal hero of the classical world, a world of tragic heroes that is fraught with uncertainty. For all his god-like achievements and lineage, Hercules is like anyone else in the realm of death, a mere mortal unable to escape his fate. The irony is that although he is divine, he suffers a mortal fate, a fact that made him a figure of great empathy, especially to slaves and the poor in ancient Rome. Ovid, depicts the death of Hercules as an unfortunate event. Having survived his labours, the son of Zeus believes that happiness and freedom, the two entitlements of mortals, are finally within his grasp. He marries a young woman, Deinara, and settles down to a life of peace and tranquillity that he had only dreamed of. Deinara decides to present her new husband with a beautiful shirt, but unbeknownst to her, it has been dipped in the one substance lethal to the hero, the blood of a centaur. (Having murdered a centaur earlier in his career, Hercules has long been the target of the other centaurs, who wait patiently for the perfect moment to serve up their revenge.) This classical equivalent of kryptonite, according to Ovid, burns away Hercules' flesh:

> With his customary courage, he suppressed his groans as long as he could, but when his suffering was beyond endurance, he flung over the altars, and filled wooded Oeta with his cries. He tried to tear off the deadly garment with all speed. But wherever the cloth was dragged away, it dragged his skin with it and, horrible to tell, either clung to his limbs, resisting all attempts to pull it off, or left lacerated flesh, revealing his massive bones. His blood, saturated by the burning poison, hissed and boiled, like a white hot iron plunged into icy water. There was no limit to his agony: greedy flames sucked in his heart, dark perspiration poured from his whole frame, his scorched sinews crackled, and the hidden pestilence melted his bones.

Ovid depicts the scene in all its gaudy and horrific detail. It's one of the major moments of transformation in a book full of transformations—the conversion of a god into a tragic mortal:

> Now the flames had gained strength, and were roaring as they spread in all directions, attacking limbs that heeded them not at all, and a hero who despised them. The gods were afraid for earth's champion, till Jupiter, perceiving their anxiety, addressed them in these welcome words: "The fear which you display displeases me, and with my whole heart I freely congratulate myself that I am called ruler and father of a people who do not forget their benefactors."

The gods fear that they, like Hercules, have the potential to become mortal. His death is a stern warning to them. What it also does is remind humans that even immortals, supposedly immune to tragedy, can be tragic. And it's a reminder for those who live in Ovid's dysfunctional universe that even immortality has its limits.

What emerges from the fires that consume Hercules is his true nature. All else, especially his flaws and weaknesses, is consumed, and there is a profound sense that this final test proves he is a survivor whose true essence is heroic:

> Meanwhile Vulcan had stripped Hercules of whatever
> fire could ravage, and the form of the hero was left, quite
> unrecognizable, retaining none of his likeness to his mother,
> but only the signs of his descent from Jove. Just as a serpent
> renews its youth, sloughing its old age with its skin, and is left
> fresh and shining with its new scales, so when the Tirynthian
> hero had put off his mortal shape, the better part of him
> grew vigorous, and he began to appear greater than before, a
> majestic figure of august dignity.

As a final compensation, Hercules' heroic shape is swept up and set among the heavens, as a reminder to others that to strive for the heroic is to reach for the stars. In the classical world, to be set among the stars is the same as being taken up bodily into heaven in the Judeo-Christian world; it's a symbolic conquest of death, where the hero achieves everlasting life, permanence, and the isolated security of residing a safe distance from the mortal realm. At the core of the semi-divine or divine hero is the idea that he can overcome death in some way, even after experiencing it, and that death strips away the mortal condition and leaves him to his true nature. If death is the most pervasive fear of mankind, the vanquishing of death represents a long-desired order in nature, a return to man's original paradisal state.

The birth of Jesus in the stable at Bethlehem.

Milton reminds his readers in the opening lines of *Paradise Lost* that mankind's disobedience brought death and disorder into the world, and that death will reign "till one greater Man / Restore us, and regain the blissful Seat." For Milton, that "one greater Man" is the protagonist of the New Testament, Jesus. Jesus first appears in the Gospel of Matthew, where like any good epic hero he is introduced by his lineage. This is not simply an epic convention; the editors of the New Testament want to locate Jesus in history, to portray him as a bridge between the past and the future. St. Paul, in his Epistle to the Philippians, attempts to cast Jesus as both a historical personage and a figure at the centre of a story of miracles, divinity, and the discourse between heaven and earth:

Who, being in the form of God, thought it not robbery to be equal with God:

An unusual profile depiction of the Virgin Mary, the human presence in heaven, and the baby Jesus. Here, she is portrayed reading a book, another peculiarity among Madonna and Child images, as it suggests that she is learned. Perhaps she is reading Virgil's Fourth Eclogue, which some believe foretells the coming of Christ.

But made himself of no reputation, and took upon him the form of a servant, and was made in the likeness of men:

And being found in the fashion as a man, he humbled himself, and became obedient unto death, even the death of the cross.

Wherefore God also hath highly exalted him, and given him a name which is above every name:

That at the name of Jesus every knee should bow, of things in earth, and things under the earth;

And every tongue should confess that Jesus Christ is Lord, to the glory of God the Father.

Jesus—like Odysseus or a Christian saint—is willing to become a servant and negate himself to achieve his desired goals. According to St. Paul, he is someone who is willing to debase himself to attain his triumph. Jesus is willing not only to make order out of chaos, but to establish a new order of his own devising, an order that will return us to our lost proximity to God. This return, which requires faith in him, is intended to extend the heroic franchise to all people, not just to the chosen few. And that franchise includes his own triumph—the triumph of life over death.

As a literary work, the New Testament, especially the four Gospels, tells the story of a character who is heroic. The pattern of the *acta sanctori*, or record of holiness, so evident in the lives of the saints, is told and retold throughout those four books to show that to achieve divinity in life, the hero must learn to adapt his talents to the world. The reader is reminded of Jesus' birth, his education, his temptations, his journey, his death (or *nekusis*), and his final triumph.

The mysterious paradox at the heart of the story is that Jesus, the son of God, is of the highest divine nature, yet he is born in the lowest possible circumstances. The extremes of position in his story—the divine in the mortal, the servant in the king, the champion of eternal life experiencing a real death—supports Luke's assertion that "with God nothing shall be impossible." Jesus is a vehicle for the work of God in the world. He is a reminder that the God who grew more and more remote in Old Testament is still an active force in the world through his "only begotten son." Jesus undergoes a series of transformations—by becoming flesh, then experiencing the Transfiguration, where he reveals his divine nature, and then metamorphosizing into a source for eternal life, salvation, goodness, and mercy through the Resurrection. The protean aspects of these transformations suggest that Jesus, as an obedient instrument of God's will, exists not merely as a person but as an idea, a force of the imagination. This is, perhaps, what underlies the Gospel of John, which is the one book that sets out to tell the story not of a venerable hero, but of a man who is transfigured from flesh into concept. Jesus, in the Gospel of John, rises above all his mortal conditions to become an imaginative construct, a hero of the mind rather than of the world or the flesh. John emphasizes this point from the very beginning of his version of Jesus' story not with a creation story but with a re-creation statement:

In the beginning was the Word, and the Word was with God and the Word was God.

The same was in the beginning with God.

All things were made by him; and without him was not any thing made.

In him was life; and the life was the light of men.

And the light shineth in darkness and the darkness comprehended it not.

Jesus seen here in an allegory of the Eucharist, or perhaps the moment from Matthew when he multiplies the loaves and fishes to feed the multitudes. The parallels between the two events are part of the constant sense of foreshadowing in the Gospels.

John then tells us that Jesus was "not that Light, but was sent to bear witness of that Light." As an observer of the grand metamorphosis that takes place in the life of Jesus, John attempts to show the parallel between the creation of the world as depicted in Genesis and the recreation of the world that the son of God will effect through his life, teachings, and philosophy. John's gospel is a story about seeing, as if seeing is believing. But the seeing takes place in the mind of the reader, not in the action of the plot. John conjures the language of the visual in phrases like "Come and see," "Behold," and "I saw." This idea of vision, of bearing witness, resides at the heart of the term "apocalypsis," which is drawn from the Greek word *apokalupsis,* meaning "uncover" or "reveal." Apocalypse in this sense suggests not the end of the world, as it has come to mean in contemporary parlance, but the end of an old style of perception, or the beginning of a new way of looking at things.

The life of Jesus, as portrayed in the other three Gospels, has elements of the fantastic, which implies that Jesus exists between two worlds. Indeed, his life is a unique combination of the heroic and the fantastic, a hero story that in many respects outstrips all other hero stories, while still adhering to the expected pattern. Jesus is born of a mortal mother who is herself heroic, in that she is chosen by God for a special purpose. Luke tells us that Mary is a female *phaulos,* a servant and a handmaid of God who has been chosen because her "soul doth magnify the Lord." God tells her that she "has found favour" with Him, and that she will conceive a child "who shall be called the Son of the Highest: and the Lord God shall give unto him the throne of his father David." Great pains are taken throughout the Gospels to show that Jesus is of royal lineage. Yet, like Hercules, he is reduced by circumstances; he is not a deity looking down on the world from above, but a mortal looking up at the world from the lowest possible position.

Jesus' journey consists of two separate series of events: his temptation in the desert and his mission work as a teacher. The forty-day period that he spends in the wilderness is an epic journey into himself, whereby he is tested by the devil and learns how to respond both morally and anagogically. When the devil, in Matthew 4:3, asks, "If thou be the Son of God, command that these stones be made bread," Jesus replies, "Man shall not live by bread alone, but by every word that proceedeth from the mouth of God." The suggestion is that what will sustain humanity after Jesus has passed from event into legend is his ideas and own body—what he can give of himself in this world and continue to provide long after he no longer exists in the flesh. What Jesus does is to remove himself from the realm of the tangible by not only speaking in parables and metaphors, but by translating the tangible into the conceptual. Jesus rejects all tangibilities because his domain resides beyond mere things. His mission, he continually states, is not to rearrange the world, but to alter the way the world is perceived. His eventual triumph over death is both physical and imaginative, because death is all a matter of perception, a pointer to the eternal path of possibility. He wants to turn the world, as it has been known, on its head—to create a nobility of human dignity, elevating those who had once had no hope of seeing a better world. He articulates this new world in Matthew 5:3–12: This passage is not a reiteration of the Ten Commandments in Exodus, but a message for the *phaulos* of the world—the poor, the meek, the peaceful, the hungry. Jesus is creating a new kind of nobility, the nobility of human dignity, in which he elevates those who once had no hope of seeing a better world:

Blessed *are* the poor in spirit: for theirs is the kingdom of heaven.

Blessed *are* they that mourn: for they shall be comforted.

Blessed *are* the meek: for they shall inherit the earth.

Blessed *are* they which do hunger and thirst after righteous-ness: for they shall be filled.

Blessed *are* the merciful: for they shall obtain mercy.

Blessed *are* the pure in heart: for they shall see God.

Blessed *are* the peacemakers: for they shall be called the children of God.

Blessed *are* they which are persecuted for righteousness' sake: for theirs is the kingdom of heaven.

Blessed are ye when *men* shall revile you, and persecute *you*, and shall say all manner of evil against you falsely, for my sake.

Rejoice, and be exceedingly glad: for great *is* your reward in heaven: for so persecuted they the prophets which were before you.

The message is quite clear: suffering does have a purpose. It opens the pathway to heaven if an individual is willing to look beyond himself, to abandon his pain and neediness in the pursuit of a larger reality. And the universe that is being proposed is not tragic. It is a world that is open to all, where every person who can prove himself worthy of human dignity counts. The means of proving your worth, the test of the hero that Jesus perceived in everyone, is faith. Believe in my ideas, he says, and the door beyond yourself will be open to you. There is a positive end to existence, a reward, a chance at a better life beyond this one, and it is a life that lies within each individual. The kingdom of heaven, he tells his disciples, is "within you." The hardest thing to imagine, as many authors will remind their readers, is yourself. But Jesus says that is where you should start looking for heaven, the land of heroic recognition and reward. Heroism is found not during a great adventure across wine-dark seas or ever-retreating horizons, but in the depths of your own being.

The question, then, is, How do we get there? In *The Divine Comedy,* Dante suggests that the path to heaven lies within the imagination. His journey through the layers of Christian afterlife is not merely a quest to reconnect with his lost love, Beatrice, but also a struggle to return home—home to God, as Boethius defines it in *The Consolation of Philosophy.* It is a route he can traverse only by conquering his own fears and failings. In Canto I of the *Inferno,* Dante finds that his way back to his native Florence, from which he has been exiled on pain of death, is blocked by three beasts: the leopard, the lion, and the wolf. The leopard is a metaphor for the sins of expediency, the moment that overcomes an individual and ruins him. The lion represents the sins of strategy, the ego that overcomes an individual and blinds him, like Oedipus, to the painful realities of the world and of himself. The wolf is a symbol of the sins of strategy, those premeditated plots in which an individual turns against God and nature and rejects the divine grace that is extended through the Christian message. Dante's *Divine Comedy* is almost a statement in psychoanalysis; he must, in the words of the Renaissance morningstar Petrarch, "turn an inward eye upon himself." Once he becomes aware, in the *Inferno* and the *Purgatorio,* of the catalogue of human failings and the price individuals must pay to redeem themselves, he literally rises above himself and soars to the very threshold of God. It is no accident of poetry that Dante puts Christ not at the right hand of God but in the sphere of soldiers, crusaders, and martyrs. This is the same sphere where Dante encounters his legendary ancestor Cacciaguida, a crusader who died in the service of Christianity. When he meets Christ, however, Dante cannot offer any description. Words fail him in the presence of the one who was "the word" made flesh:

> With my whole heart, and in that tongue which all
> Men share, I made burnt-offering to the Lord,
> Such as to this new grace was suitable,
>
> And ere the sacrificial fire had soared
> Forth of my breast, I knew my prayer had sped
> Accepted, and found favorable accord;
>
> For such bright splendours, and so ruby-red
> With two rays appeared, "O Eloi,"
> I cried, "that giv'st them thus the accolade!"
>
> As, white between the two poles of the sky
> Gleaming, and decked with great and lesser stars,
> Riddle of sages, shines the Galaxy,
>
> E'en so, constellate in the depth of Mars,
> Those rays displayed the venerable sign
> Traced in a circle by the quadrant-bars.

Jesus carrying the cross along the Via Dolorosa on his way to his Crucifixion, from an early seventeenth-century engraving.

Here memory beats me, and my wits resign
Their office, for that cross so flashed forth Christ
As beggars all similitude of mine;

But whoso takes his cross and follows Christ
Will pardon me this gap in my narration
When lightening through Heav'n's brightening, he sees Christ.

Though words fail the redoubtable poet, the suggestion he makes is that each person perceives his or her own version of Christ. Jesus becomes the ultimate hero, in that he can become whatever an individual needs to see in him. He's the every-hero whose power lies in the flexibility of interpretations people bring to him as a character.

A large part of this flexibility resides in the fact that Jesus speaks in metaphors—the figurative language of poetry, a type of language that begs for a variety of interpretations. Christianity has always made a clear distinction between the process of spreading the gospel, called *krygma,* and *theologia,* the philosophical debate and interpretation of Jesus' ideas. Metaphors give the message of *krygma* its range and the content of *theologia* its depth. Speaking in metaphors is Jesus' armour. While characters like Aeneas or King Arthur are outfitted with weapons, Jesus is armed with poetry, images, and figurative language that is powerful in its ability to speak to actualities while at the same time addressing extremely abstract concepts. The idea is mightier than any sword, and Jesus has an arsenal of ideas that appear to turn the world upside down while building on phrases, prophecies, and statements of wisdom that occurred earlier in the Bible.

For all his power and intelligence, Jesus, as the New Testament says, sacrifices himself to redeem mankind. The New Testament transforms the idea of confronting death into a process by which the hero conquers death to offer life to others. In the scene of his agony in the Garden of Gethesemane, on the eve of his Crucifixion, Jesus questions whether his mortal death is necessary:

> And he went a little further, and fell on his face, and prayed, saying, O my Father, if it be possible, let this cup pass from me: nevertheless not as I will, but as thou wilt.

Nonetheless, Jesus is obedient to the will of the Father. Obedience, as Milton tells us in *Paradise Lost,* is the key to making the universe run according to the laws of God and nature. God, the Father, according to Milton and Boethius, has a plan for the world—He wants us to fall, because only then will we grow closer to Him through the grace and knowledge that comes from Christ's sacrifice. We will then return to our original state brighter and wiser for having experienced history, and evil. The thanatic force of darkness and destructiveness will be defeated once and for all, and order will prevail over chaos.

The idea of confronting death, as the eminent theologian Joseph Ratzinger wrote in *Introduction to Christianity* in the 1960s, was a process by which God, through his son, came to understand the ultimate human fear, the fear of loneliness. Ratzinger, who later became Pope Benedict XVI, writes:

> In my view it is only at this point that we come face to face
> with the problem of what death really is, what happens when
> someone dies, that is, enters the fate of death. Confronted with
> this question we all have to admit our embarrassment. No one
> really knows the answer because we all live on this side of death
> and are unfamiliar with the experience of death. But perhaps
> we can try to begin formulating an answer by starting again
> from Jesus' cry on the Cross, which we found to contain the
> heart of what Jesus' descent into hell, his sharing of man's mortal
> fate, really means. In this last prayer of Jesus, as in the scene on
> the Mount of Olives, what appears as the innermost heart of his
> Passion is not any physical pain but radical loneliness, complete
> abandonment. But in the last analysis what comes to light here
> is simply the abyss of loneliness of man in general, of man who
> is alone in his innermost being. This loneliness, which is usually
> thickly overlaid but is nevertheless the true situation of man, is
> at the same time in fundamental contradiction with the nature
> of man, who cannot exist alone; he needs company. That is why
> loneliness is the region of fear, which is rooted in the exposure
> of a being that must exist but is pushed out into a situation with
> which it is impossible for him to deal.

What Jesus' death and resurrection suggest is that the spirit of God is never lost to the world, even in the deepest moments of despair and loneliness. This light in the darkness, this presence of order in the midst of chaos, is presented as a form of triumph when Jesus, the ultimate conquering hero, rises from the dead.

At the conclusion of *Paradise Regained,* Milton's sequel to *Paradise Lost,* the great struggle between good and evil is finally resolved, with good triumphing and evil being vanquished. Milton says that mankind cannot regain the original earthly paradise, but that something far greater awaits, a newer and better situation in which maker and creation can converse not as subject and object, but as closer partners who have grown together through knowledge and understanding:

> For though that seat of earthly bliss be fail'd,
> A fairer Paradise is founded now
> For Adam and his chosen Sons, whom thou
> A Saviour art come down to re-install,
> Where they shall dwell secure, when time shall be
> Of Tempter and Temptation without fear.

In the idea that God—"the eternal Father and maker of all things," as the poet Caedmon called him in the earliest English poem—can be everlasting is the suggestion that life is never shut down or shut out. Death is never total. If the hero exists to comfort those who herald him or believe in him, then the ultimate comfort is that offered against the ultimate fear.

The desire to perceive the infinite in the expression of life can be seen in the concept of God that Jesus represents in the Gospels. The fact that God cannot be seen, let alone fathomed, is not a problem for those who choose to believe that the universe is guided by a structure that prevents it from collapsing into disorder and chaos. Life itself, as anatomists will point out, is the presence of order in the face of extremely long odds. Each individual, they will insist, is a mathematical miracle, the combination of all the right things in all the right places and at all the right times to enable that individual to be alive and conscious and interactive with his environment. For those who believe that the universe is mediated by a presiding spirit and not just a mathematical code, there is the idea that a heroic and creative consciousness is beyond everything. This spirit is the God who explains Himself to Job and makes the universe run as an elaborate and complex miracle. In his Letter to the Hebrews, St. Paul argues that God, the spirit of life and order, is active throughout the universe, even though His presence is not always discernible:

> Cast not away therefore your confidence, which hath great recompense or reward.

> For yet have need of patience, that, after ye have done the will of God, ye might receive the promise.

> For yet a little while, and he that shall come will come, and will not tarry.

> Now the just shall live by faith: but if any man draw back, my soul shall have no pleasure in him.

> But we are not of them who draw back into perdition; but of them that believe to saving of the soul.

> Now faith is the substance of things hoped for, the evidence of things not seen.

The idea that the source of order in the universe, the hero who makes structure out of chaos, cannot be seen is hard for most people to accept. Everyone wants to put a face on God, and no two individuals' ideas of God are alike. In *Confessions,* St. Augustine looked for God in everything he saw, hoping to catch a glimpse of his face:

> But what is my God? I put my question to the earth. It answered, "I am not God," and all things on earth declared the same. I asked the sea and chasms of the deep and the living things that creep in them, but they answered, "We are

not your God. Seek what is above us." I spoke to the winds that blow, and the whole air and all that lives in it replied, "I am not God." I asked the sky, the sun, the moon, and the stars, but they told me, "Neither are we the God whom you seek." I spoke to all the things that are about me, all that can be admitted by the door of the senses, and I said, "Since you are not my God, tell me about him. Tell me something of my God." Clear and loud they answered, "God is he who made us."

What Augustine realizes is that God is the spirit of creation, the imagination behind the workings of the universe, the pervasive force of life that drives everything that exists. He is both simple and complex at the same time. As St. Augustine perceived Him, God was a paradox, the container and the contained, that which lives in things but also lives beyond them. In Job 38, the long-suffering servant of God asks why his faith has been so tested by a deity to whom he has been unwaveringly faithful. God's answer, stretching over three chapters, is His greatest monologue in the Bible, and it suggests that He is not only the creator of the universe, but also the manager, chief engineer, and keeper of order. Job answers,

I know that thou canst do everything, and that no thought can be with-holden from thee.

Who is he that hideth counsel without knowledge? Therefore have I uttered that I understood not; things too wonderful for me, which I knew not.

God possesses infinite knowledge, and with infinite knowledge comes infinite responsibility. Mary Shelley, in *Frankenstein,* uses a similar relationship between the creator and his creation as a metaphor for the

God, in a rare depiction, seated in glory in heaven.

need for humans to practise responsibility. The Daemon curses his creator, Victor Frankenstein, for his absence and for his resignation of care. Frankenstein, however, only plays God. The weight of responsibility is too much for him, and unlike Job's God, who not only created the mechanisms of the universe but also operates them, Frankenstein proves a poor manager. For Job, God's extensiveness—his limitless capabilities and boundless energy, the force that makes the universe exist—is an expression of creativity, the order that prevails against chaos. To desire to understand God, from Job's point of view, is to comprehend why things happen as they do. Job does not want to *be* God; he only wants an explanation. The explanation he receives is that there is something in the universe that is larger than human suffering or comprehension. Job marvels at the creativity and the breadth of God's works, and resigns himself to a sense of awe and wonder.

Given the chance to look upon God, if only for an instant, Dante, at the conclusion of the *Paradiso,* is suddenly struck speechless. For the poet who found words to describe the degradations of hell and the privations of purgatory—who conversed with villains, saints, and heroes in order to better understand humanity in all its complexity— the presence of God is too overwhelming for language. Language, literature, and even the figurative reach of metaphor are all only systems, and God exceeds all systems because He is not a system in Himself, but the boundless creativity that cannot be contained by all He creates. God not only exceeds his capabilities, He is the excess:

> How weak are words, and how unfit to frame
> My concept—which lags after what was shown
> So far, 'twould flatter it to call it lame!
> Eternal light, that in Thyself alone
> Dwelling, alone, dost know Thyself, and smile
> On Thy self-love, so knowing and so known!

As Dante moves beyond words and comprehension into the realm of pure anagogy, he realizes that God is the self-knowledge that can make and maintain order in the midst of a chaotic universe. As a hero, God does not desire to become more than Himself because He already is all that He can be. He is the goal that underlies the heroic drive towards certainty, the peace of mind and spirit that never needs to be restless because it has found its home and is the creator of that home.

Language, image, and the ability to organize them into stories are the means by which we come both to see ourselves and to see beyond ourselves. The real hero, when all is said and done, is the story itself— our ability to share with one another through narrative and expression. I take considerable solace in the idea of *logos,* the word made flesh, the idea made into a story, and the means by which a story can be told. In Greek, *logos* originally meant "to speak," as if speaking, telling ourselves stories and sharing those stories with others, can reveal something that we can know and grow by. God, of course, cannot be explained. He can only be alluded to through metaphors. But at least those figurative constructs, the building blocks of literature, point us in the general direction of what we want to become. Each of us possesses the capacity to dream and to explore ourselves through the power of our imaginations. And where will the imagination take us? Anywhere we might want to go, from our everyday lives to the very threshold of divinity. If we allow our imaginations to have free rein, we may be intrigued by the sense of connection, accidental or otherwise, that we encounter. I would like to think that the divinity that is continually described in literature is not merely a representation of the infinite, but an expression of the finite that is so easily overlooked as we dream of bright heavenly kingdoms.

THE CHAMPIONS OF OUR IMAGINATIONS

S o what, then, is the hero? In 1921, shortly after the First World War, the poet Rainer Maria Rilke found himself alone and in a profoundly introspective mood in Paris, where he struggled with the outcomes of a life that had offered him only isolation. Prior to the war, he had experienced the death of his close friend, the sculptor Paula Becker-Modersohn; the failure of his marriage to another artist, Clara Westhof; and the mad descent of the world from gentility into a barbaristic militarism. To search for the meaning of his own life, Rilke had taken up residence in a small castle at Duino, in northern Italy. There, he penned a series of elegies, called *The Duino Elegies,* the sixth of which dealt with the idea of the hero:

The hero is strangely close to those who died young.
Permanence does not concern him. He lives in continual
ascent, moving on into the ever-changed constellation of
perpetual danger. Few could find him there. But Fate, which
is silent about us, suddenly grows inspired and sings him into

the storm of this onrushing world. I hear no one like *him*. All
at once I am pierced by his darkened voice, carried on the
streaming air.

The hero, for Rilke, is a figure of elevated isolation, an outcast who
is like no other person because he has struggled with what life has
dealt him. He is Christ and Hercules, figures who must overcome
their obstacles regardless of their outcast state. Rilke's hero continues
to strive and to struggle because he believes that somehow his struggling will give him increase as he trudges onward. That was Rilke's
view before the First World War. The ensuing years transformed his
vision.

By 1921, Rilke had constructed an entirely different view of the
heroic nature. In his quiet and isolated pursuit of knowledge, he
realized that the act of inspiration, inexplicable as it often is, represented the presence of something far greater within him. In one of
his *Sonnets to Orpheus*, penned in 1921, he tried to put into words the
complex question of the nature of the hero:

> Wonders happen if we can succeed
> in passing through the harshest danger;
> but only in a bright and purely granted
> achievement can we realize the wonder.
>
> To work *with* Things in the indescribable
> relationship is not too hard for us;
> the pattern grows more intricate and subtle,
> and being swept along is not enough.
>
> Take your practiced powers and stretch them out
> until they span the chasm between two
> contradictions . . . For the god
> wants to know himself in you.

Rilke suggests that the hero is that spark of divinity or breath of inspiration that each of us possesses—a hero within us that never ceases to amaze and never fails to believe in itself. It sings of the determination not only to survive but to grow and to learn, and to foster that spirit in others by becoming the person our imaginations tell us we can be. The authors of the past left maps to lead us through the dark and labyrinthine passages of life's puzzle, all in the certain belief that we will encounter what we already possess: the courage to become ourselves.

Whether in the lightless labyrinth or, like Dante, on that road midway through life, the hero finds himself constantly challenged by what he does not or cannot know. As he struggles against monsters like the mythic heroes did or slogs through the mud of the trenches like Wilfred Owen did, he is engaged in the process of problem-solving. The questions of the universe are infinite, and the hero wrestles with them, physically, mentally, and spiritually.

Every hero narrative has three parts to it: the hero himself, the puzzle he must solve, and the monster he must confront to assert his claim to greatness. This three-part structure is repeated over and over in Western literature. In Homer, Odysseus faces the wine-dark sea and Poseidon. In the stories of the saints, there is a divinely inspired figure of faith, the world he or she must struggle through, and the devil. In *Jane Eyre,* Brontë's protagonist must find her way through the maze of class structure and society, facing down both the madwoman in the attic and the reticence within her own soul. In the Superman legend, the city of Metropolis is a contemporary labyrinth, and the forces of crime Superman must fight are his metaphorical monsters. (No matter how many criminals Superman overcomes, there always seem to be more waiting in the wings so his hero pattern can be repeated, proving time and again that his goodness and his strength really are super.) Whatever his situation, the hero remains constant in his desire for success. And the stakes are high: success equates with life and failure with death.

In the story of Theseus, as recounted by Ovid in *Metamorphoses,* the young Athenian prince knows that his fate is sealed, and logic argues that he resign himself to it. There seems to be no way out of the labyrinth, and the monster has a record of consecutive triumphs. But Theseus understands that failure is not an option. As he faces the monstrous Minotaur, the very personification of death, he chooses life, even though it's a remote possibility at best.

Something in Theseus tells him that there is an alternative to death. The demand to decide how our own personal narrative is going to conclude is one of the greatest human motivators, after love and hunger. It resides at the heart of hope, democratic society, and critical thought. As long as there are alternatives, the hero, as an imaginative structure, continues to be plausible. If there remains one possibility to allow the hero to survive, as Freud argues, then why can there not be others? What limits the number of options? Why not an infinite number, a divine storehouse of solutions, a veritable kingdom where every answer can be found? Perhaps one of the greatest roles the hero plays in our imaginations is to act as an essential metaphor that points us toward the divine, to that "world without end."

If the concept of the hero in human consciousness shows us anything, it is that we live in constant need of possibilities; the "zero option" is not tolerable to us. In his famous Nobel Prize speech of 1949, William Faulkner talked about the challenge that he saw facing mankind. With the advent of nuclear arms at the conclusion of the Second World War and the spread of the technology behind atomic weaponry, the possibility for the conquest of *Thanatos* over *Eros* loomed. Faulkner concluded that mankind was in a precarious position, and that humanity now had the god-like power to destroy itself. He realized that his chief obligation as a writer was to swear a fealty to life. He recognized that literature not only serves that broad, vague concept called civilization, but also ultimately acts in obedience to the universal, biological rule that life will always find a way for itself. The small sound still refuting death even after "the last ding-dong of doom" had tolled was the voice of the imagination crying out for the grand human narrative to continue. In pronouncing that "man will not merely endure, he will prevail," Faulkner sounded a triumphant note for the heroic spirit that he witnessed among those who simply persevered. At the conclusion of *The Sound and the Fury,* he offered to Dilsey, the black nursemaid of the Compson family, a simple tribute when he wrote that "she endured." The world, to Faulkner and so many other writers, is a battleground between both good and evil and life and death. As long as life can eke out a victory, there is always the potential that we will see something beyond the mere struggle for existence—that we will escape the bonds of time and mortality. In its most refined sense, the heroic can be defined as that moment in a narrative when the forces of life make a stronger assertion than death.

Paget Toynbee, Dante's biographer, tells the story of how *The Divine Comedy* was completed. When Dante died—from a mosquito bite and a fever—it appeared that the final three cantos of the *Paradiso* had not been written. His friends and readers mourned not only the poet's untimely passing but also the fact that although he had brought them through the fires of hell and the anxious miasma of purgatory, he had not been able to bring them to the threshold of God. Like Moses, who was unable to enter the Promised Land, Dante had brought his readers to the edge of high heaven, only to fall short of that moment when "the vision" would be complete. About three months after the poet's death, however, his son, Jacopo, had a dream in which his father appeared to him and told him that the poem had indeed been finished. Dante told Jacopo that he would find the missing pieces in the dead poet's room in his recently vacated residence in Ravenna. Jacopo raced across the city to his father's former house and woke the new tenant in the middle of the night. The two men turned the room upside down, to no avail. On the verge of despair, Jacopo is said to have turned and looked at a worn and threadbare tapestry that hung on the wall. There seemed to be nothing in the tapestry to give him a clue. At that moment, however, his mind made a tremendous leap. He realized that his father had been writing about the world of the insubstantial that lies not only within the imagination but *behind* human experience. The tenant and the younger Alighieri lifted the tapestry and started to tap against the panelling on the wall. One panel revealed a hollow sound, and they pressed on it. When it gave way, they found the final three cantos of *The Divine Comedy*. Dante *had* taken his readers to the threshold of God. What is more, he had, through an act of the imagination, spoken to the world from beyond death. He had completed his vision of infinite possibilities and set out a marked pathway for others to follow in their own imaginations.

Whether this legend is true is not the point. The story serves as a useful metaphor for what literature does, and as an explanation for why literature itself may be the hero when all is said and done. Literature serves to put a pattern and a structure on human experience. It organizes our dreams, our thoughts, our experiences, and our emotional lives, and contextualizes them in such a way as to create connections. On a very simple level, a narrative is any series of facts or events which, when juxtaposed, form a larger idea. I would like to think that the hero is someone who makes order out of chaos and holds a story together, who engages with, experiences, and connects material that would otherwise be random in our imaginations. But the hero is only a metaphor for something larger. Ultimately, he serves the same purpose as literature itself—that is, to make order and meaning out of the chaos of time, the immeasurable blur of history, and the constant entrances and exits of characters on life's stage. And if our stories enable us to plumb the enormous depths of who we are, I would like to think that we are never lost in our own narratives. I would like to imagine that someone very much like us is there to guide us as we seek the answers to our questions and the solutions to our problems.

Acknowledgments

B ooks such as this require the heroic efforts of many individuals, each of whom contributes in his or her own way to the final product. I am indebted to the following individuals for their kindness, good offices, gracious assistance, moral support, energy, and enthusiasm. A sincere thank-you to Ted Hackborn and Mark Tearle for their photographic skills. I owe a special thanks to my student Robin Parkes, of Laurentian University in Barrie, for giving me his permission to use his grandfather's photograph of Keith Douglas on parade with Winston Churchill in North Africa. In my search for artwork for this book, I was nobly assisted by Richard Darling of the Toronto Antique Centre, Guenther Dreeke of the Dickinson Gallery, Don Lake of D. E. Lake Antique Prints and Books, and the employees of Alexandre Antiques, all of Toronto. Fred Addis, Adde and Bette Walker, Treasa O'Driscoll of Barrie and Orillia—my thanks to you all for your support and belief in this project. Thank you to Dora Goh of the Ontario Multicultural History Association of Toronto, Brian O'Riordan, Barry Callaghan, Austin Clarke, and Tomson Highway. To my spiritual mentor, Father Robert Madden of

St. Michael's College, I offer my sincerest blessings and expressions of appreciation. Terry O'Malley, Jim Wilson, and Father Eusebio Tubale of Notre Dame College in Wilcox, Saskatchewan, must be remembered with thanks, as must Sister Vicky. Thanks to Dr. Cherylyn Cameron, Fred Fallis, Jean Payne, Mary Whittaker, and Dr. Donald Dennie. I also thank my colleagues and the students of the Laurentian University B.A. Program at Georgian College, as well as Dr. Mimi Marrocco of the St. Michael's College Continuing Education Program at the University of Toronto and my students at St. Michael's College for their support, encouragement, and friendship. This book became a reality because of the kindness and belief of Iris Tupholme of HarperCollins. Special thanks are owed to my agent deluxe, Bruce Westwood of Westwood Creative Artists, and to his colleagues Carolyn Forde and Natasha Daneman. It is great to have champions on my side. To my team at HarperCollins, a very special thanks: to Barbara Bower, my publicist, and the sales and marketing team; to Alan Jones for his remarkable talents; and to Noelle Zitzer, Nita Pronovost, and Sharon Kish, for their care and detail. Most of all, I offer my heartfelt thanks to my editor, Jim Gifford, who was a paragon of patience, goodwill, and humour right through the very thick of things. We strove together. Janice Weaver's skills held the secret to the completion of this book, and I am forever indebted to her for finding the way through the labyrinth of ideas and language I presented to her. In the end, my closest champions, those who pulled the oars with me when it seemed that the darkness of the *nekusis* would overtake me, were the ones who guided me home. Thanks to all of you—my uncle, Dr. E. G. Meyer; my mother, Margaret Meyer; my late father, Homer Meyer; my sister, Dr. Carolyn Meyer; my wife, Kerry; and my daughter, Katie—for teaching me the true meaning of the hero. And to those who read my previous book and cheered me on with your encouragement and good wishes, you too are all my heroes.

Selected Bibliography

Aristotle. *Poetics* in *Classical Literary Criticism*. Trans. T. S. Dorsch. Harmondsworth, UK: Penguin, 1975.

———. *The Nicomachean Ethics*. Trans. J. A. K. Thomson. Harmondsworth, UK: Penguin, 1976.

Beckett, Samuel. *Waiting for Godot: A Tragicomedy in Two Acts*. New York: Grove, 1982.

Bede, the Venerable. *A History of the English Church and People*. Trans. Leo Sherley-Price. Harmondsworth, UK: Penguin, 1974.

Beowulf: A New Verse Translation. Trans. R. M. Liuzza. Peterborough, ON: Broadview Press, 2000.

Boethius. *The Consolation of Philosophy*. Trans. V. E. Watts. Harmondsworth, UK: Penguin, 1976.

Brontë, Charlotte. *Jane Eyre*. Ed. Margaret Smith. Oxford, UK: Oxford University Press, 2000.

Bunyan, John. *The Pilgrim's Progress*. Ed. Roger Sharrock. Harmondsworth, UK: Penguin, 1987.

Burns, Robert. *Poems: Selected*. Eds. William Beattie and Henry W. Meikle. Harmondsworth, UK: Penguin, 1977.

Byron, George Gordon. *The Selected Poetry of Lord Byron*. Ed. Leslie A.
Marchand. New York: Modern Library, 2001.

Campbell, Joseph. *The Hero with a Thousand Faces*. Princeton, NJ: Princeton
University Press, 1968.

Carlyle, Thomas. *On Heroes, Hero-Worship and the Heroic in History*. Ed. Carl
Niemeyer. Lincoln, NE: University of Nebraska Press, 1966.

Cervantes, Miguel de. *Don Quixote*. Trans. Edith Grossman. New York: Ecco
Press, 2003.

Chaucer, Geoffrey. *The Canterbury Tales*. Trans. Nevill Coghill.
Harmondsworth, UK: Penguin, 1973.

——. *Love Visions*. Trans. Brian Stone. Harmondsworth, UK: Penguin, 1983.

Cohen, Leonard. *Beautiful Losers*. Toronto: McClelland and Stewart, 1966.

Dante. *The Comedy of Dante Alighieri the Florentine: Cantica I: Hell (L'Inferno)*.
Trans. Dorothy L. Sayers. Harmondsworth, UK: Penguin, 1972.

——. *The Comedy of Dante Alighieri the Florentine: Cantica III: Paradise
(Il Paradiso)*. Trans. Dorothy L. Sayers and Barbara Reynolds.
Harmondsworth, UK: Penguin, 1976.

——. *The Divine Comedy, II. Purgatorio, Part 2*. Trans. Charles S. Singleton.
Princeton, NJ: Princeton University Press, 1991.

de Lorris, Guillaume, and Jean de Meun. *The Romance of the Rose*. Trans.
Harry W. Robbins. New York: E. P. Dutton, 1962.

de Voragine, Jacobus. *Golden Legend*. Trans. Christopher Stace.
Harmondsworth, UK: Penguin, 1998.

Eliot, T. S. *Collected Poems, 1909–1962*. London: Faber and Faber, 1983.

The Epic of Gilgamesh. Trans. N. K. Sandars. Harmondsworth, UK: Penguin, 1973.

Euripides. *Herakles*. Trans. Tom Sleigh. Oxford, UK: Oxford University Press,
2001.

Faulkner, William. *Light in August*. New York: Vintage, 1972.

Flaubert, Gustave. *Madame Bovary*. Trans. Geoffrey Wall. Harmondsworth,
UK: Penguin, 2003.

Frye, Northrop. *Anatomy of Criticism*. Princeton, NJ: Princeton University
Press, 1957.

Goethe, Johann Wolfgang von. *Faust: Part I*. Trans. Randall Jarrell. New York: Farrar, Strauss and Giroux, 1999.

——. *Faust: Part II*. Trans. Philip Wayne. Harmondsworth, UK: Penguin, 1959.

Greene, Graham. *The End of the Affair*. Harmondsworth, UK: Penguin, 1975.

Hamer, Richard, ed. and trans. *A Choice of Anglo Saxon Verse*. London: Faber and Faber, 1970.

Homer. *Iliad*. Trans. Robert Fagles. Harmondsworth, UK: Penguin, 1991.

——. *Odyssey*. Trans. E. V. Rieu. Harmondsworth, UK: Penguin, 1973.

James, William. *The Varieties of Religious Experience*. Ed. Martin E. Marty. Harmondsworth, UK: Penguin, 1985.

Kempis, Thomas à. *The Imitation of Christ*. Trans. Leo Sherley-Price. Harmondsworth, UK: Penguin, 1977.

Kennedy, John F. *Profiles in Courage*. New York: HarperPerennial, 2000.

Langland, William. *Piers Ploughman*. Trans. J. F. Goodridge. Harmondsworth, UK: Penguin, 1977.

Machiavelli, Niccolò. *The Prince*. Trans. George Bull. Harmondsworth, UK: Penguin, 1999.

Marchand, Leslie A., ed. *Selected Poetry of Lord Byron*. New York: Modern Library, 2001.

Marlowe, Christopher. *The Complete Plays*. Ed. J. B. Steane. Harmondsworth, UK: Penguin, 1976.

Miller, Arthur. *Death of a Salesman*. Ed. Gerald Weales. New York: Penguin, 1996.

Milton, John. *Paradise Lost*. Ed. Merritt Y. Hughes. Indianapolis, IN: Odyssey Press, 1962.

——. *Paradise Lost and Paradise Regained*. Ed. Christopher Ricks. New York: Signet Classics, 1968.

Owen, Wilfred. *The Collected Poems of Wilfred Owen*. Ed. C. Day-Lewis. London: Chatto and Windus, 1963.

Ratzinger, Joseph. *Introduction to Christianity*. London: Search Press, 1971.

Rilke, Rainer Maria. *The Selected Poetry of Rainer Maria Rilke*. Trans. Stephen Mitchell. New York: Vintage, 1989.

Seneca. *Four Tragedies and Octavia*. Trans. E. F. Watling. Harmondsworth, UK: Penguin, 1970.

Shakespeare, William. *Hamlet, Prince of Denmark*. Ed. Willard Farnham. Harmondsworth, UK: Penguin, 1985.

———. *The Life of Henry V*. Ed. John Russell Brown. New York: Signet Classics, 1998.

———. *A Midsummer Night's Dream*. Ed. Russ McDonald. Harmondsworth, UK: Penguin, 2000.

———. *The Tragedy of Hamlet, Prince of Denmark*. Ed. Edward Hubler. New York: Signet Classics, 1963.

———. *The Tragedy of Richard the Third*. Ed. Mark Eccles. New York: Signet Classics, 1998.

Sophocles. *The Theban Plays*. Trans. E. F. Watling. Harmondsworth, UK: Penguin, 1973.

Virgil. *Aeneid*. Trans. W. F. Jackson Knight. Harmondsworth, UK: Penguin, 1977.

Ward, Geoffrey C., and Ken Burns. *Baseball: An Illustrated History*. New York: Alfred A. Knopf, 1994.

Whitman, Walt. *Song of Myself* (unabridged). New York: Dover, 2001.

Yeats, W. B. *W. B. Yeats: A Critical Edition of the Major Works*. Ed. Edward Larrissy. Oxford, UK: Oxford University Press, 1997.

Index

Henry V (King of England), **52**
Henry VIII (King of England), 123
Hera, 103, 117, 217, 228
Hercules, 16, 32, 33, 103, **104**, 154, 195, 200,
    227–28, **229**, 234
    death of, 234–36
    labours of, 228–33
Hercules furens, 113
Hero, 1, 110
"hero"
    etymology of, 28
    OED definitions of, 30–31, 35–36, 39, 190
hero
    anti-hero, 19, 26, 64, 70–71, 86
    classical categories, 49–51
    common, 43–73
    in death, 33–34, 60
    divine, 6–7, 33, 233, 236
    infernal, 109–49
    and masks, 36–37, 38
    saintly, 151–85
    supernatural, 38, 223–36
    tragic, 75–108
    in underworld, 60, 103, 205–10
    wandering, 147–48
hero, concepts of
    Campbell's, 19–20
    Carlyle's, 16
    Christian, 22–23
    Freudian, 21
    Frye's, 22–27
    Jungian, 19
    Milton's, 145
    Shakespeare's, 78–79
hero narrative, three-part structure, 17, 257
hero pattern, 18, 21, 23, 41, 60, 257
Heroic Age, 32, 196
heroic transformation, 3, 4, 11, 33, 35, 149,
    160, 224, 235, 240
heroine, 28
Hickcock, Wild Bill, 231
Holy Grail legend, 166, **167**, 219
Homer, 177, 186, **187**, 193, 216
    Iliad, 32, 33, 59–62, 132, 179, 190,
      193–96, 220, 223
    Odyssey, 19, 25, 68, 106, 114, 146,
      147–48,153, 178, 196, 202, 204, 206,
      215. *See also* Odysseus.
Horace, 58
hubris, 95, 117, 144, 145
humanists, 129
Hydra, 20, 228

infernal hero, 109–49
Irish mythology, 32

Jackson, Gentleman George, 109
James, Henry, 164
James, William
    The Varieties of Religious Experience, 162,
      164–66, 168, 184
Jason, 25, 31, 32, 199–200
Jesus Christ, 6–7, 22, 25, 31, 131, 172–3,
    191–92, 205, 218, 225, 237, 246
    as divine hero, 237–43, 246–48
    life of, in Gospels, 177–85,
Job, 80, 251–52
John Paul II (Pope), 151–52
Johnson, Samuel, 17
    Lives of the Poets, 39
journey theme, 201–6
Joyce, James
    Dubliners, 71
    Ulysses, 19, 26, 68
Judeo-Christian universe, 80, 81, 92, 118, 236

Keats, John, 59
Kent, Clarke. *See* Superman.
Kennedy, John F.
    Profiles in Courage, 39
Knights of the Round Table, **167**, 213–14
Knox, John, 17
Kolbe, Maximilian, 151, 161, 164, 184
krygma, 247
Kyd, Thomas
    The Spanish Tragedy, 85, 91

Lafayette, Marquis de, 66
Lancelot, 25
Langland, William
    Piers Ploughman, 212–13, 215
latria, 165
Lawrence, D. H.
    Women in Love, 179
Leander, 1, 110
Leonardo (da Vinci), 39
Leroux, Gaston, 37
Levertov, Denise, 62
Lewis, C. Day, 53
Lewis, C. S.
    A Preface to Paradise Lost, 148–49
logos, 253–54

quest theme, 149, 195, 219, 244
The Quest for the Holy Grail, 20, 213–14
Quince, Peter, 50

Rank, Otto
 The Myth of the Birth of the Hero, 18–19, 28
Raphael (Sanzio), 39
Ratzinger, Joseph. *See* Benedict XVI.
Red Crosse Knight (*The Faerie Queene*), 204, 205, 216
Renaissance world-view, 39, 86, 98–99, 120–21, 129
Revelations, Book of, **182**, 183
Richard III (King of England), 124
Rilke, Rainer Maria
 The Duino Elegies, 255–57
 Sonnets to Orpheus, 255
Rochester, Bertha (*Jane Eyre*), 69, 116
Rochester, Edward Fairfax (*Jane Eyre*), 37, 69, 114–17
Rolle, Richard, 210
"romance," 218
romance hero, 218–19, 231
Romulus and Remus, 157
Roosevelt, Franklin D., 43
Rousseau, Jean-Jacques, 17
 The Social Contract, 68

"saint," 152
St. Andrew Kim, 160
St. Augustine, 217
 Confessions, 4, 96, 250–51
St. Catherine, 164–65
St. George, **150**, 217
St. Jerome, 163
St. John (the Evangelist) 182. *See also* under Gospels.
St. Lucy, 164
St. Luke. *See under* Gospels.
St. Mark. *See under* Gospels.
St. Martin de Porres, 160
St. Matthew, 180. *See also* under Gospels.
St. Michael, 154
St. Nicholas, 154–55
St. Paul, 180, 181, 237, 239, 250
St. Sebastian, 162
St. Thomas, 152–53
St. Ursula, 154–55

St. Valentine, 101, 156–59
saintly hero, 151–185
 categories of, 153–164
 contemporary, 161–64
 historical, 159–161
 legendary, 154–59
 mythic, 153–54
Sancho Panza, 49
Santa Claus, 156
Satan (*Paradise Lost*), 37, 141–46, 147, 148
Sauron (*Lord of the Rings*), 21
Saxo Grammaticus
 Historica Danica, 84
Seneca
 Octavia, 94, 102
Senecan tragedy, 60, 93, 95, 127
Shakespeare, William, 8, 9, 17, 55–56, 74, 75, 81
 Coriolanus, 91
 Hamlet, 26, 48, 75–88, 90–95, 97–98, 99, 100–101, 103, 105, 107, 201
 Henry V, 25–26, 51, 53
 King Lear, 80, 91, 106, 155
 Macbeth, 143, **145**
 A Midsummer Night's Dream, 50
 Othello, 80, 85
 The Tragedy of Richard III, 125–28
Shaw, George Bernard, 141
Shelley, Mary
 Frankenstein, 37, 130, 140, 224, 251–52
Shelley, Percy Bysshe, 144
Shuster, Joe
 "The Reign of Superman," 223–24, 225
Sibyl, 140
Siegel, Jerry
 "The Reign of Superman," 223–24, 225
Sir Gawain and the Green Knight, 213, 231
Sophocles
 Antigone, 36, 80–81, 100–2, 105
 Oedipus the King, 36, 89. *See also* Oedipus.
Spenser, Edmund
 The Faerie Queene, 204, 206, 217
spoudaios, 48–49, 53, 60, 63, 70, 77, 100, 131
Starveling, Robin, 50
Strachey, Lytton
 Eminent Victorians, 39
Suetonius, 38
Sullivan, Barry, **99**
Superman (character), 38, 224–226, 257
superman myth, 225, 226
supernatural hero, 223–36